W9-BAF-814

Craig Kielburger

Marc Kielburger

Deepa Shankaran

©2008 Me To We Books
233 Carlton Street
Toronto, Ontario
Canada M5A 2L2

TAKE MORE ACTION! How To Change The World

HOME
Preface, Contents

LEVEL I
Global Citizenship: Around the World, Across the Street

LEVEL II
Becoming Global Citizens: A Question of Choice

TAKE MORE ACTION! How To Change The World

HOME	**LEVEL I**	**LEVEL II**
Preface, Contents	Global Citizenship: Around the World, Across the Street	Becoming Global Citizens: A Question of Choice

A MESSAGE FROM MARC AND CRAIG KIELBURGER

For over a decade, the young people of Free The Children and Me to We have been actively and passionately engaged in changing the world through volunteerism and the movement for social justice. Free The Children has grown from a small group of students into the world's largest network of children helping children, with over one million youth involved in its projects and campaigns. Leaders Today, founded to help Free The Children participants reach their leadership potential, has since expanded into the Me to We movement, now empowering more than 350,000 young people every year with the skills and the spirit to be active global citizens. Our journey through social activism has been both challenging and uplifting, and we have had to learn many lessons the hard way. Through this book, and the *Take Action!* series, we hope to share what we've learned with you.

Level III The Seven Steps to Social Action: Taking It to the Next Level	**Level IV** The How-To Guide: The Global Citizen's Toolbox	**Level V** Sources And Resources, End Notes

We discovered the most important of these lessons not long ago, when we were leading a group of young volunteers into the heights of the Andes mountains in Ecuador to help construct a school for a rural community. We were excited about the experience and the opportunity to share our resources with our new friends, but when we discovered what a challenge it would be to build the school with our own hands, we began to doubt our ability to complete the construction in time.

The elders of the community, however, reassured us that it was possible. They taught us about the *minga*, a tradition of the Puruhae indigenous people that has survived for hundreds of years. It meant that, although this single community would be the only one to benefit from the school, hundreds of people from all over the region would come together to make it stand. Elderly women carried bags of cement to lay the foundation; children who would never be able to attend the school helped to put up the walls of its new classrooms; farmers gave up three precious days at the peak of the growing season to make sure that the job got done.

TAKE MORE ACTION! How To Change The World

HOME	LEVEL I	LEVEL II
Preface, Contents	Global Citizenship: Around the World, Across the Street	Becoming Global Citizens: A Question of Choice

Level III
The Seven Steps to Social Action:
Taking It to the Next Level

Level IV
The How-To Guide:
The Global Citizen's Toolbox

Level V
Sources And Resources,
End Notes

When we asked what moved them to make such sacrifices even though they had nothing to gain from the project, they told us that some things are sacred, and among them are children and education. These values are fundamental to any community and its future, and take precedence over the individual's needs and wants. For a people with few possessions, these values proved to be their greatest resource, because they connected and united the Puruhae through all challenges and times.

We went to that village to provide an education for the community, but we realized that we had a lot to learn too. Many communities around the globe are small and struggling, but survive because they believe so deeply in the value of supporting one another. Working alongside them puts our own struggles into context, and teaches us that we are all part of something larger than our individual lives and that our well-being is connected to that of others. When we begin to think about the world as a single community and focus our energy on making it stronger, we become conscious of our power to make a difference.

In this guide to social involvement, you will discover what it means and what it takes to be a global citizen. You will learn how to break down and tackle even the most difficult social problems, and how to channel your passion for a better world into concrete actions—big and small. You will also begin to develop and hone the skills that will make your vision and actions speak louder, and discover how other young people, just like you, are taking up the challenge of confronting injustice in thoughtful, creative ways. We know that being a true global citizen is not easy—we have to confront the harsh reality that we are often part of the problems that we see. But we can be inspired by the knowledge that we are also part of the solution—with every action we take, we have the chance to make a positive change.

When dealing with tough issues by yourself, it is easy to feel powerless and alone. But as an African proverb holds, "When spider webs unite, they can tie up a lion." When we come together as a minga—as citizens of a global community—we can tie up the roots of injustice and secure a happier, more sustainable world. This consciousness and solidarity begins with us, with youth. This is our challenge, as individuals and as a generation: Will we sit back and allow others to create the future, or will we build the world we want to see, starting today?

We are the generation we've been waiting for. ***Let's get started!***

TAKE MORE ACTION! How To Change The World

HOME	LEVEL I	LEVEL II
Preface, Contents	Global Citizenship: Around the World, Across the Street	Becoming Global Citizens: A Question of Choice

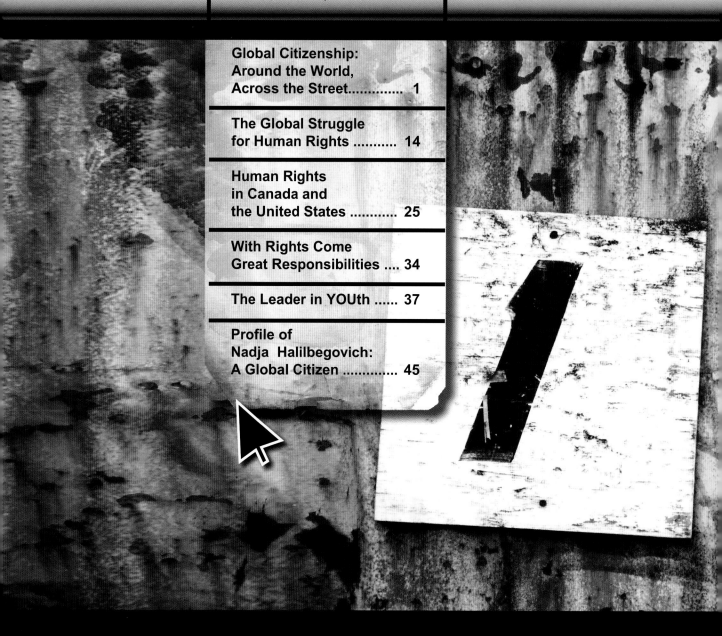

GLOBAL CITIZENSHIP: AROUND THE WORLD, ACROSS THE STREET

Julia Butterfly Hill sat almost 180 feet up in a tree in the ancient redwood forest in California, from December 10, 1997, to December 18, 1999. That's 738 days. Straight. Seriously.

"I didn't come from a background of activism," said the 23-year-old woman from Arkansas. But when she was climbing and hiking through the valleys and mountains of the US west coast, she learned that much of the majestic old-growth forests, thousands of years old, were under threat from clearcut logging. "I fell to the ground and started crying," she said, "and immediately got involved."

"IT'S NOT THAT WE CAN MAKE A DIFFERENCE.
IT'S THAT WE DO MAKE A DIFFERENCE.
THE KIND OF CHANGE WE MAKE IS UP TO US.
EACH AND EVERY ONE OF US HAS THE POWER TO HURT
OR TO HEAL, TO BE THE HERO OR THE DESTROYER,
WITH EVERY MOMENT, OF EVERY BREATH, OF EVERY
DAY."

—Julia Butterfly Hill
(b. 1974)
Social activist

TAKE MORE ACTION!   How To Change The World

HOME	LEVEL I	LEVEL II
Preface, Contents	Global Citizenship: Around the World, Across the Street	Becoming Global Citizens: A Question of Choice

Julia chose her favorite tree, named it "Luna," and climbed up to perch in its branches—not planning to break any world tree-sitting records, but having simply promised herself that she would not come down without a guarantee that the 1,000-year-old tree would survive. She remained focused when lumber workers tried to frighten her down, and braced herself against the devastating sight of beautiful trees crashing to the ground around her. When security guards swore at her, Julia sang back. When she began to doubt that she could continue, she learned, from watching Luna and the other trees, to stand firm and grounded during storms, yet be willing to bend. Finally, after two long years, a deal was reached with the Pacific Lumber/Maxxam Corporation. Julia had succeeded in saving Luna, along with acres of land surrounding it.

THE ERA OF THE GLOBAL CITIZEN

Do you have to spend two years in a tree to make a difference? Of course not! The point of Julia's story—and of this book—is that anybody can make a difference. You don't have to be a genius at math or public speaking or have a history of volunteering since the age of five. Each and every one of us can do huge things. Mother Teresa, Nelson Mandela and Rosa Parks, for instance, were all regular people who changed the world in extraordinary ways. But you don't have to be the next Mother Teresa to make a difference. You only have to be you, and make the unique difference that only you can.

Julia is only one among a tide of young people, in every part of the globe, who are working to realize their ideals in concrete ways. They stand firm and grounded during the tough storms, yet are willing to bend and change, to make the world a better place. Since the inception of Free The Children in 1995, we have witnessed many important actions by thousands of youth who have joined the ranks of our worldwide network. For example:

- In Toronto, Canada, young people came together in their efforts to provide emergency relief to children in Afghanistan. They collected over 10,000 school and health kits and thousands of blankets, items of clothing and toys to deliver to refugees in need.
- In Rio de Janeiro, Brazil, young people launched a campaign that was instrumental in pressuring the government to commit one million dollars toward a nationwide program to combat exploitative child labor. The group also persuaded dozens of teachers to volunteer their time to teach basic literacy skills to child laborers and convinced many corporations to donate school and health supplies to rural learning centers.

Julia Butterfly Hill braved the intense winds and cold of two harsh winters, suffering from frostbite on her fingers and toes during her sit in the 1,000-year-old tree she named Luna.

TAKE MORE ACTION! How To Change The World

Home Preface, Contents	**Level I** Global Citizenship: Around the World, Across the Street	**Level II** Becoming Global Citizens: A Question of Choice

- In Munich, Germany, young people created the Children Paint Their Dreams initiative, encouraging their peers around the world, particularly those living amid the upheaval of war, to express their fears and dreams through art. An exhibition of artwork collected by the group has traveled the world, raising awareness of the hardships and the hopes of the world's children.
- In Calcutta, India, youth helped to gather evidence of the trafficking of children to the Middle East for use as drug carriers and to ride racing camels. Presenting their findings before the Indian government and courts, they convinced the President of India to send a representative to Saudi Arabia to negotiate the release of the enslaved children.

These examples are a tiny few compared with the overwhelming number of stories of people who continue to make a difference in their communities and the world. Throughout the continents, young people are seeking ways to promote solidarity, or unity—an awareness of how interconnected we are as a human race. This solidarity dissolves the borders between countries and deepens our understanding of the concept of "citizenship." Based on the Latin *civitas*, meaning people in a city or community, the word "citizen" was first used to refer to one who was granted specific rights and responsibilities as a member of a state or nation. More and more, however, we are coming to realize that we are not only members of our nations, but also of our world as a whole.

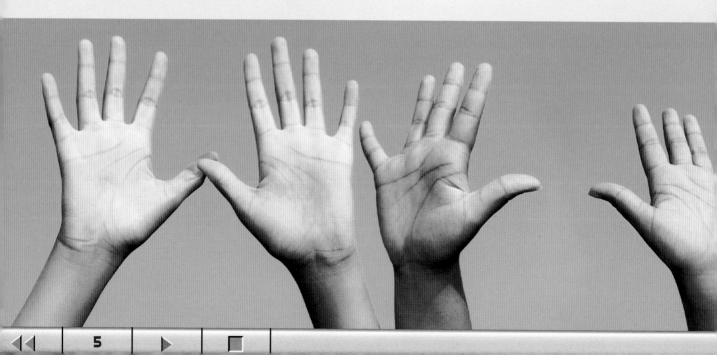

Noteworthy:

"WE HAVE LEARNED THAT WE CANNOT LIVE
ALONE, AT PEACE; THAT OUR OWN WELL-BEING
IS DEPENDENT ON THE WELL-BEING OF OTHER
NATIONS, FAR AWAY.... WE HAVE LEARNED TO
BE CITIZENS OF THE WORLD, MEMBERS OF THE
HUMAN COMMUNITY."

—Franklin D. Roosevelt
(1882-1945)
Former President of the United States

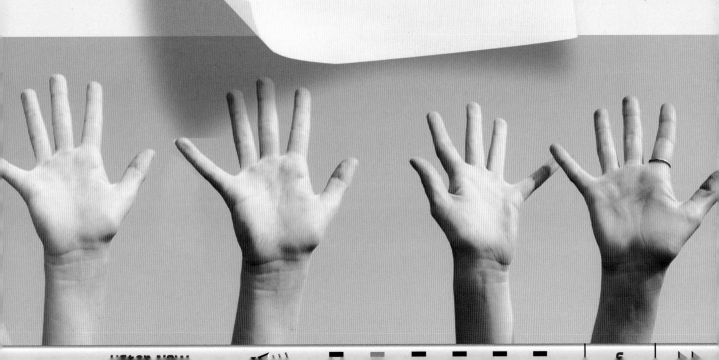

TAKE MORE ACTION! How To Change The World

| **Home**
Preface, Contents | **Level I**
Global Citizenship:
Around the World, Across the Street | **Level II**
Becoming Global Citizens:
A Question of Choice |

Welcome to the era of the global citizen, of rapidly growing numbers of people—especially youth—turning a critical eye to the evening news, speaking out for justice, coming up with creative ways to address the causes of human suffering and taking action for the well-being of others. Theirs is a vision of the world as a global community, in which there are no outsiders. It comes from the knowledge that we are all human, and we have only one planet to share, so the problems and struggles and issues that used to be "over there"—other people's hunger, other people's wars—become our own. When one person suffers, we all suffer. When one of us does not survive, a part of us all is lost. When the environment is hurting, we all feel the effects. In other words, we share this world with at least six billion neighbors, and we need to look out for one another.

In this age of the internet and 24-hour news stations, it is no longer possible to claim ignorance as an excuse for not acting to resolve the inequalities and injustices around us. We are exposed to these realities every day. We have all seen thousands of images of famine, poverty, refugees, environmental destruction and war. But somebody else is taking care of those problems, right? Don't we have the United Nations or charities to do something about them? Plus, many young people think, "I'm just a student. I can't vote. And these issues are way too huge—how am I supposed to stop wars? I don't control companies. I'm not a president or prime minister."

Global citizenship means recognizing that the world's problems are massive and overwhelming, but that you can make a difference, and more importantly, you *do*.

You may be thinking, "I had nothing to do with creating these problems. I've just been sitting here, minding my own business, trying to get decent marks or hanging out with my friends. I shouldn't be responsible for solving them."

Level I > Global Citizenship: The Era Of The Global Citizen

Level III	**Level IV**	**Level V**
The Seven Steps to Social Action: Taking It to the Next Level	The How-To Guide: The Global Citizen's Toolbox	Sources And Resources, End Notes

Keep in mind, however, that the most serious problems our world faces have grown out of the accumulated actions of millions of people, many of whom are simply going about their lives with the best of intentions. Your own daily routine just may play a part. For instance, have you ever:

- Thrown something away when it could have been recycled or composted?
- Bought brand-name clothing from a company with a reputation for exploiting its workers?
- Walked past a homeless person and pretended not to see him or her?
- Told a racist joke?
- Joined in teasing the unpopular kid at school?
- Driven the car to school?
- Used a printer for only one side of a page?
- Rented a violent movie?
- Taken an extra-long shower?

The fact is that small, negative actions like these do add up. The same is true, however, for small, positive actions. This brings us to the second key point of this book: The actions you take to make a difference do not have to be huge. They can be easy, meaningful actions that change the world in little ways each day—like smiling at a neighbor or bringing your lunch in a reusable container instead of a plastic bag. Just as Julia Butterfly Hill said, we make a difference every moment, with every action we take. The question is whether our difference is for the better or for the worse.

TAKE MORE ACTION! How To Change The World

HOME	LEVEL I	LEVEL II
Preface, Contents	Global Citizenship: Around the World, Across the Street	Becoming Global Citizens: A Question of Choice

Let's try that list again. Have you ever:

- Carried a glass bottle all the way home to put into the recycling bin?
- Worn a shirt without any logos or (even better) with a positive message?
- Given a homeless person a cup of coffee or a warm smile?
- Made an effort to be friends with a student of a different culture?
- Stuck up for someone who was being teased?
- Walked or ridden your bike to school?
- Printed on both sides of a page?
- Rented a documentary or a movie with a serious message?
- Turned the shower off as you shampoo to save water?

We are all responsible in some way for the state of our world. Thinking globally leads us to consider how every action we take locally affects our six billion neighbors and the Earth that we all share. It reveals that our choices are incredibly powerful instruments for effecting change, whether negative or positive. And when more and more people become aware of this power and commit to using it with passion and with purpose, it is the beginning of a healthier world.

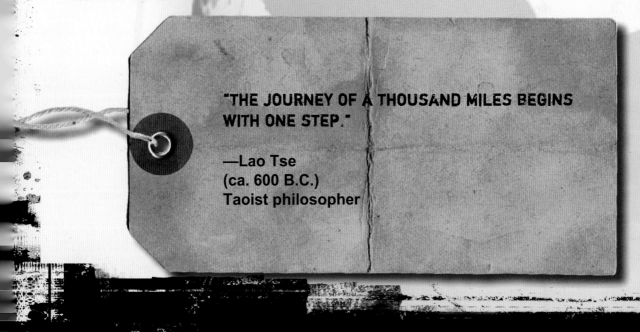

"THE JOURNEY OF A THOUSAND MILES BEGINS WITH ONE STEP."

—Lao Tse
(ca. 600 B.C.)
Taoist philosopher

Taking concrete action could mean speaking to others about an issue that is important to you.

TAKE MORE ACTION! How To Change The World

| HOME
Preface, Contents | LEVEL I
Global Citizenship:
Around the World, Across the Street | LEVEL II
Becoming Global Citizens:
A Question of Choice |

A global citizen:

- Takes an interest in global issues, asks questions about established assumptions and practices and questions the answers provided
- Cares about what he or she believes is right and wrong, just and unjust
- Lives and acts in a way that reflects these beliefs
- Carefully considers every action he or she takes and how it impacts all neighbors around the globe
- Strives for a more just and sustainable world, celebrating diversity and solidarity in this mission

This is the essence of global citizenship, which makes the difference between living in a world that we just accept and taking concrete action—small and large—to create the world that we want. This could mean living in a tree for two years, or participating in a canned food drive, or offering a kind word to someone who looks discouraged. It means bringing our actions into line with our values: not merely blaming others and complaining about the problems that we see, but also believing that a better world is possible and working to make it real. It is about discovering that if we want our world to change, the change has to begin with us.

Throughout this book, you will discover a range of issues, problems, stories, ideas, actions and solutions that will help you to develop your values. Values are the beliefs you hold about what is really important and how they guide your choices and behavior. Your values evolve over the entire course of your lifetime—they come from the general beliefs of your society and from the personal experiences and thoughts that shape your own unique perspective. We all have values, but being a global citizen means promoting and acting in accordance with your values in seeking a happier, more just society. As you read on, reflect occasionally on what your values are and how they can contribute to your community, your country and your world.

TAKE MORE ACTION! How To Change The World

HOME	LEVEL I	LEVEL II
Preface, Contents	Global Citizenship: Around the World, Across the Street	Becoming Global Citizens: A Question of Choice

WE HOLD THESE TRUTHS

EVIDENT; THAT ALL MEN A

EQUAL, THAT THEY ARE ENDO

CREATOR WITH CERTAIN

RIGHTS, AMONG THESE AR

AND THE PURSUIT OF HAP

TO SECURE THESE RIGHTS

ARE INSTITUTED AMON

SOLEMNLY PUBLISH AND

THESE COLONIES ARE A

OUGHT TO BE FREE AND

Level I > Global Citizenship: The Global Stuggle For Human Rights

Level III	**Level IV**	**Level V**
The Seven Steps to Social Action: Taking It to the Next Level	The How-To Guide: The Global Citizen's Toolbox	Sources And Resources, End Notes

THE GLOBAL STRUGGLE FOR HUMAN RIGHTS

If global citizenship entails working together for a world that reflects our values, it would make sense for us to agree on some common values that we could all promote and defend. Perhaps the most common value we share as a human race is the "golden rule," which holds that we should treat others as we ourselves would like to be treated.

This principle of fairness and mutual respect has been the foundation of global human rights, influencing beliefs, laws and institutions for centuries. As early as 1215, England's Magna Carta, a charter granted by King John, established rights for all its citizens. In 1776, the Fathers of the American Revolution, led by Thomas Jefferson, declared it a "self-evident" truth that "all men are created equal," and soon followed this with an advanced, ever-evolving Bill of Rights in their Constitution. The early days of the French Revolution led to the Declaration of the Rights of Man and the Citizen in 1789.

These legislative landmarks, however, were still exclusive of women, non-whites and the poor. Never before had the international community declared that every human being had rights—and stated these rights clearly—until the horrors of World War II compelled them to do so.

World War II (1938-1945) was one of the most devastating, deadly wars in history. Millions

"INJUSTICE ANYWHERE IS A THREAT TO JUSTICE EVERYWHERE."

—Martin Luther King, Jr.
(1929-1968)
Baptist minister, civil rights leader

"WE'VE HEARD ENOUGH TALK ABOUT SOLIDARITY AND SYMPATHY; WHAT WE WANT TO KNOW IS, WHERE'S THE JUSTICE?"

—Stephen Lewis
(b. 1937)
Former United Nations Secretary General's Special Envoy on HIV/AIDS

TAKE MORE ACTION! How To Change The World

HOME	LEVEL I	LEVEL II
Preface, Contents	Global Citizenship: Around the World, Across the Street	Becoming Global Citizens: A Question of Choice

of people were killed because they were Jewish, Gypsies, political enemies, disabled or homosexual. They were systematically executed in concentration camps during the Holocaust. Millions of people were killed on the battlefield. A hundred thousand more were wiped out in a matter of minutes by nuclear bombs that fell on Hiroshima and Nagasaki, Japan. At the end of that war, the human race made itself a promise—a promise to its children: *Never Again*. Never again would we allow our differences to divide us in a way that violated our basic common values. Never again would we allow such atrocities to be committed against anyone, for any reason.

In 1945 (before the end of World War II), delegates from 50 countries gathered in San Francisco to create the United Nations (UN), with a vision of international co-operation, peace and security. In the words of the first article of the UN Charter, signed on June 26, 1945, the new worldwide organization would work toward "promoting and encouraging respect for human rights and for fundamental freedoms for all without distinction as to race, sex, language or religion." This statement meant that every person on Earth was entitled to the rights that enforced his or her dignity and value, but was also responsible for granting these rights to others. It was intended to unite us all in building a more peaceful, equitable and humane world.

And we have followed that rule ever since—right? Not quite.

TAKE MORE ACTION! How To Change The World

Home	**Level I**	**Level II**
Preface, Contents	Global Citizenship: Around the World, Across the Street	Becoming Global Citizens: A Question of Choice

International Law at a Glance

Simply put, international law is a set of rules and norms that regulates the conduct of states in the international system or community. Its highest judicial authority is the International Court of Justice, which was established in the United Nations Charter.

International law is derived from two sources: treaties and customary practices, through which states establish rights and responsibilities that govern their relationships with one another.

An international treaty is a source of international law when it is signed and ratified by countries. The treaty becomes legally binding only to those countries that choose to sign and ratify it. "Signed" means that a country says "This sounds good in principle," and "ratified" means "We agree to be legally bound by this treaty." Examples of treaties are the United Nations Charter, the International Covenant on Civil and Political Rights and the United Nations Convention on the Rights of the Child.

In addition to international treaty law, there also exist rules and norms that are the result of long practice among states, known as international customary law.

Because there are rarely any serious repercussions for violating international law, countries that are parties to a treaty sometimes do not live up to their obligations. Until they are willing to commit to truly upholding rights themselves, and find a way to enforce the law, we continue to use international law more as a form of moral expression and pressure.

Enforcement mechanisms are within reach, however. The World Trade Organization (WTO) has very strict rules regarding international economics and trade, and it enforces them by imposing financial penalties against countries that violate the rules. Many people hope that some day, human rights, gender equality, the environment and other social issues will have the same enforceable backing of international law as economics and business.

LeveL III
The Seven Steps to Social Action:
Taking It to the Next Level

LeveL IV
The How-To Guide:
The Global Citizen's Toolbox

LeveL V
Sources And Resources,
End Notes

In 1948, the UN General Assembly (the branch of the UN with representatives from every member country) adopted the Universal Declaration of Human Rights to embody the most basic values that we share, and to express with one united voice that these rights are not to be violated. This document succeeded in bringing the language and concept of justice, equality and fundamental freedoms to the attention of the world.

However, it has not yet been successful in realizing the ideals it envisioned. Genocides (the systematic killing of an identity group) of millions of people in countries such as Cambodia (1975-1979) and Rwanda (1994) have gone unchecked by the global community. Wars, terrorism and torture continue to rage uncontrollably throughout the world. Hundreds of thousands of children have no access to clean water or an education.

Our promise of "Never Again" has yet to be fulfilled. But it can be fulfilled as global citizens commit to taking action to realize the dream of universal human rights. Following are a few key articles of the Universal Declaration of Human Rights, and a word on what work remains to be done.

Noteworthy:

"I DREAM OF GIVING BIRTH TO A CHILD WHO WILL ASK, 'MOTHER, WHAT WAS WAR?'"

—Eve Merriam
(1916-1992)
Author

TAKE MORE ACTION! How To Change The World

HOME	**LEVEL I**	**LEVEL II**
Preface, Contents	Global Citizenship: Around the World, Across the Street	Becoming Global Citizens: A Question of Choice

From the Universal Declaration of Human Rights

Article 1: All human beings are born free and equal in dignity and rights.

Girls and women in many societies are denied their rights to adequate health care, nutrition and education, and are routinely exposed to sexual abuse, violence and forced marriage. Around the world, individuals are denied basic needs and freedoms and are exposed to violence and exploitation simply because of their skin color, ethnic background, religion or other identity group.

Article 3: Everyone has the right to life, liberty and security of person.

According to the UN High Commissioner for Refugees, in 2006 nearly 32.9 million people in more than 150 countries were internally displaced, stateless, refugees or asylum-seekers. Forced to flee their homes because of armed conflict or natural disasters, these people are pushed into unstable conditions, without shelter or land to grow food. In many countries, political opponents or members of targeted groups are routinely jailed without trial, tortured or killed.

Article 4: No one shall be held in slavery or servitude.

The UN Office on Drugs and Crime reports that between 600,000 and 800,000 men, women and children are trafficked every year for the purposes of bonded and forced labor in factories, agriculture or domestic servitude. Many of these workers are also physically confined, threatened with violence and sexually exploited.

Article 5: No one shall be subjected to torture or to cruel, inhuman or degrading treatment or punishment.

According to the International Rehabilitation Council for Torture Victims, torture continues to be practiced regularly in up to 100 countries. Individuals who speak out against torture in their own countries are often subject to repression and harassment, and are even tortured themselves.

LeveL I > Global Citizenship: The Global Stuggle For Human Rights

LeveL III	**LeveL IV**	**LeveL V**
The Seven Steps to Social Action: Taking It to the Next Level	The How-To Guide: The Global Citizen's Toolbox	Sources And Resources, End Notes

Article 7: All are equal before the law and are entitled without discrimination to equal protection of the law.

An estimated thirty-two million Americans—a number equal to the population of Canada—report having been targeted and singled out for criminal suspicion by law enforcement or security officials because of their race, ethnicity religion or nationality. Racial profiling disproportionately affects Aboriginal, African and Hispanic minority groups, and following September 11, 2001, the targeting of Muslims, Sikhs and people of South Asian and Middle Eastern descent has substantially increased.

Article 20: Everyone has the right to freedom of peaceful assembly and association.

Millions of workers in the United States, including farm workers, domestic workers and immigrant workers, do not have collective bargaining rights under any law, and thus cannot negotiate with their employers to determine wages, hours, rules and working conditions. In many countries, unions are illegal and union leaders are jailed, beaten or murdered for attempting to organize for their rights.

TAKE MORE ACTION! How To Change The World

HOME	LEVEL I	LEVEL II
Preface, Contents	Global Citizenship: Around the World, Across the Street	Becoming Global Citizens: A Question of Choice

Article 21: Everyone has the right to take part in the government of his/her country, directly or through freely-chosen representatives.

According to the Inter-Parliamentary Union, women, who make up more than 52 percent of the world's population, hold only 17 percent of seats in parliament worldwide. Billions of people live under dictatorships, one-party governments or corrupt democracies. They are either denied the vote or their votes are virtually ignored. In such countries, political candidates are frequently threatened, jailed or killed during elections.

Article 23: Everyone has the right to work, to free choice of employment, to just and favorable conditions of work and to protection against unemployment.

Despite strong economic growth in recent years, global unemployment remains at a record high, at a rate of 6.3 percent, or 195.2 million people without work. A lack of decent and productive jobs means that 1.37 billion working people have to survive on less than US$2 per day. The employment gap between women and men persists in both quantity and quality of available work. In 2006, only 48.9 percentof women over the age of 15 were working, compared to 74 percent of men.

Article 26: Everyone has the right to education.

UNICEF reports that despite a global increase in educational enrolment, over 115 million children of primary school age are growing up without a basic education. For every 100 boys out of school, there are 115 girls who are out of school.

Nearly sixty years after these rights were recognized, we are still struggling to uphold their ideals. Development experts agree that in order to target violence and conflict at their root, we need to undertake a massive international effort to reduce poverty, illiteracy and injustice, and to promote democratic principles and human rights. As global citizens, we must make this our mission as we begin to take action within our local, national and global communities.

TAKE MORE ACTION! How To Change The World

| **HOME** Preface, Contents | **LEVEL I** Global Citizenship: Around the World, Across the Street | **LEVEL II** Becoming Global Citizens: A Question of Choice |

"HOW LOVELY TO THINK THAT NO ONE NEED WAIT A MOMENT, WE CAN START NOW, START SLOWLY CHANGING THE WORLD!"

–Anne Frank
(1929-1945)
Diarist, Holocaust victim

LeVeL III
The Seven Steps to Social Action:
Taking It to the Next Level

LeVeL IV
The How-To Guide:
The Global Citizen's Toolbox

LeVeL V
Sources And Resources,
End Notes

Prominent Human Rights Activists

The protection of human rights is not automatic—it requires the vigilance, passion and action of all citizens. Within our borders and beyond, there are millions of people whose rights are threatened or non-existent, and around the world, many individuals dedicate their lives to the struggle for the human rights of those most in need. Here are some of these activists.

Stephen Lewis

Stephen Lewis was the leader of the Ontario New Democratic Party, and later the Canadian Ambassador to the United Nations, where he struggled to bring the plight of poor countries, especially in Africa, into the sight lines of the world. From 2001 to 2006, he served as the United Nations Secretary General's Special Envoy on HIV/AIDS. He began researching the scope of the pandemic and advocating with an unparalleled passion for the governments of the world to take immediate action to help those most desperately in need of treatment and aid.

Muhammad Yunus

Muhammad Yunus is the founder of the Grameen Bank, an institution that provides small "microcredit" loans to the poorest of the poor in rural Bangladesh, with a vision for economic and social development from below. When his PhD in Economics left him with no insight into the lives of the poor, he decided to make himself useful, "not as an economist, but as a human being." He founded the Grameen Bank to offer small collateral-free loans to people whom traditional banks refused to serve. Since 1983, the Bank has given loans to nearly 7 million poor people, most of whom are women, and 99 percent of whom repay their loans. More than half of the borrowers have lifted themselves out of poverty, and the bank's success has inspired thousands of similar microcredit programs around the world.

Shirin Ebadi

Shirin Ebadi is a lawyer and activist who has spoken out for the promotion of human rights and democracy in Iran. She was the first female judge in her country, and served as president of the Tehran city court from 1975-79. Following the revolution in 1979, she was forced to resign, as such positions were no longer open to women. Her campaigns for the rights of Iranian women and children frequently brought her into conflict with the authorities. Ebadi established a law practice, often taking on politically sensitive legal cases and championing the reform of family laws in Iran concerning divorce and inheritance legislation.

TAKE MORE ACTION! How To Change The World

HOME	LEVEL I	LEVEL II
Preface, Contents	Global Citizenship: Around the World, Across the Street	Becoming Global Citizens: A Question of Choice

HUMAN RIGHTS IN CANADA AND THE UNITED STATES

Because the Universal Declaration of Human Rights is more a statement of ideals than an effective guarantee of our fundamental rights and freedoms, we rely on our individual countries to protect our human rights. Canadians and American are among the best-protected people in the world because our rights and freedoms are guaranteed under the Canadian Charter of Rights and Freedoms and the United States Bill of Rights. However, overcoming racism, discrimination and inequality has not always been easy, and the struggle continues today.

Level III	**Level IV**	**Level V**
The Seven Steps to Social Action: Taking It to the Next Level	The How-To Guide: The Global Citizen's Toolbox	Sources And Resources, End Notes

Human Rights Events in Canada

1885: A discriminatory $50 head tax is placed on immigrants from China. The tax is later raised to $500 in 1903, before a complete ban on immigration from China is imposed from 1923 to 1947.

1916: Women are granted the right to vote and run in provincial elections in Manitoba. The federal government follows suit in 1918, and Québec is the final province to do so in 1940. Women cannot be appointed to the Senate until the 1929 "Persons Case."

1947: Canadians of Asian descent are granted the right to vote and run in federal elections. First Nations peoples have to wait until 1960.

1960: Prime Minister John Diefenbaker passes the Canadian Bill of Rights. For the first time, all Canadians are guaranteed specified rights and freedoms in law. The Bill of Rights, though, applies only to federal laws, and because it is not entrenched in the Constitution, it does not have the power to automatically overrule other federal laws.

1977: Canadian Human Rights Act is passed, prohibiting discrimination in federal employment and services.

1982: Prime Minister Pierre Trudeau leads the repatriation of the Canadian Constitution, including an enshrined Charter of Rights and Freedoms.

1993: Four years after Audrey McLaughlin becomes the first female leader of a federal political party (NDP), Canada has its first female Prime Minister (Kim Campbell), Deputy Prime Minister (Sheila Copps), MP (Jean Augustine, who is African Canadian), Secretary of State (Ethel Blondin-Andrew, who is from the Dene First Nation) and provincial premier (Catherine Callbeck, Prince Edward Island).

2002: Canadian forces are deployed to Afghanistan to serve under US command in the US-led "War on Terror." This is a controversial combat assignment for Canadian soldiers, who traditionally assume peacekeeping positions.

TAKE MORE ACTION! How To Change The World

HOME	LeveL I	LeveL II
Preface, Contents	Global Citizenship: Around the World, Across the Street	Becoming Global Citizens: A Question of Choice

The Canadian Charter of Rights and Freedoms

The Charter of Rights and Freedoms is generally acknowledged as one of the greatest social and political achievements in Canadian history. By being entrenched in the newly repatriated Canadian Constitution, its provisions supersede all federal and provincial legislation and policies. It guarantees the fundamental rights and freedoms of Canadians, and it gives the judicial system the power to declare a law or policy unconstitutional, and therefore invalid, if it violates the Charter. Some of the major articles of the Charter include:

Section 2: Everyone has the following fundamental freedoms:
   a) freedom of conscience and religion;
   b) freedom of thought, belief, opinion and expression […];
   c) freedom of peaceful assembly; and
   d) freedom of association.

Section 3: Every citizen of Canada has the right to vote […].

Section 6 (2): Every citizen of Canada [...] has the right:
   a) to move to and take up residence in any province; and
   b) to pursue the gaining of a livelihood in any province.

Section 7: Everyone has the right to life, liberty and security of the person […]

Section 9: Everyone has the right not to be arbitrarily detained or imprisoned.

Section 15 (1): Every individual is equal before and under the law and has the right to the equal protection and equal benefit of the law without discrimination and, in particular, without discrimination based on race, national or ethnic origin, color, religion, sex, age or mental or physical disability.

LeveL I > Global Citizenship: Human Rights In Canada And The United States

| **LeveL III** The Seven Steps to Social Action: Taking It to the Next Level | **LeveL IV** The How-To Guide: The Global Citizen's Toolbox | **LeveL V** Sources And Resources, End Notes |

Prime Minister Trudeau watches as Queen Elizabeth Ii signs the Constitution into law on April 17, 1982, on Parliament Hill.

TAKE MORE ACTION! How To Change The World

HOME	LEVEL I	LEVEL II
Preface, Contents	Global Citizenship: Around the World, Across the Street	Becoming Global Citizens: A Question of Choice

The Charter puts two limits on the rights and freedoms within it. First, in Section 1, it declares that the rights and freedoms are "subject only to such reasonable limits prescribed by law as can be demonstrably justified in a free and democratic society." In other words, if it can be shown that a law violating any right or freedom is justified, that law is valid. Such a case happened in Canada (Human Rights Comm.) v. Taylor (1990), when the Supreme Court of Canada ruled that restricting hate propaganda is a reasonable limit on the freedom of expression.

The second limit on the rights and freedoms in the Charter is included in Section 33: the "notwithstanding clause" that allows provincial or federal legislatures to overrule the Charter. This clause is only meant to be used in extreme circumstances, and such a law must be renewed every five years.

LeveL I > **Global Citizenship: Human Rights In Canada And The United States**

LeveL III
The Seven Steps to Social Action:
Taking It to the Next Level

LeveL IV
The How-To Guide:
The Global Citizen's Toolbox

LeveL V
Sources And Resources,
End Notes

Human Rights Events in the United States

1789: The first ten amendments to the Constitution are passed by Congress, then ratified two years later. Known as the Bill of Rights, they guarantee the rights and liberties of all citizens.

1865: Slavery is abolished in the United States by the 13th Amendment to the Constitution. A number of Southern states respond by enacting "black codes" designed to limit the civil rights of newly-freed slaves.

1920: Women are granted the right to vote by the 19th Amendment to the Constitution.

1964: The Civil Rights Act outlaws segregation in US schools and public places and establishes the Equal Employment Opportunity Commission.

2001: Following the terrorist bombings of the World Trade Center on September 11, President Bush launches the War on Terror with the invasion of Afghanistan. The USA PATRIOT ACT (the Uniting and Strengthening America by Providing Appropriate Tools Required to Intercept and Obstruct Terrorism Act) is signed into law, and is quickly criticized as a threat to civil liberties.

2003: The United States leads the invasion of Iraq, with profound humanitarian consequences for the Iraqi civilian population. Detainees at the Abu Ghraib and Guantanamo prisons are subjected to human rights violations.

TAKE MORE ACTION! How To Change The World

HOME	LEVEL I	LEVEL II
Preface, Contents	Global Citizenship: Around the World, Across the Street	Becoming Global Citizens: A Question of Choice

The United States Bill of Rights

The Bill of Rights is a defining symbol in the history of American government and law. It evolved from the debates surrounding the adoption of the Constitution in 1789, during which opponents to the draft argued that it would put too much power in the hands of the central government. In an effort to secure the rights of individual citizens, the First Congress proposed a series of amendments to the Constitution that presented the essential rights and liberties guaranteed to all Americans. In 1791, the first ten amendments were ratified by three-quarters of the state legislatures and became known as the Bill of Rights. Some of these rights included:

- 1: Freedoms: religion, speech, press, peaceable assembly, petition
- 4: Right to be secure against unreasonable searches and seizures
- 5: Rights in criminal cases
- 6: Right to a fair trial
- 8: No excessive bail imposed, nor cruel and unusual punishments inflicted
- 9: Rights retained by the People shall not be disparaged or denied by rights set out in the Constitution

Traditionally, the United States provides federal constitutional guarantees for civil and political rights (such as the rights to expression, assembly and due process), but does not support economic and social rights (such as the right to education, health care and an adequate standard of living) in either foreign or domestic policy.

Universal Human Rights and Responsibilities

Rights	Responsibilities
Article 1: All human beings are born free and equal in dignity and rights. **Article 7:** All are equal before the law and are entitled without discrimination to equal protection of the law	Standing up to discrimination and injustice; celebrating cultural and other differences
Article 3: Everyone has the right to life, liberty and security of person	Obeying your country's laws
Article 13: Everyone has the right to freedom of movement and residence within the borders of each state	Caring for, appreciating and protecting our beautiful environment, coast to coast to coast
Article 18: Everyone has the right to freedom of thought, conscience and religion **Article 19:** Everyone has the right to freedom of opinion and expression	Expressing opinions on issues that you care about freely and passionately while respecting the opinions, rights and freedoms of others
Article 20: Everyone has the right to freedom of peaceful assembly and association	Active participation in your community, especially volunteering, helping and getting to know other people
Article 21: Everyone has the right to take part in the government of his/her country, directly or through freely chosen representatives	Voting in elections; researching and discussing the issues at election time; supporting the campaign of a local candidate

TAKE MORE ACTION! How To Change The World

Home	**Level I**	**Level II**
Preface, Contents	Global Citizenship: Around the World, Across the Street	Becoming Global Citizens: A Question of Choice

de·moc·ra·cy

government by the people,

equality, opportunity, freedom

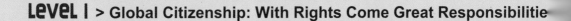

WITH RIGHTS COME GREAT RESPONSIBILITIES

Being a citizen of any society—including the global society—is an interdependent relationship. Along with the right to enjoy Earth's resources and the freedoms promised to us in the Universal Declaration of Human Rights, comes a fundamental responsibility to treat the world and its inhabitants with respect, and to actively work to create the future that we want to see. As Article 29 of the Universal Declaration states, "everyone has duties to the community in which alone the free and full development of his personality is possible."

Our democratic social system is built upon the values of equality, respect, freedom, peace and rule of law. These values come together to protect us from harm and help us fulfill our life goals. If no one contributed by fulfilling his or her social responsibilities, our society would simply not be capable of providing those cherished freedoms. If no one voted, we would have no government. If no one respected the law, no one would be safe. If no one paid taxes, we would have no schools, no hospitals, no roads, no garbage pickup or fire department, among other things.

Not having the vote does not excuse young people from their responsibilities to society. Civic participation in a democracy should happen a lot more often than once every four or five years!

"DEMOCRACY IS NOT A SPECTATOR SPORT."

—**Marian Wright Edelman**
(b. 1939)

TAKE MORE ACTION!   How To Change The World

Home	**Level I**	**Level II**
Preface, Contents	Global Citizenship: Around the World, Across the Street	Becoming Global Citizens: A Question of Choice

Today We March... Tomorrow We Vote.

"IT IS SO MUCH EASIER
SOMETIMES TO SIT DOWN AND
BE RESIGNED THAN TO RISE
UP AND BE INDIGNANT."

—Nellie McClung
(1873-1951)
Suffragist, politician

LeveL III
The Seven Steps to Social Action:
Taking It to the Next Level

LeveL IV
The How-To Guide:
The Global Citizen's Toolbox

LeveL V
Sources And Resources,
End Notes

Citizenship, in essence, is social responsibility in action. Remember, the rights that we have today were not given—they were won after years of long, difficult struggle against unfair attitudes and laws. Throughout this book, you will find issues, ideas and skills to help you create your vision of an ideal world, and start working toward it as an informed and inspired global citizen.

TIP

Voting is only one way to influence government. Other methods include signing or starting petitions, writing letters to your Member of Parliament or Member of Congress and to the editors of newspapers or magazines, attending town hall meetings held by government representatives and getting involved in the local riding association of your favorite political party. See the Plugging Into the Political System section in the How-To Guide for more ideas.

Take Action!

- Examine the full United Nations Universal Declaration of Human Rights. Which rights do you value the most? Why? Are there rights you value that are not included in the document? Discuss these rights with a partner.
- Select one of the human rights listed in the Universal Declaration and research the world's progress on making that right a reality. Answer the following questions:
    In which countries is that right being violated?
    How is it being violated, and how many people are affected?
    What efforts have been made to enforce that right?
    What organizations are working to report violations and advocate for better enforcement?
- Write a letter to your Member of Parliament or Member of Congress to express your concern about the human right you researched above. Ask what your government has done and can do to ensure better enforcement. See the Plugging Into the Political System section (page 247) for more details.
- Brainstorm all the ways you have fulfilled your responsibilities as a global citizen today, this week and this year. Come up with three more ways that you can add to your list starting today.

TAKE MORE ACTION!
How To Change The World

HOME	LeVeL I	LeVeL II
Preface, Contents	Global Citizenship: Around the World, Across the Street	Becoming Global Citizens: A Question of Choice

THE LEADER IN YOUTH

You do not have to wait to start making a positive difference in the world. You do not have to put it off until you pull up your grades or are old enough to vote, drive, graduate from high school or get a part-time job. You do not have to be perfect to change the world. You only have to be willing to change, to try to make a difference and encourage the people around you to do the same. The world needs you now, just as you are. As a young person. The time for letting adults do all the work to build the world that we are going to inherit has long passed. We are not called upon only to be the leaders of tomorrow; we must also be the leaders of today!

"THERE IS A VITALITY, A LIFE FORCE, AN ENERGY, A QUICKENING, THAT IS TRANSLATED THROUGH YOU INTO ACTION.
AND BECAUSE THERE IS ONLY ONE YOU IN ALL TIME, THIS EXPRESSION IS UNIQUE.
IF YOU BLOCK IT, IT WILL NEVER EXIST THROUGH ANY OTHER MEDIUM AND WILL BE LOST.
THE WORLD WILL NOT HAVE IT.
IT IS NOT YOUR BUSINESS TO DETERMINE HOW GOOD IT IS, NOR HOW IT COMPARES WITH OTHER EXPRESSION.
IT IS YOUR BUSINESS TO KEEP THE CHANNEL OPEN."

—Martha Graham
(1894-1991)
Dancer, choreographer, teacher

Level I > Global Citizenship: The Leader In YOUth

Level III
The Seven Steps to Social Action:
Taking It to the Next Level

Level IV
The How-To Guide:
The Global Citizen's Toolbox

Level V
Sources And Resources,
End Notes

Within this book, you will find a number of examples of youth, just like you, who one day decided that something had to be done about a problem and that they were ready to take on the challenge. You will meet Cheryl Perera, who traveled to Sri Lanka to document the rise of child labor and exploitation in that country; and Jean-Domenic Lévesque-René, who fought to ban the use of pesticides in Québec after discovering their link to his own cancer.

You will also learn about Dalal Al-Waheidi, who grew up amid war and uncertainty in the Middle East, and remains devoted to promoting a culture of peace and dialogue.

Young people have the power to be a "beacon of freedom, a beacon of justice and a beacon of light to the world," declared Hafsat Abiola, a young human rights activist from Nigeria. Committed to the empowerment of women and youth, Hafsat founded an organization called the Kudirat Initiative for Democracy (KIND), named for her mother, to continue the legacy of her parents, whose courageous struggle for freedom and justice in Nigeria led to their assassination. Speaking to her young peers at an international assembly in San Francisco, she urged them to use their "inner light to do amazingly beautiful work … If this connects with others, the internal light will become external, and you can set our whole planet aglow."

TAKE MORE ACTION! How To Change The World

| HOME
Preface, Contents | LeveL I
Global Citizenship:
Around the World, Across the Street | LeveL II
Becoming Global Citizens:
A Question of Choice |

Identifying your gifts

Everyone has something unique to contribute to the world, even though we sometimes don't have the confidence to admit it. Think about what you love to do, or what interests you. Whether it's sports, or art, or hanging out with friends, what lights you up is often where you'll find your gift, and it can inspire other people to search for their own gift. We are all gifted in some way, but not in every way—so we have to share our talents to help one another, to lift one another up. Ask yourself: What are my gifts and talents, and how can I use them to make a difference in the world?

GIFT	SERVICE
Good listener	Join a peer-counseling group; be known among your friends as the one who is always there to help them through difficult times.
Physical strength	Shovel your elderly neighbor's driveway; stick up for the students getting bullied at school (without violence, of course!).
Bilingual	Tutor other students in one of your languages; help new immigrants who speak that language to adjust and get settled.
Good writer	Start a school newspaper devoted to social issues; draft letters to Members of Parliament for a social cause.
Good speaker	Run for student council and create positive change; speak at your school or a place of worship about an issue that concerns you.
Outgoing	Reach out to welcome new students; be the spokesperson for a social action group at school; recruit new members.
Athletic	Organize a sports tournament to raise awareness and funds for charity.
Musical	Organize a charity concert or open-mike night at school, with the participation of local bands; write a song about an issue, or put together a whole CD!
Artistic	Start a community mural project that invites participants to express their thoughts about an issue in a group painting; design greeting cards to sell during the holidays as a fundraiser for charity.

When we all put our gifts and talents together, we become a team of world-changing, difference-making, global citizens. Seek out others with gifts that are different from yours, and discover how powerful you can be as a team!

✪team teaching
work cooperatively
single group of stude
team·work (tēm′wər
which individual in
ciency; coordinated
with a team
tea party a social g

TAKE MORE ACTION! How To Change The World

HOME	LEVEL I	LEVEL II
Preface, Contents	Global Citizenship: Around the World, Across the Street	Becoming Global Citizens: A Question of Choice

Craig Kielburger's Gifted Story

I was doing a CBC interview a few years ago for a television show that was taking a look at youth who had accomplished a great deal very early in their lives. One other guy was being interviewed with me. He was 19, had already completed his master's degree and PhD and was working at a pharmaceutical company. He told the host and myself on air that he was "gifted." He had discovered this fact in Grade 3, when he passed a special IQ test where you circle a number of boxes on sheets of paper. They were then run through a computer to determine how gifted or average you are.

Several times throughout the conversation, this guy explained his many accomplishments in terms of being "gifted." He must have said the word "gifted" at least ten times during the interview. Finally, the host turned to me and asked, "Are you gifted, Craig?" I looked at her, then at him, and shook my head, "no."

Later that day, I was still thinking about the interview when I went back to the Free The Children office. As I looked around at the remarkable young people who work with us, I realized that I had given the host the wrong answer. I saw our webmaster, whom we all consider to be incredibly gifted when it comes to designing websites that are visited by millions of people around the world. I saw our young writing staff, who are so talented at translating our passion and energy into words that inspire others to become involved. I saw our wonderful student volunteers who are gifted at organizing, raising funds and communicating with others. I thought of all of the young people I know who are gifted in art, or music, or sports, or who are compassionate listeners, terrific in business matters, or at making others laugh. As a matter of fact, I couldn't think of a single person I knew who wasn't gifted.

I realized that each one of us is born with special gifts or talents, but no single person is gifted in all ways. We are all pieces of a complex puzzle, a mosaic. And only by sharing our special gifts or talents can we complete it, and create a happier and more fulfilling world.

"WHAT LIES BEHIND US AND WHAT LIES BEFORE US ARE TINY MATTERS COMPARED TO WHAT LIES WITHIN US."

—Ralph Waldo Emerson
(1803-1882)
Lecturer, poet, essayist

TAKE MORE ACTION! How To Change The World

HOME Preface, Contents	LEVEL I Global Citizenship: Around the World, Across the Street	LEVEL II Becoming Global Citizens: A Question of Choice

Take Action!

- Finish these sentences: "People always say to me, you are so good at _____!" and "In my spare time, I love to _____." Next, write down as many of your gifts, skills and strengths as you can (aim for at least ten). Come up with a way that you can use each one to help make a difference in your community.

- Choose one particularly useful gift from your list and offer it to a school club or social justice organization. If they do not need the kind of help you are offering right now, offer to help in a way that uses another of your skills, or find an organization that can use your gifts to their fullest.

- Dream big now! Envision a way for you to use your most potent gift full-time, for the rest of your life. Identify a career that would allow you to use your unique gift for the betterment of the world. Describe your "dream job" in 250 to 300 words.

TAKE MORE ACTION! How To Change The World

HOME	LEVEL I	LEVEL II
Preface, Contents	Global Citizenship: Around the World, Across the Street	Becoming Global Citizens: A Question of Choice

PROFILE

Nadja Halilbegovich: A Global Citizen

When Nadja Halilbegovich was 12, her vision of the world changed forever. In 1992, the violent regional conflict in the former Yugoslavia spread to Sarajevo, the capital of Bosnia, Nadja's homeland. Sarajevo became a city plagued with danger and death, where the sounds of sirens and grenades were constant. Nadja was injured when a bombshell exploded close to her home, and her family was forced to take shelter for months at a time in the basement of their apartment building. Although physically trapped and wounded, Nadja was determined to free and nourish her mind and soul.

By recording her thoughts in a diary, Nadja maintained the courage to dream—of escaping the fighting and hatred, of the things she wanted to do, and the person she wanted to become. But the daily realities of war tested her strength. Nadja drew from the courage of her parents, and fought against words of pessimism and misery by replacing them with poems of hope and peace. Nadja used her artistic talents to inspire her fellow Bosnians to keep their hope alive. She read excerpts of her diary entries and poetry on national radio and shared her music with her choir in schools and hospitals.

Today, Nadja lives in Canada and recently published her diaries as *My Childhood Under Fire: A Sarajevo Diary*. Surviving the conflict has made her grateful, not bitter, and committed to achieving a peaceful future. She is an activist against injustice and intolerance, speaking out for the children of Bosnia who did not survive. In 2002, as a member of Free The Children's Embracing Cultures project, she traveled to more than 150 schools across North America to share her experience of the war as an example of what can happen when differences between human beings are not valued and respected, and how crucial it is to move beyond merely tolerating other cultures to actively and wholeheartedly embracing them.

Nadja's story proves that, even in the worst of conditions, hope can prevail.

LeveL III
The Seven Steps to Social Action:
Taking It to the Next Level

LeveL IV
The How-To Guide:
The Global Citizen's Toolbox

LeveL V
Sources And Resources,
End Notes

• **What attributes of a global citizen do you find in Nadja?**

• **Which of these attributes do you possess? Which would you like to develop?**

• **Is having hope essential to being a global citizen? Write out a statement that will inspire you to maintain your hope for a better world, even when you face a difficult issue.**

TAKE MORE ACTION! How To Change The World

| HOME | LEVEL I | LEVEL II |
| Preface, Contents | Global Citizenship: Around the World, Across the Street | Becoming Global Citizens: A Question of Choice |

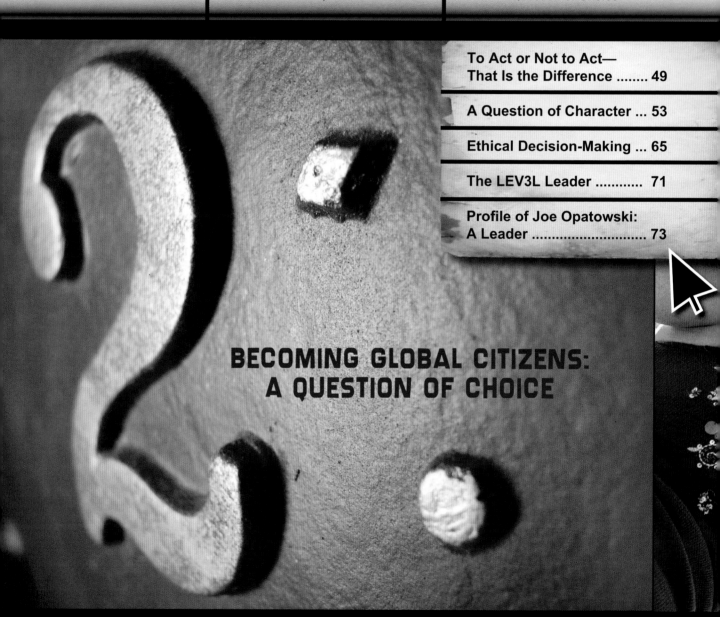

BECOMING GLOBAL CITIZENS: A QUESTION OF CHOICE

TAKE MORE ACTION! How To Change The World

HOME	LEVEL I	LEVEL II
Preface, Contents	Global Citizenship: Around the World, Across the Street	Becoming Global Citizens: A Question of Choice

TO ACT OR NOT TO ACT–THAT IS THE DIFFERENCE

In 1995, Canadian General Roméo Dallaire was leading the United Nations peacekeeping force in Rwanda, a country in East Africa. He was desperately troubled by evidence that something terrible was about to happen—something horrifying and inhuman. Following a political struggle that had erupted between the two tribal groups, extremists within the Hutu majority were planning a massive, merciless attack on the country's Tutsi minority.

Dallaire communicated with the United Nations Security Council, made up of the five most powerful countries (the United States, the United Kingdom, France, Russia and China) and ten others. He repeatedly stressed that immediate action had to be taken to avert an all-out genocide, with deaths expected in the millions. More troops were needed, and they required the authorization to take all necessary action to stop the impending devastation. But the Security Council forced Dallaire to back down. Ten Belgian soldiers from Dallaire's unit were killed, and the entire UN force was removed from Rwanda. In the following months an estimated 800,000 Tutsis were massacred—raped, beaten, chopped up with machetes and buried in mass graves.

It was exactly as Dallaire had forewarned. The world stood by and did nothing.

LeveL II > Becoming Global Citizens: To Act Or Not To Act—That Is The Difference

LeveL III
The Seven Steps to Social Action:
Taking It to the Next Level

LeveL IV
The How-To Guide:
The Global Citizen's Toolbox

LeveL V
Sources And Resources,
End Notes

**A UNICEF official called General Roméo Dallaire (below)
"the one shining beacon" during the tragedy in Rwanda.**

"FIRST THEY CAME FOR THE JEWS,
AND I DID NOT SPEAK OUT,
BECAUSE I WAS NOT A JEW.
THEN THEY CAME FOR THE COMMUNISTS,
AND I DID NOT SPEAK OUT,
BECAUSE I WAS NOT A COMMUNIST.
THEN THEY CAME FOR THE
TRADE UNIONISTS,
AND I DID NOT SPEAK OUT,
BECAUSE I WAS NOT A TRADE UNIONIST.
THEN THEY CAME FOR ME,
AND THERE WAS NO ONE LEFT,
TO SPEAK OUT FOR ME."

—Pastor Martin Niemöller
(1892-1984)
Lutheran pastor, former
president of the
World Council of Churches

TAKE MORE ACTION! How To Change The World

HOME	LEVEL I	LEVEL II
Preface, Contents	Global Citizenship: Around the World, Across the Street	Becoming Global Citizens: A Question of Choice

"MEN ARE ALL ALIKE IN THEIR PROMISES. IT IS ONLY IN THEIR DEEDS THAT THEY DIFFER."

—Molière
(1622-1673)
Playwright, philosopher

General Dallaire has since spoken out powerfully against the inaction of the United Nations, especially the members of the Security Council. The Rwandan genocide was preventable, he said, and so were many others that have happened since the famous "Never Again" promise following the Holocaust and World War II.

The sheer size of global problems like these often makes us feel powerless, useless, helpless—that's why most people do not help. It is important to understand, however, that major struggles like these often start out as small issues. Conflicts escalate into wars when individuals stand by and do nothing. The Hutu and Tutsi once lived as neighbors and as friends. Individuals in their communities failed to take a stand when violence against neighbors began; the international community failed to take a stand when the massacres occurred. We are always told that our actions have consequences, but inaction has a consequence too. When we stay silent or look the other way, we are bystanders to a problem, and we contribute to making it worse.

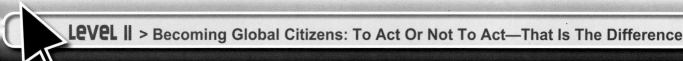

Level II > Becoming Global Citizens: To Act Or Not To Act—That Is The Difference

Level III	**Level IV**	**Level V**
The Seven Steps to Social Action: Taking It to the Next Level	The How-To Guide: The Global Citizen's Toolbox	Sources And Resources, End Notes

Jody Williams, who won the Nobel Peace Prize in 1997 for her leadership in the struggle to ban landmines, once said, "compassion without action is meaningless." In our own lives, we are challenged on a daily basis to take a stand for the rights of others.

- Have you ever seen someone being bullied at school?
- Have you ever disagreed with something that your government was doing?
- Have you ever found out that the maker of your favorite food, clothing line or other product exploits its workers or pollutes the environment?
- Have you ever seen someone wrongly accused or punished in class?
- Have you ever seen an image of a malnourished child on television?

Each of these scenarios is an opportunity to act. Instead of closing our eyes, walking away or asking, "Where's the TV remote?" we can ask ourselves, "What can I do?" In many cases, we fail to help not because we do not care, but because we do not understand what should be done, we are afraid to get involved too deeply or we don't believe that we have what it takes to do anything useful about it. We can easily forget our own guilt when we notice that no one else is helping either, but when everyone assumes that someone else will take charge, no one does anything.

TAKE MORE ACTION! How To Change The World

HOME	LEVEL I	LEVEL II
Preface, Contents	Global Citizenship: Around the World, Across the Street	Becoming Global Citizens: A Question of Choice

What if the world were made up of only bystanders? What if there were no leaders to take up the challenges that the rest of us choose to shy away from? Slavery would still be legal in the United States. No woman, Chinese person or First Nations person would have the right to vote in Canada. Black South Africans would still be cruelly oppressed under apartheid. As young people, we have far greater power than we think we do. This is our world to build in the image that we want to see. There is no more time to wait around for a superhero to drop from the sky. We have the gifts. We have the skills. We have a heartbeat. It's time to choose. Who are you waiting for?

A QUESTION OF CHARACTER

It is often said that "character" is who you are when no one is watching. It is what you do when there are no expectations of you, no incentives and no rewards. It is the choices you make when you are free to do whatever you want, without consequence or judgment. From this perspective, character is how your actions measure up to your values when it matters to no one else—how tall you stand when you alone are in the room. This aspect of character is called "integrity."

Maintaining this integrity in the face of a challenge often requires courage. When injustice, wrongdoing or need stare you in the face, do you flinch or take it on? One of the most famous images of the twentieth century is that of a lone figure standing defiantly in front of a massive advancing tank in China's Tiananmen Square in June 1989. A pro-democracy uprising had prompted the Chinese Army to clear the square, and hundreds of unarmed civilians, including children and elderly people, were shot dead by troops firing into the crowd. Standing before the tank, the young man refused to back down from the ideals he had come there to defend. As the tank moved to avoid him, he kept in front of it, challenging the troops to run him down.

Finally, the tank just stopped. For its integrity and courage, this extraordinary act will never be forgotten.

LeveL II > Becoming Global Citizens: A Question Of Character

LeveL III	**LeveL IV**	**LeveL V**
The Seven Steps to Social Action: Taking It to the Next Level	The How-To Guide: The Global Citizen's Toolbox	Sources And Resources, End Notes

"ALL THAT IT TAKES FOR EVIL TO TRIUMPH IS FOR GOOD PEOPLE TO DO NOTHING."

—Sir Edmund Burke
(1729-1797)
Statesman, lecturer, author

Courage means having the inner strength to do what is right or necessary in spite of fear.

TAKE MORE ACTION! How To Change The World

HOME	LEVEL I	LEVEL II
Preface, Contents	Global Citizenship: Around the World, Across the Street	Becoming Global Citizens: A Question of Choice

LeVeL II > Becoming Global Citizens: A Question Of Character

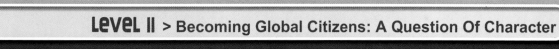

LeVeL III	LeVeL IV	LeVeL V
The Seven Steps to Social Action: Taking It to the Next Level	The How-To Guide: The Global Citizen's Toolbox	Sources And Resources, End Notes

To help us better understand the concept of character as a combination of integrity and courage, we turn to Mahatma Gandhi (1869-1948), a leader in the movement to free India from British rule, and one of the most famous advocates of non-violent action to achieve social change. His two most famous quotations reflect the two key components of character: "I live my message" and "You must be the change you wish to see in the world."

On integrity: living your message

Can you imagine what people would have thought if Martin Luther King, Jr., had gone home after his celebrated "I Have a Dream" speech and had a fistfight with a white neighbor? What if former US vice president Al Gore, a global climate change activist, showed up to work in a gas-guzzling SUV? As leaders and global citizens, when we speak up for an issue we care about, people listen. But they also watch us very closely to make sure we practice what we preach. When we violate our own message through our actions, our leadership is called into question, both by those who support us and those who oppose us. They call us hypocrites and say, "You have no integrity." They would be right. Consider how you would evaluate the character of someone who:

- Runs a peer group about substance abuse, but gets drunk every weekend
- Warns her children never to smoke, but goes through a pack of cigarettes a day
- Demonstrates at peace rallies, but settles a heated argument after school with a fistfight
- Directs a campaign against stereotypes and discrimination, but tells blonde jokes
- Complains about global warming, but drives to school every day instead of biking or taking public transit or the school bus

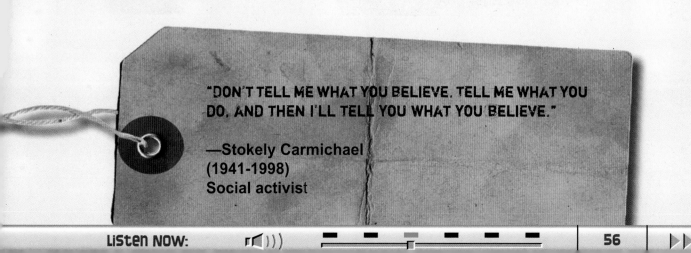

"DON'T TELL ME WHAT YOU BELIEVE. TELL ME WHAT YOU DO, AND THEN I'LL TELL YOU WHAT YOU BELIEVE."

—Stokely Carmichael
(1941-1998)
Social activist

TAKE MORE ACTION! How To Change The World

HOME	LEVEL I	LEVEL II
Preface, Contents	Global Citizenship: Around the World, Across the Street	Becoming Global Citizens: A Question of Choice

Even the greatest leaders have found themselves compromising their integrity at times; they are human and imperfect, just as we are. Leadership means striving to bring your actions into line with your values, and challenging others to do the same, in order to improve not only your society, but also yourselves.

For example, Gandhi's struggle for Indian independence involved not only opposition to British colonialism, but also to the Indian caste system (a deep-rooted and discriminatory social hierarchy). He challenged Indians to recognize that, just as the British could no longer oppress them, they could no longer oppress their own. For Gandhi, and those who joined him, the simultaneous development of the moral person and the moral society was key.

It may be difficult to change your own attitudes and habits once you take on a social issue. If you are against war and violence, can you stop playing violent video games or watching violent movies? If you are against unfair trade for farmers in Africa, can you stop eating your favorite chocolate bar, or drinking your favorite latte? The good news is that when you make a sacrifice that people know is very hard for you, they are more likely to be inspired to follow your example and make similar sacrifices in their own lives.

When, as leaders, we are conscious of our own behavior, others are able to understand our values and aspire to our example. To maximize your effectiveness and your impact as a leader, it is crucial that you not only believe in and deliver your message. You must also, truly, live your message.

LEVEL II > Becoming Global Citizens: A Question Of Character

LEVEL III	**LEVEL IV**	**LEVEL V**
The Seven Steps to Social Action: Taking It to the Next Level	The How-To Guide: The Global Citizen's Toolbox	Sources And Resources, End Notes

TAKE MORE ACTION! How To Change The World

Home	**Level I**	**Level II**
Preface, Contents	Global Citizenship:	Becoming Global Citizens:
	Around the World, Across the Street	A Question of Choice

Level II > Becoming Global Citizens: A Question Of Character

Level III
The Seven Steps to Social Action:
Taking It to the Next Level

Level IV
The How-To Guide:
The Global Citizen's Toolbox

Level V
Sources And Resources,
End Notes

On courage: being the change

Have you ever looked back at a situation and thought, "I really should have had the courage to do something about that"? The character of a global citizen is determined in part by making choices that require courage—to lead by example and to stand up for a better world when no one else will.

As the leader of the pro-democracy movement in Burma (now called Myanmar) since the brutal repression of a 1988 uprising, Aung San Suu Kyi was placed under house arrest for six years, unable to see her family, and restricted in her freedom to travel and speak even after her release. Yet she continued her struggle and has drawn international attention to the plight of her nation.

For her determined efforts as an activist in the Green Belt movement in Kenya, an environmentalist network that planted over 30 million trees and provided work to tens of thousands of women, Wangari Maathai received death threats, and was beaten and repeatedly arrested. Labeled as an elitist, a man-hater, and a subversive, she was also abandoned by her husband, who complained that she was "too educated, too strong, too successful, too stubborn and too hard to control." Maathai knew that as an outspoken woman, she would be an easy target for persecution, but she refused to compromise. "I knew in my mind I was doing the right thing," she says. "I knew that the people who were going against me were not going against me for a good purpose. I knew that they were trying to justify their corruption and misgovernance."

After over two decades of struggle, Maathai was vindicated—in 2005, she became the first African woman to be awarded the Nobel Peace Prize.

"THE WORLD BREAKS EVERYONE AND AFTERWARD MANY ARE STRONG AT THE BROKEN PLACES."

—Ernest Hemingway
(1899-1961)
Author

TAKE MORE ACTION! How To Change The World

| **Home** Preface, Contents | **Level I** Global Citizenship: Around the World, Across the Street | **Level II** Becoming Global Citizens: A Question of Choice |

Creating change is not easy. The "status quo," or the existing state of affairs, is deeply ingrained in social attitudes and practices. It is also perpetuated because it serves the interests of powerful people. Many sacrifices have been made before our time to create the amazing society in which we live. The least we can do to honor those who have struggled in the past is to continue to work toward an even better world. So have the courage to not simply talk about the change you wish to see in the world, but also to be the change.

We choose our own battles, and often simply breaking with accepted social norms requires significant doses of courage, especially around others who do not understand, and who may mock, disrespect or exclude us. Courage at the high school level could mean putting your "cool" factor on the line by befriending a bullied student, speaking out against an offensive joke or joining a social action group.

Standing up for what you value is not an easy task, but it can be a very rewarding one. There is an old saying that if you can find a path with no obstacles, it probably doesn't lead anywhere. Think about the heroes you admire, throughout history, in the movies and in real life. All of them had the courage to take a stand. We tend to look at the negative consequences of standing out from the crowd, but we should focus instead on another crucial point: Courage is something that people respect, and it can inspire them to stand up alongside you.

In the end, your character is on display with every action you take, whether people are watching or not. You have to look at yourself in the mirror at the end of every day and be proud of who you are and the choices you make. What will make you proud today?

"COURAGE CAN'T SEE AROUND CORNERS, BUT GOES AROUND THEM ANYWAY."

—**Mignon McLaughlin**
(1913-1983)
Author, humorist

LEVEL II > Becoming Global Citizens: A Question Of Character

LEVEL III	**LEVEL IV**	**LEVEL V**
The Seven Steps to Social Action: Taking It to the Next Level	The How-To Guide: The Global Citizen's Toolbox	Sources And Resources, End Notes

Sharing the Spotlight

You've probably heard of most of these stars, but did you know that they have been working hard to turn the spotlight onto important social issues? More and more, world celebrities are using their fame to spread positive messages and rally people to action.

Take a look at what they have been up to, behind and in front of the scenes:

TAKE MORE ACTION! How To Change The World

| HOME
Preface, Contents | LEVEL I
Global Citizenship:
Around the World, Across the Street | LEVEL II
Becoming Global Citizens:
A Question of Choice |

Bono

Lead singer of the band U2, Bono is a vocal social activist who has rallied numerous actors and artists to his causes. As spokesman for the Jubilee 2000 Debt Relief Campaign, now called Drop the Debt, he advocates for a major initiative that would wipe out the $90 billion debt owed by the world's poorest nations to the richest nations and promote trade reform and a commitment from pharmaceutical companies to provide free HIV drugs to African countries.

Oprah Winfrey

Oprah Winfrey has founded numerous charities, including Oprah's Angel Network, a philanthropic organization that, among many projects, grants scholarships for minority students, builds homes for Habitat for Humanity and has constructed 60 schools in 13 countries with Free The Children. In January 2007, she opened the Oprah Winfrey Leadership Academy for Girls, an education program in South Africa.

Angelina Jolie

Serving as the United Nations High Commissioner for Refugees' Goodwill Ambassador, actress Angelina Jolie traveled to refugee camps in more than 20 countries, including Pakistan, Kosovo, Sudan and Chad. She visited refugees and internally displaced persons and helped raise awareness of and support for their rights. Beyond her UNHCR commitments, she has become an outspoken advocate for the protection of refugee rights, addressing global political and economic leaders on the issue.

Mira Nair

Indian director Mira Nair won an Academy Award nomination for her film *Salaam Bombay!*, which profiles the lives of street children in Mumbai (Bombay). Her many thought-provoking films have shed light on the struggles of marginalized groups, addressing such issues as the plight of sex workers in Mumbai, racial tensions between the African-American and Indian-American communities in the American South and the experience of Cuban refugees in the United States.

Many more public figures, such as Richard Gere, K'naan, Dikembe Mutombo, Vince Carter and Michael Moore, are using their fame to draw attention to urgent social issues. Research celebrities whom you admire for their talent, and find out how they are using it to make a difference!

LeveL III
The Seven Steps to Social Action:
Taking It to the Next Level

LeveL IV
The How-To Guide:
The Global Citizen's Toolbox

LeveL V
Sources And Resources,
End Notes

Take Action!

1. Think of one prominent world leader or a leader in your community and one person in your own life whose character you admire. What actions have they taken that reveal their character? Which of their character traits would you most like to develop yourself?

2. Describe a time when you demonstrated global character (as in making a difference in the world), either when no one was watching or when everyone was watching. How did you feel making that choice? How do you feel now, looking back?

3. Brainstorm ways you can improve your integrity—in what ways do you not always live your values or your message? Brainstorm courageous ways of making a difference at school or in your community— what would be the consequences of putting yourself on the line? What would be the consequences of *not* acting?

Commit to act on one item from each list and go for it.

TAKE MORE ACTION! How To Change The World

HOME	LEVEL I	LEVEL II
Preface, Contents	Global Citizenship: Around the World, Across the Street	Becoming Global Citizens: A Question of Choice

ETHICAL DECISION-MAKING

Doing the right thing is not always easy. Right and wrong are not always clear-cut, and most situations do not allow us the time to sit down and debate the fine line. While making an ethical decision is not always a simple matter, it is always a crucial one, because what we say and do determines not only the shape of our own lives, but also the lives of others.

"Ethical," "moral," and "principled" are all various ways of saying "according to your values." They provide us with a general code of conduct that we can follow to keep our actions true to our values. But we cannot always just plug our values into a specific situation and get a printout of the right answer. This section will offer some helpful guidelines and tools that you can use to chart your way through the sea of ethical dilemmas that life throws us.

The CARE model of global citizenship

Although perceptions of right and wrong sometimes differ among people, generations, cultures, and ways of life, a number of values do seem to resonate across social divisions and national borders. The CARE Model of Global Citizenship represents a set of core values that unite them all, despite the many differences that exist among them. They are the values at the core of global citizenship, and they have very little to do with the diverse groups to which we belong, and everything to do with our common humanity.

Using the CARE model as a guide to your actions, you can enhance your effectiveness as an active participant in the world. As you continue to develop your skills as a leader and a global citizen, revisit this model occasionally to make sure that the actions you take reflect your values. This list is by no means exhaustive, and we encourage you to add or subtract from it as you think about your own values and the things that matter most to you.

LeveL II > Becoming Global Citizens: Ethical Decision Making

LeveL III	LeveL IV	LeveL V
The Seven Steps to Social Action: Taking It to the Next Level	The How-To Guide: The Global Citizen's Toolbox	Sources And Resources, End Notes

Compassion

Have empathy for everyone involved: Try to see a situation from all perspectives and to truly understand and take into account the feelings, needs, and motives of others in making your decisions, even when you do not agree with them personally. Show caring by being attentive to people's various needs, especially emotional needs, and by treating everyone with kindness, concern, and generosity, regardless of outcomes.

Action

Take initiative to act, showing that you are ready to do what it takes to reach a solution. Have courage and the strength of mind to control fear and act firmly in the face of difficulties, to do the right thing even when it may be unpopular, and to resist peer pressure to fall in line with accepted but questionable practices. Display perseverance in reaching for your goals Never give up or lose focus on what you have set out to do. Be a shameless optimist, seeing beauty, hope, and opportunity in any given situation. Dream big and unapologetically.

Responsibility

Be trustworthy and reliable; be accountable for all your actions and only make commitments that you can and will honor. Above all, be honest—honesty breaks down barriers and allows for finding pure, true, sustainable solutions. Display your integrity. Be sincere and back it up by living your message. Help. When in doubt, seek opportunities that allow you to contribute and give of yourself to someone in need.

Equality

Strive for fairness by being sensitive to the needs of each individual, seeking solutions that leave everyone better off. Show respect so that others can see it. Treat all people with honor, courtesy, dignity, civility, and esteem. Do not just accept personal and cultural differences—celebrate them. Listen to what others have to say, and be open to the fact that you can learn from them. Always be prepared to agree to disagree in order to salvage a relationship. You will always be better off when you consider your personal relationships to be more important than being right.

TAKE MORE ACTION! How To Change The World

HOME	LeveL I	LeveL II
Preface, Contents	Global Citizenship: Around the World, Across the Street	Becoming Global Citizens: A Question of Choice

Putting CARE into action

Sometimes we focus so much on upholding one ethical principle that we end up compromising another principle. For example, we might persevere so much in an effort to get a job done that we fail to be compassionate with our teammates, or we might try to be fair to everyone in a group, but end up not meeting anyone's needs. In situations that pit your values against each other, it's easy to get confused and not know what to do.

Remember, character is putting your values into action as best as you can. All that can be asked is that you do your best and that you be honest. If you still find yourself totally stumped by an ethical dilemma, try one (or more) of the following four Take Action Ethics Tests. They can help clarify a situation and lead you toward an answer that leaves your conscience clear and strengthens your character.

Take Action Ethics Tests
- **Golden Rule**: Are you treating others as you would want to be treated?
- **Public Scrutiny**: Would you be comfortable if your reasoning and final decision were to be publicized on the front page of your local newspaper?
- **Kid-on-Your-Shoulder**: Would you be comfortable if your younger brother or sister were observing you?
- **Voice of Reason**: Would the most ethical person you know applaud your decision?

When you are working as part of a team, it is important to treat each person with respect, no matter how rushed you might be.

TAKE MORE ACTION! How To Change The World

HOME	LEVEL I	LEVEL II
Preface, Contents	Global Citizenship: Around the World, Across the Street	Becoming Global Citizens: A Question of Choice

Take Action!

Using the **CARE** Model, the Take Action Ethics Tests, and your own judgment, consider how you would deal with the following scenarios. Share your reasoning and final decision with a partner and discuss them. How did your ethical decision-making processes differ? How did the difference affect the outcome? Now try to develop a compromise approach with your partner, and join with another pair to share and discuss the different processes and outcomes.

1. You are among new friends at a party, and the person you have a crush on asks you if you want to go outside together to smoke a joint. You know that this person has had serious problems with drugs in the past, and has been proudly clean for several months. If you try to help discourage this person from using them now, you will lose your chance to be alone with him or her and may possibly cause him or her to lose interest. What do you do?

2. You and your friend are both interested in the same internship, and you decide to both apply for it. After seeing your friend's résumé, you realize that your friend has a lot more experience than you, so you make up a few things on your own résumé to ensure that you qualify as well. As a result, you are selected for the internship and your friend is not. Do you admit that you were dishonest, even if this means that you will lose your work opportunity and perhaps also your friend?

3. A close friend of yours confesses to you that he is contemplating suicide, and then swears you to secrecy. You agree because you want him to know that he can trust you. If you tell someone, you may lose his trust, and possibly make him feel more alone. If you keep the secret, your friend's life may be in danger. What do you do?

4. At the start of your summer holidays, you are attending a protest at a factory that supplies the army with weapons that are believed to have horrific, long-term effects on large numbers of innocent people. The police have warned that anyone who trespasses on factory property will receive an automatic two-month jail sentence. Several people, including one of your friends, begin to climb the gate, but the others say they do not want to jeopardize their summer break, or to have criminal records that may prevent them from getting a job in the future. Do you climb or stay?

5. You are responsible for an anti-terrorism task force that will protect the civilians of your country from harm. You have apprehended a known terrorist and have knowledge that he has been involved in planning an attack that is set to occur within days. He refuses to reveal the plans to you. Someone on the force suggests that torturing him will force him to speak. Do you agree and violate the prisoner's human rights because this may save the lives of other people?

"EXPERIENCE IS NOT WHAT HAPPENS TO A
MAN. IT'S WHAT A MAN DOES WITH WHAT
HAPPENS TO HIM."

—Aldous Huxley
(1894-1963)
Author

TAKE MORE ACTION! How To Change The World

HOME	LeveL I	LeveL II
Preface, Contents	Global Citizenship: Around the World, Across the Street	Becoming Global Citizens: A Question of Choice

THE LEV3L LEADER

Among the young people who work with Free The Children and Me to We, there is a concept called Level 3, or "LEV3L." It means seeing every choice and every action as a chance to change the world, and realizing that change has to begin with each one of us.

Level 3, we believe, is not merely something we do; it is a way of life. Level 3 is the courage to dream, the passion to believe, and the intensity to act. It is the energy that allows us to make the ordinary extraordinary, to change our lives, the lives of others, and the world around us. It means striving to live our values every single day as socially conscious and responsible global citizens.

Sound intimidating? Sure it is, and that is why there are also Levels 1 and 2. Level 1 is first becoming socially involved in little ways. This can mean smiling at a student whom others exclude or reject, recycling your plastic water bottle or refraining from telling and laughing at racist jokes. Level 2 is taking your commitment to a higher level in your thoughts, actions, and words. It may include speaking to that student whom others exclude, refilling your plastic bottle with drinking water for a month or objecting when you hear a racist joke.

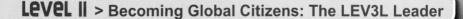

LeveL III	**LeveL IV**	**LeveL V**
The Seven Steps to Social Action: Taking It to the Next Level	The How-To Guide: The Global Citizen's Toolbox	Sources And Resources, End Notes

However, when you are ready and committed and psyched—we mean *really* ready, *really* committed, and *really* psyched—you can "punch it up a click" to Level 3.

Level 3 means doing things that most people would never dream of doing, and that some people would even make fun of you for—but remembering that everything you do is part of something bigger, and that there is no time off from your values or how you live your life. Level 3 may include inviting that student whom others exclude on a social outing with you and your friends, organizing a drive in the cafeteria for reusable bottles or setting up a team to organize a multicultural event in your school.

No matter what level you are operating on (and it will change from day to day, moment to moment, depending on how much sleep you've had or if you have a test next period), you are changing the world. Our challenge to you, though, is to be more at Level 3 more of the time, as much as you can!

TAKE MORE ACTION! How To Change The World

HOME	LEVEL I	LEVEL II
Preface, Contents	Global Citizenship: Around the World, Across the Street	Becoming Global Citizens: A Question of Choice

PROFILE

Joe Opatowski: A Leader

Growing up, Joe Opatowski was a class clown who scored high marks and was involved in volunteer work, but his heart was not always in it. The fighting and turmoil in his family seemed to drown out everything else in his life. On the outside, Joe pretended things were fine, but deep down he was beginning to crumble, and his life took a self-destructive turn.

When Joe was 15, he attended a summer camp hosted by Free The Children—initially, he signed on only because he was promised by a friend there would be "tons of girls." But while there, he began to experience a shift in attitude, and began to warm up to the idea of helping others.

Through Free The Children, Joe was given the opportunity to volunteer in Riverton, Jamaica, a town built inside a garbage dump. There, he met children wearing rags and suffering from malnutrition—a level of poverty far beyond what he had ever seen back home. Joe had nothing to offer them but his time and energy, but he gave it purely, and from the heart.

Giving them piggyback rides and watching their faces light up, he realized how intimately his own happiness could be connected to theirs. He discovered that helping people find a life worth living brought meaning to his own life.

When he returned home and became more involved in Free The Children, Joe realized that he had some serious things to figure out. He knew that he could not continue to live self-destructively if he hoped to be a mentor and empower young people to change the world.

With his extraordinary charisma and positive outlook, unique ideas and ability to make everyone he met believe in themselves, Joe became a powerful motivational speaker, inspiring young people to make a difference in the lives of others. After graduating from high school, he began touring North America, eventually speaking to more than 150,000 young people about issues such as youth violence, poverty, and compassion.

On October 29, 2004, Joe was making the long drive home from a series of speaking engagements in New York State. What happened next isn't entirely certain, but somewhere along that drive home his car was hit by an oncoming vehicle. In a sudden fleeting moment, the world lost a truly special individual far too soon.

Hundreds of e-mails and letters poured in from all over the world. Joe's enthusiasm and loving nature had touched many people's lives, and the memorial that followed was less a mournful farewell than a celebration of his accomplishments and the overwhelmingly positive philosophy by which he lived.

LeVeL III
The Seven Steps to Social Action:
Taking It to the Next Level

LeVeL IV
The How-To Guide:
The Global Citizen's Toolbox

LeVeL V
Sources And Resources,
End Notes

- What choices—good and bad—did Joe make on his path toward becoming a leader? How do you evaluate Joe's character? How does he display integrity and courage?

- Describe a time when you acted at Level 3 (it could be in sports, in school, at home or with friends). How did it feel? What were the consequences, both good and bad, of putting yourself on the line? Was it worth it?

- In your life, who do you look up to for their courage and integrity? What qualities do they display that make you admire their character?

TAKE MORE ACTION!　How To Change The World

HOME	LEVEL I	LEVEL II
Preface, Contents	Global Citizenship: Around the World, Across the Street	Becoming Global Citizens: A Question of Choice

THE SEVEN STEPS TO SOCIAL ACTION
TAKING IT TO THE NEXT LEVEL

TAKE MORE ACTION! How To Change The World

HOME	LEVEL I	LEVEL II
Preface, Contents	Global Citizenship: Around the World, Across the Street	Becoming Global Citizens: A Question of Choice

Turning Passion Into Action

In April 2001, over 35,000 people poured into the streets of Québec City to voice their views at the opening of a new round of global trade negotiations. Among them were students, teachers, clergy, social workers, small business owners, farm workers, feminists, environmentalists, and others from every kind of background. They stood together in solidarity for fair labor standards, environmental protection, and basic human rights.

Young people made up nearly one-third of the crowd. They sang, chanted, blew whistles, shook tambourines, and danced to the beat of drums. There were jugglers among them, stilt walkers, mimes, and puppeteers. Their spirit was as strong as their statement, and their commitment to the issue was clear. They were protesting the inequalities of globalization and standing up for human rights everywhere.

Young people are at the forefront of a number of campaigns in which international and domestic problems, and their solutions, overlap.

Level III
The Seven Steps to Social Action:
Taking It to the Next Level

Level IV
The How-To Guide:
The Global Citizen's Toolbox

Level V
Sources And Resources,
End Notes

Are these issues that you care about too? The good news is that you don't have to go to a protest somewhere far away or spend a day on stilts to change the world. As a global citizen, you can start taking action in your classroom, your community, and even right in your home. It all begins with a dream and a daily effort, as Noam Chomsky, a famous activist, writer and linguist from the Massachusetts Institute of Technology (MIT) wrote:

"There are no magic answers, no miraculous methods to overcome the problems we face, just the familiar ones: honest search for understanding, education, organization, action."

The path to change he describes is simple and direct. It reveals the steps followed by social activists everywhere who know that a better world will come when we work hard to create it. Global citizens around the world use the steps outlined in this section to break down complex, overwhelming issues with small, manageable actions that turn their passion into concrete social change. If you want to make a difference, these steps will show you how to:

1. *Find your passion*
2. *Research the reality*
3. *Build your dream team*
4. *Meet around the round table*
5. *Set a mission*
6. *Take action!*
7. *Bring in the fun!*

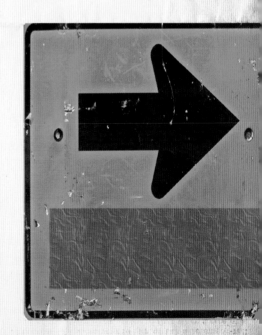

Take Action!: A Guide to Active Citizenship outlined the Seven Steps to Social Involvement. Hopefully, they led you to discover new skills and success. Now it's time to take it to the next level, to make your vision for a better world speak louder. Whether you are experienced as an active global citizen, or just beginning, you can use the Seven Steps to help you focus your efforts, overcome obstacles and put creative solutions into action.

No matter what your issue or level of commitment, if you have 20 minutes or 20 years, from getting healthier options at your cafeteria to fighting AIDS in Africa, you can follow these Seven Steps to reach your goals!

TAKE MORE ACTION! How To Change The World

Home	**Level I**	**Level II**
Preface, Contents	Global Citizenship: Around the World, Across the Street	Becoming Global Citizens: A Question of Choice

STEP ONE: FIND YOUR PASSION

A great fire begins with a small spark. Every social movement begins the same way, when one person's passion lights up a crowd.

Passion is about finding your purpose, what inspires and awakens something inside you. Every person has an issue that is close to the heart—something that makes him or her angry, frustrated or sad: a pet peeve or a news story that hurts to watch.

Sometimes we discover it suddenly, like Craig Kielburger did when he was flipping through the newspaper for the comics one morning and instead read a headline that changed his life: "Battled Child Labor, Boy 12, Murdered." Being 12 years old himself at the time, Craig felt an instant connection to the story of this boy in Pakistan, Iqbal Masih. He had never heard about the issue of child labor before that day, but he knew he had to do something to help.

What is it that moves *you*? Think about your own life and the problems that you see.

Have you ever:

- Experienced or witnessed discrimination because of race, gender, age, height, weight, clothes, appearance or any other reason?
- Noticed garbage littering the parks that you spend time in?
- Felt unsafe walking home alone at night?
- Watched a nearby wooded area disappear because of a new building development or housing project?
- Read an article or seen a television program that made you say, "That's not right!" or "Why do people let that happen?"

Many people around the world face the same struggles. These social issues, such as racism, poverty, pollution, and conflict, are global, even though they may vary in severity in different regions. It is important to understand the global reach of these problems, but our actions can target their local occurrences. When you think globally and act locally, you work at the level of real solutions, where you can see an immediate and definite impact.

TAKE MORE ACTION! How To Change The World

| **HOME** | **LEVEL I** | **LEVEL II** |
| Preface, Contents | Global Citizenship: Around the World, Across the Street | Becoming Global Citizens: A Question of Choice |

For example:

If you want to end world poverty, you might start by gathering a group of friends to distribute food and health items to the homeless in your city, or order some extra food when dining out and take it "to go" to give to someone who asks you for change on the street, or organize a clothing drive for people in need in your community.

If you want to promote fair labor standards, you can become involved in the No Sweat Campaign. This campaign ensures that clothes that bear your school's logo are not made through exploitative practices. You can cut out the labels from the clothes that you buy and include them in letters to the companies who make them. You can tell the companies that you will not buy any more clothing from them until you see a copy of their codes of conduct and are satisfied that their labor standards are acceptable.

If you are concerned about the issues of war and intolerance, you can organize a workshop on the human realities of a recent war and present it to your school, or make friends with a student of a different culture from yours.

If you are concerned about climate change, you can start a bike co-op in your community. You and your friends fix up old bikes and sell them cheaply to promote sustainable transportation. You can write a letter to encourage your local authorities to establish or improve bike lanes or the public transit system, and urge your government to make a clear commitment to cut greenhouse gas emissions.

It doesn't matter how you start making a difference; just as these issues are global, they are all interconnected. For example, the poverty of many communities around the world is often a result of unfair global trade policies, consumer demand for cheap food and products, and lower taxes (which mean less money for schools, hospitals, and social programs to help those in need). And the inequalities and injustices produced by these factors are often at the root of violence and war.

It is important to understand that social problems exist because of one another; they are interconnected and inseparable. But working for change does not mean tackling all of these problems at once. It means, rather, that by working on one problem, you are really working on all of them! At the core, what counts is that you are involved and that you care. Choose an issue that is meaningful to you. This is the key to unlocking your passion and to starting a project that you are committed to seeing through.

LEVEL III
The Seven Steps to Social Action:
Taking It to the Next Level

LEVEL IV
The How-To Guide:
The Global Citizen's Toolbox

LEVEL V
Sources And Resources,
End Notes

If you saw this photograph in a newspaper, what would you think?
Describe the circumstances of this image.

TAKE MORE ACTION! How To Change The World

HOME	LEVEL I	LEVEL II
Preface, Contents	Global Citizenship: Around the World, Across the Street	Becoming Global Citizens: A Question of Choice

GLOBAL ISSUES AT A GLANCE

Unsure of what issue to choose? This section will give you a glimpse of some of the most challenging problems our world faces today. What you discover here may inspire you to expand your knowledge by doing your own research into one of these social problems, or finding another issue that really moves you. Check out the Sources and Resources in Part 5 for organizations that are working on these issues. You can contact them for more information and for ideas on how to get involved.

HIV/AIDS

HIV (human immunodeficiency virus) is a contagious virus that gradually breaks down the immune system, weakening the body's ability to fight infection and disease. The final stage of HIV is called AIDS (acquired immune deficiency syndrome). Many people with AIDS die from various illnesses that their immune systems are unable to combat. HIV/AIDS cannot be spread through casual contact. It may be transmitted through the exchange of bodily fluids in sexual contact, or by sharing infected needles and syringes. A mother can also pass the virus on to her child during pregnancy, childbirth or breast-feeding.

AIDS is a pandemic, a disease causing great concern in every region of the world. At the end of 2006, 39.5 million people were living with HIV—the highest number of people on record. Nearly two-thirds of cases were concentrated in Sub-Saharan Africa, and 59 percent of these were women. Although antiretroviral drugs (ARVs) are an effective treatment, the cost of these drugs remains high for many low and middle income countries.

HIV/AIDS is bound up in global inequalities. Poverty, gender injustice, social exclusion, and a lack of access to information and education increase the vulnerability of certain populations to infection, and reduce their opportunities for treatment. In Canada, Aboriginal peoples are disproportionately affected by the virus, and in the United States, racial and ethnic minority groups are over-represented among the country's HIV-positive. On a global scale, young people (15-24 years of age) represented 40 percent of new HIV infections among adults 15 years and older in 2006.

Because HIV/AIDS is closely related to aspects of sexuality that are considered taboo in many cultures and religions, people continue to react to it with fear, resentment or denial. Awareness and prevention initiatives must aim not only to reduce transmission, but also to reduce stigma and discrimination against people living with HIV/AIDS.

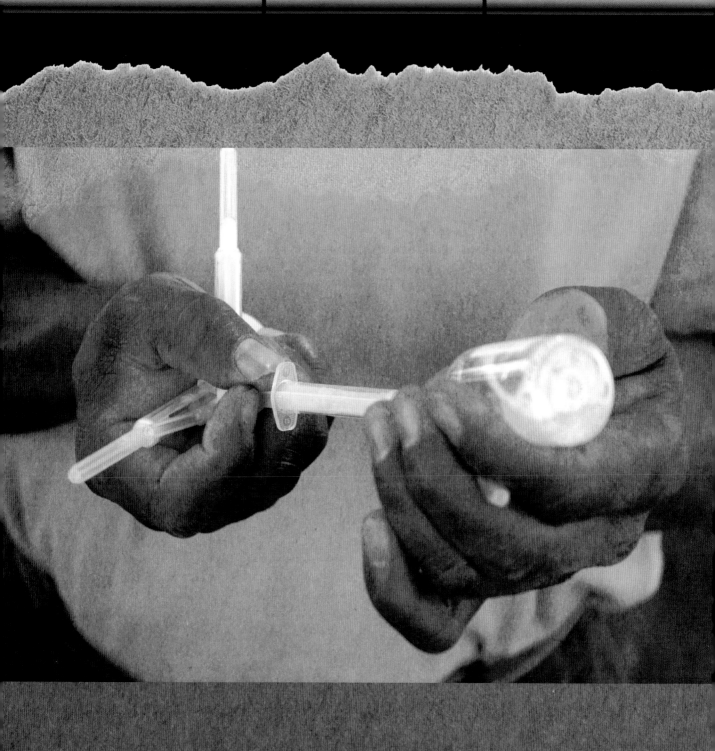

TAKE MORE ACTION! How To Change The World

HOME	LEVEL I	LEVEL II
Preface, Contents	Global Citizenship: Around the World, Across the Street	Becoming Global Citizens: A Question of Choice

Gender inequality

In virtually every country in the world, women face social, legal, political, and economic discrimination simply because they are women. Laws, customary practices, and traditions restrict women's access to employment, education and health care, and their participation in public life. Although women produce half of the world's food, they earn only 10 percent of the world's income and own less than one percent of the world's property. UNESCO estimates that of the 781 million illiterate adults in the world, two-thirds are women. This inequality puts women at a greater risk of poverty—consequently, the vast majority of the world's poor are women.

In many countries, abuses against girls and women are systematic and widely tolerated. According to Amnesty International, one in three of the world's women will be beaten, coerced into sex or otherwise abused in her lifetime. Discrimination against the girl child is equally widespread, with 60 million girls missing from the world because they were aborted, or killed as infants simply because they were girls.

Advocates for women's human rights have long been working to confront gender inequality around the world. Their efforts have secured the adoption of the Convention on the Elimination of All Forms of Discrimination against Women (CEDAW) in 1979, the UN Beijing Platform for Action in 1995, and UN Security Council Resolution 1325 on Women, Peace and Security in 2000, which recognized that women not only as victims of war but also as agents of peace.

Governments have repeatedly pledged to uphold women's rights as a key to ending poverty and promoting sustainable development. But because women are under-represented where economic and political decisions are made, these verbal commitments have not yet translated into tangible resources to meet the goal of gender equality.

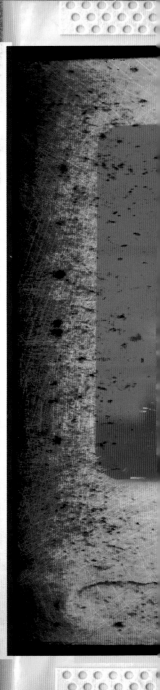

TAKE MORE ACTION! How To Change The World

HOME	LEVEL I	LEVEL II
Preface, Contents	Global Citizenship: Around the World, Across the Street	Becoming Global Citizens: A Question of Choice

Climate change

The ecosystems of our planet Earth possess a natural balance in which the elements of air, water, land, and plant and animal habitats co-exist and support one another. However, these systems are not invincible. Human activity and patterns of energy consumption are disrupting the stability of the planet as a whole. Industries, cars, and households contribute to carbon emissions through the burning of coal, oil, and natural gas.

These emissions thicken the blanket of greenhouse gases around the earth, and result in what is known as the "greenhouse effect," an increase in global temperatures. Climate monitoring indicates that the average global temperature has increased more in the last century than over the past 1,000 years.

The effects of climate change could include rising sea levels (as the ocean absorbs more than 80 percent of the climate's heat), more frequent and intense storms, changes in wind patterns and precipitation, the extinction of species, worsening droughts and crop failures, and a wider reach of diseases, such as malaria.

LeveL III
The Seven Steps to Social Action:
Taking It to the Next Level

LeveL IV
The How-To Guide:
The Global Citizen's Toolbox

LeveL V
Sources And Resources,
End Notes

Concern over global warming led to the Kyoto Protocol in 1997, which called for reductions in carbon dioxide emissions. Though heralded by its proponents as a landmark agreement to mitigate climate change, the protocol was criticized by its opponents as being inequitable and costly to implement. The United States, the world's largest producer of greenhouse gases, has rejected the protocol altogether.

Climate change is intimately connected with global inequalities and complex issues such as economic development, population growth, and poverty. While industrialized countries in North America and Western Europe, as well as Japan, are disproportionately responsible for the carbon emissions that cause global warming, the world's poorer nations bear the brunt of the disastrous consequences, as they have few resources to cope in the face of droughts, disease, food and water scarcities, storms, and mass migrations. Climate change will thus deepen global economic and social inequalities between rich and poor nations, and halt progress toward the Millennium Development Goals.

TAKE MORE ACTION! How To Change The World

HOME	LEVEL I	LEVEL II
Preface, Contents	Global Citizenship: Around the World, Across the Street	Becoming Global Citizens: A Question of Choice

| **Level III**
The Seven Steps to Social Action:
Taking It to the Next Level | **Level IV**
The How-To Guide:
The Global Citizen's Toolbox | **Level V**
Sources And Resources,
End Notes |

Racism and Minority Rights

Racism is a set of unjustified or oversimplified beliefs about a group of people based on their racial or ethnic origin, often as perceived through physical attributes (such as skin color). Attitudes of fear, hate or resentment toward the group in question are frequently part of a racist ideology. Along with the differentiation comes the assumption that one group is superior to, or should hold power over, another. When racist attitudes are expressed through actions, this is called "discrimination."

Throughout history, racism has resulted in slavery, anti-immigration legislation, civil rights violations (i.e., denial of access to voting, education or employment), apartheid and genocide. Around the globe, refugees, migrants, and internally displaced persons are the victims of racial discrimination and violence—with racism as both the cause and the result of forced displacement. In three-quarters of the major armed conflicts around the world in 2006, specific minority groups were key targets.

In almost every region of the world, there is a growing suspicion of "otherness," or difference. Minorities are not only singled out for exclusion, but are also labelled as threats to society. Over the past decade, industrialized nations have introduced a series of restrictive policies targeting asylum seekers, refugees, and migrants. Members of minority groups in these countries often face harassment, arbitrary detention, and abusive treatment by the justice system.

Although it is inequality, and not diversity itself, that gives rise to tension and conflict, racism is often used as a tool in the struggle for political power. Securing a lasting peace means working to accommodate differences, through negotiation, dialogue, and the equal participation of all members of society.

TAKE MORE ACTION!   How To Change The World

HOME	LEVEL I	LEVEL II
Preface, Contents	Global Citizenship: Around the World, Across the Street	Becoming Global Citizens: A Question of Choice

Violence and crime among young people

An alarming number of young people are exposed to or resorting to violence, in the form of assaults, fights, threats, bullying, gang violence, destruction of property or date violence. An overwhelming majority of those who engage in violence against young people are roughly the same age as their victims. There is a close connection between youth who are victimized and youth involved in crime.

Some young people turn to crime as a survival or escape tactic from problems such as poverty, homelessness, domestic violence or substance abuse. These circumstances can make it challenging for young people to withstand negative peer pressure.

Much of public perception is shaped by the media, which often focuses on youth offences rather than on youth achievements. When teens are excluded or labeled as criminals, they can be moved to disconnect themselves even further from this society by turning to delinquent behavior. Across Africa, juvenile crime is primarily associated with poverty, hunger, unemployment, and a lack of opportunity. And in transition countries, crime rates among youth have risen over 30 percent since 1995.

Many of the inequalities that contribute to crime in the first place also carry over into the justice system. Overall, youth of racial or ethnic minorities are more likely than white youth to be sent to detention and corrections facilities and to be transferred to adult court—often for the same offences. Some states have instituted strict and punitive systems for young offenders, who are routinely exposed to violence and arbitrary detentions by the police.

For young people facing social and economic exclusion, effective programs and solutions must go beyond punitive methods to include early childhood interventions, educational and leadership programs, job and skills training, as well as reintegration programs.

TAKE MORE ACTION! How To Change The World

HOME	**LEVEL I**	**LEVEL II**
Preface, Contents	Global Citizenship:	Becoming Global Citizens:
	Around the World, Across the Street	A Question of Choice

LeveL III	**LeveL IV**	**LeveL V**
The Seven Steps to Social Action: Taking It to the Next Level	The How-To Guide: The Global Citizen's Toolbox	Sources And Resources, End Notes

Military Expenditure and Social Development

Every year, armed violence kills over half a million people and yet, every year, eight million more guns enter the marketplace. Many people argue that war and violence are inevitable, yet they are the result of a conscious choice to devalue human life.

While international aid to developing countries has dwindled in recent years to a sum of $103.9 billion, global military spending has been steadily on the rise. In the decade since 1996, military expenditure increased by 34 percent, to reach a peak of $1.11 trillion in 2005—that's equal to $173 per person. The military expenditure of the United States accounts for 48 percent of the global total, while the UK, France, Japan and China account for four to five percent each.

Many governments invest more in building armies and weapons than they do in providing for the basic needs of their people, such as education, health care, and communication systems. In Latin America, Asia, Africa and the Middle East, many countries have a yearly military budget of $22 billion—a sum that could provide education to every child in their nation, and cut child mortality rates by two-thirds by 2015.

At the turn of the twentieth century, 10 percent of war deaths and injuries were suffered by non-military personnel. In the new, brutal warfare that marks the twenty-first century, the victims are far more likely to be non-combatants than soldiers. In recent conflicts, nearly 70 percent of casualties have been suffered by civilians—most often women and children.

The proliferation of guns and weaponry is intimately related to human rights abuses and the cycle of poverty. Not only do instability and conflict increase in the absence of social protection systems, but the abundance of weaponry also fuels armed conflict, crime, state violence and domestic abuse, and destroys advances toward social development.

TAKE MORE ACTION! How To Change The World

| **HOME** Preface, Contents | **LEVEL I** Global Citizenship: Around the World, Across the Street | **LEVEL II** Becoming Global Citizens: A Question of Choice |

Children's Rights

The United Nations Convention on the Rights of the Child, ratified by 192 UN member countries, declares that children have the right to be kept safe from neglect, cruelty, and exploitation, and underlines the basic human rights to which all children are entitled:

- The right to survival and to the resources necessary for survival such as food, water, and shelter
- To develop to the fullest of their potential
- To protection from harmful influences, abuse, and exploitation of any kind
- To participate fully in the family, cultural and social life of their communities

Yet the rights of children continue to be violated in every region of the world. The situation is most critical in poorer regions, where socially excluded children (especially girls and ethnic minorities) are among the most vulnerable. Globally, almost 11 million children under the age of five die every year, mostly of easily preventable causes—more than five million of them from malnutrition. Nearly 120 million children in developing countries are not in primary school.

Child labor is both a cause and a consequence of poverty. Millions of children around the world are forced into exploitative activities, and are robbed of their health, their dignity, and their right to simply enjoy being a child. According to estimates by the International Labour Organization, there are 218 million child laborers worldwide, 126 million of which are engaged in hazardous work. Most children work in the informal sector, without legal or regulatory protection.

As governments fail to uphold their global commitment to children, the world continues to squander its most precious human resource. The United States is one of only two countries in the world that have not ratified the United Nations Convention on the Rights of the Child (CRC). Somalia—a country without an internationally-recognized government—is the other.

TAKE MORE ACTION!   How To Change The World

HOME	LEVEL I	LEVEL II
Preface, Contents	Global Citizenship: Around the World, Across the Street	Becoming Global Citizens: A Question of Choice

Level III The Seven Steps to Social Action: Taking It to the Next Level	**Level IV** The How-To Guide: The Global Citizen's Toolbox	**Level V** Sources And Resources, End Notes

Indigenous Rights

There are more than 370 million indigenous people in approximately 70 countries around the world. Historically displaced from their ancestral lands by colonizers and settlers, they continue to be marginalized by mainstream society, and by governments that fail to respect indigenous economic and social organizations, laws, and worldviews.

In Canada and the United States, many of the social problems faced by aboriginal communities today stem from the policy of forced assimilation and cultural destruction instituted through the boarding school system. Beginning the late 1800s, indigenous children in both Canada and the United States were forcibly removed from their homes by church and government officials and sent to residential or boarding schools; there the children experienced a range of abuses, including forced assimilation and punishing labor, as well as widespread physical and sexual abuse.

This practice, which went on well into the 1970s in Canada (the United States ended this project four decades earlier), not only denied indigenous children contact with their families, but also the right to speak their native languages and to practice their religion and cultural customs. The loss of culture, language and identity destroyed the traditional social structure of indigenous communities, and left a legacy of family violence, and drug and alcohol abuse and suicide.

Despite their diversity, many indigenous groups share a common struggle to protect their cultures, livelihoods and territories. National economic and industrial development projects uproot these communities from their livelihood base in land, forest and water resources, and often lead to further impoverishment.

The most significant international standard for the protection of indigenous human rights and freedoms is the draft United Nations Declaration on the Rights of Indigenous Peoples. Although the declaration has been under development for over 20 years, it has yet to be adopted by the UN General Assembly, due to the objections of a handful of states.

TAKE MORE ACTION! How To Change The World

HOME	LEVEL I	LEVEL II
Preface, Contents	Global Citizenship: Around the World, Across the Street	Becoming Global Citizens: A Question of Choice

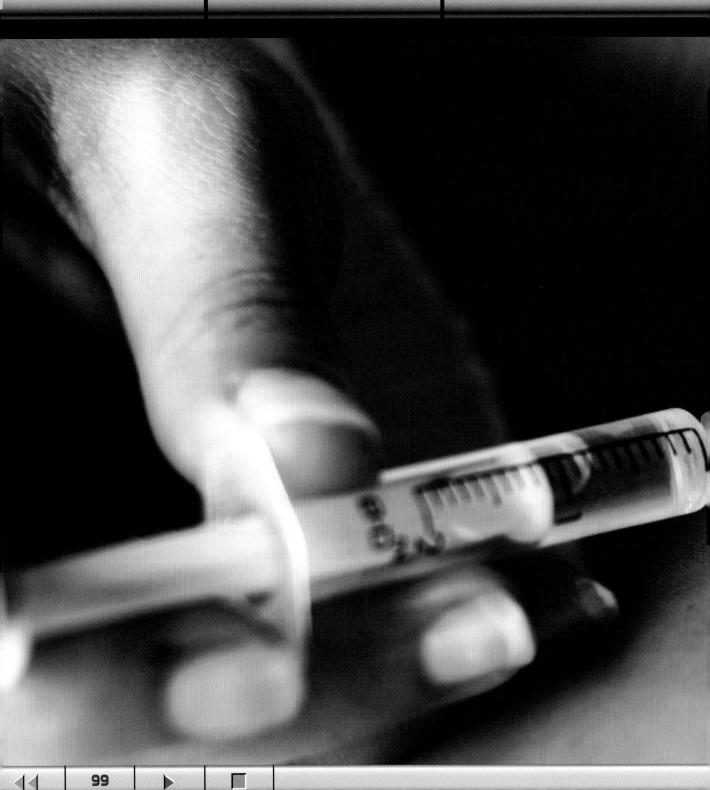

Level III The Seven Steps to Social Action: Taking It to the Next Level	**Level IV** The How-To Guide: The Global Citizen's Toolbox	**Level V** Sources And Resources, End Notes

Substance Abuse

Youth are exposed to a variety of mixed messages about drugs, alcohol and tobacco. The media often portrays these substances as attractive, and some of your peers may dismiss them as harmless, and even good for your status or image.

In the United States, 23 percent of high school students currently smoke cigarettes, and each day, 4,000 young people between the ages of 12 and 17 years take up cigarette smoking. This trend comes with a consequence. Tobacco use, however, is one of the main preventable causes of death in the world. Studies have shown that nearly 30 percent of people who begin smoking in their youth continue to smoke, and die from tobacco-related diseases at an early age. Cannabis (marijuana) is also widely used among young people. Over 30 percent of 15-year-olds in the United States have used cannabis, while in Canada the rate is over 40 percent.

The use of alcohol, tobacco and illegal drugs among youth is often linked to depression and trouble in school. Substance abuse has also been linked to teenage pregnancies, unwanted or unsafe sex, and the contraction of sexually transmitted diseases such as HIV/AIDS. Substance abuse burdens the economy and the health care system, causes family problems, and leads to crime and violence associated with drug trafficking. It affects the safety and well-being of the entire population of countries throughout the world.

Youth are a major target for advertising and marketing campaigns of alcohol and tobacco industries. Because of recent attempts to limit this kind of marketing in industrialized countries, these companies have shifted their focus to young people in developing countries and countries in transition, where similar protective measures have not yet been initiated and health services are less accessible to young people.

Taking on the challenge

Did any of these issues leap out at you and move you to take action? If not, keep searching to find a need or an injustice that stirs something inside you. The problems described here are not small, but they are not insurmountable. Throughout this book, you will meet several young people, just like you, who are using their talents, vision, and determination to create effective solutions to such problems. As you read their stories, you'll see that change can begin and grow from a single person, a single idea, a single hope for a better future.

There exist limitless possibilities for change that have not even been explored yet. Every young person has the potential to come up with a unique solution—a new way to make a difference. What will *yours* be?

TAKE MORE ACTION! How To Change The World

HOME	LEVEL I	LEVEL II
Preface, Contents	Global Citizenship: Around the World, Across the Street	Becoming Global Citizens: A Question of Choice

PROFILE

Abraham Kenmore: Paper and Pencils For All

Ever since he could remember, Abraham Kenmore felt the need to reach out and help others. Growing up in Clarence Center, NY, in a household that encouraged public service, he knew from an early age that he wanted to help others.

Abe saw how education can be a powerful tool in helping children rise out of life-threatening situations. He learned that children with access to education are less likely to be forced into hazardous child labour or expose themselves to the risk of HIV/AIDS, and more likely to achieve greater health and prosperity throughout their lives.

"Education can not only break the poverty cycle," he says, "it can start a better cycle."

A fortuitous encounter when he was eight years old turned out to be a pivotal moment in Abe's life. Abe met friends of his parents who had been regularly travelling to war-torn countries to assist children and their families in recovering from the damages of military conflicts. Abe expressed his hope to help improve the lives of children in developing nations.

The friends explained that they would soon be heading to Afghanistan, where children have little access to quality schooling as the country struggles through violent regime change. Seizing this opportunity, Abe arranged for the delivery of school supplies from the family's own home. The idea for his organization had been sparked, and a plan began to take shape.

In 2004, he founded Paper and Pencils For All (PAPFA). Since then, PAPFA has arranged the delivery of school supplies to children all over the world to places where resources are scarce, such as Afghanistan, Nicaragua, Iraq, Indonesia, India and Kenya, as well as to areas of the southern United States affected by Hurricane Katrina in 2005. In total, his work has resulted in more than 13 shipments to ten different countries.

Through this work, Abe has learned the value of stepping out of one's comfort zone and taking risks to achieve goals. Experiences such as delivering a talk to a roomful of Grade 9 students, or single-handedly editing and designing the PAPFA newsletter, have brought him greater confidence in his ability to make a positive difference. Managing a chequing account and personally signing notes of thanks to each and every donor have endowed him with tremendous responsibilities for someone so young—but Abe has managed to succeed despite the pressures.

LeVeL III
The Seven Steps to Social Action:
Taking It to the Next Level

LeVeL IV
The How-To Guide:
The Global Citizen's Toolbox

LeVeL V
Sources And Resources,
End Notes

Abe's biggest source of inspiration remains the children he is able to help. He is especially proud of the impact he was able to make in Mississippi following Katrina's devastation.

"Two boys living in a shelter had no supplies at all until PAPFA supplies arrived," he says. "My contact sent me a photograph of the two boys who were living in a gymnasium at the time. It was the first time that PAPFA school supplies had made a noticeable difference that quickly that I know of."

Despite the demands of a busy schedule, he hopes to continue leading PAPFA to help students around the world get the chance of a better future through education. He has ambitious plans for a PAPFA scholarship fund, and hopes to eventually even build schools for those children who miss out on the opportunities of education.

TAKE MORE ACTION! How To Change The World

HOME	LEVEL I	LEVEL II
Preface, Contents	Global Citizenship: Around the World, Across the Street	Becoming Global Citizens: A Question of Choice

• When Abe saw how young people just like him in developing countries lacked access to education, he felt compelled to take action. Do you think it is important to identify with an issue in order to want to help? Explain.

• Write a list of all the supplies and resources you use in school every day—including your teachers, transportation and in your extracurricular activities. How would your life be like if these were impossible to obtain? How would this affect your future possibilities? Write a short scenario imagining a life without education.

• Which problems do you feel are more important to address: those in countries overseas, or those in your own community? Explain your answer.

Staying psyched: passion boosters

To stay dedicated to your issue every single day, remember why you got involved. This is the fuel that gets you psyched up to push toward your goal with true passion. But it may be hard to remember your mission as you wake up in the morning or after a long day at school. Give yourself visible, tangible reminders of your mission that stir your memory and rekindle your passion to work harder. Your passion booster can be a sad picture of a war-affected village or a polluted river, or a beautiful picture of the ideal world as you envision it. It can be a ring or necklace you were given by someone special who shares your cause, or a quotation or poem you stick on your bathroom mirror or locker. Your passion boosters are like Popeye's spinach—they give you an instant rush of adrenalin to do whatever it takes to accomplish your goals.

Take Action!

List some of the issues that you see around your school and community. Choose three, and brainstorm four actions you can take to make a difference: two small, one medium, and one hard.

Ask two friends what issues they are passionate about. Are they different from or the same as yours? Brainstorm simple ways they can make a difference.

LeVeL III The Seven Steps to Social Action: Taking It to the Next Level	**LeVeL IV** The How-To Guide: The Global Citizen's Toolbox	**LeVeL V** Sources And Resources, End Notes

Choose Your Issue!

Choose one issue from those on pages 83-100 or come up with one of your own—the one about which you are most passionate. We will refer to your chosen issue throughout the rest of the book, so make sure it's one that you really care about. Write it down and remember it. From here on, we will equip you with the tools and skills to make a difference, before you get to the end of the book, and beyond.

Choose a passion booster that inspires you.

TAKE MORE ACTION! How To Change The World

| **HOme** Preface, Contents | **LeveL I** Global Citizenship: Around the World, Across the Street | **LeveL II** Becoming Global Citizens: A Question of Choice |

STEP TWO: RESEARCH THE REALITY

You may have heard this expression before, but pay special attention this time, because without it, your quest for a better world ends right here: *Knowledge is power*. If you want to make a difference, you have to educate yourself. You have to know what you are striving toward. Research plays a key role in any movement for social justice. It lays the groundwork for your actions in three main ways.

First, it reveals the facts about an issue. You have to know what the problem is, where and why it is happening, who is involved, and what impact it has, on whom. Second, it allows you to communicate this information to others and to rally a team to the cause. And third, it enables you to find appropriate solutions and devise effective strategies to put them in place.

Finding solutions to social issues is far more difficult than it seems. You have to learn about not only the current state of the problem, but its root causes as well—the historical, political, economic, and social factors that gave rise to and perpetuated it. Because many of the world's problems are the result of years of discrimination and injustice, becoming familiar with the

LeVeL III The Seven Steps to Social Action: Taking It to the Next Level	**LeVeL IV** The How-To Guide: The Global Citizen's Toolbox	**LeVeL V** Sources And Resources, End Notes

background is a crucial step to developing lasting solutions. As you learn more about the kinds of solutions that have been attempted in the past, you can evaluate their successes and failures to find an improved and effective plan of action.

Research also motivates you to strive harder to succeed and inspire others to become involved; the more you learn about an issue, the stronger your emotional reaction and passion to make a difference.

Knowing the complete reality of an issue is even more important when you are speaking out and taking action as a young person. Because of your age, people may be tempted to dismiss you as naïve, idealistic or uneducated. In fact, it is often ten times harder to earn credibility as a young person. Your opponents may want to tell you that you do not know what you are talking about. Prove them wrong! Show them that young people have the power to make a difference and that your passion and belief in a better world is rooted in a solid and realistic understanding of the issues and how they can be solved.

TAKE MORE ACTION! How To Change The World

HOME	LEVEL I	LEVEL II
Preface, Contents	Global Citizenship: Around the World, Across the Street	Becoming Global Citizens: A Question of Choice

Level III	Level IV	Level V
The Seven Steps to Social Action: Taking It to the Next Level	The How-To Guide: The Global Citizen's Toolbox	Sources And Resources, End Notes

What Are You Looking For?		
Type of Information	**How You Can Use It**	**Where to Find It**
Facts	• What is the problem? • Where is it happening? • When does/did it happen? • Why is it a problem and why does it happen? • Who is involved and whom does it affect? • How does it affect you, your community, and the world?	• Daily newspapers • Brochures or Web sites of organizations involved in the issue • The people who are involved and directly affected • Backgrounder sections of television news • Web sites
Statistics	"Stats" can give you an idea of the scope (size and trends) of the issue. Try to put them into a context that you and others can relate to. *For example:* "Today, more than 1 billion people around the world live on less than $1 a day, and about 2.7 billion struggle to live on less than $2 a day."	• UN organizations' yearly reports • Brochures or websites of organizations involved in the issue • Statistics Canada or the US Census Bureau • Special issues of magazines on the subject • Your own surveys
Stories	Facts and statistics are powerful in convincing people that there is a problem, but numbers can be overwhelming and do not often inspire an emotional reaction. True accounts of people affected by an issue reveal the human face of a problem, ensuring an emotional connection.	• Interviews with people affected by the issue or others who know them • Documentaries

TIP 1:

Beware when researching and citing statistics. The wording is just as important as the numbers, so understand exactly what the numbers represent. You also need to make sure that your source is reliable.

TIP 2:

Be very cautious when interviewing individuals you do not know. Avoid being alone with someone by bringing along at least two friends, or by carrying out surveys or interviews in public places in daylight.

Now that you have the information you want, you have to know how to document it. The process is called "citation," which is, basically, the act of writing down the source of the information.

A citation looks like a bibliography reference. Make sure you record the name of the writer; the title and type (book, film, newspaper) of the source; the year the information was published or the date of the airing (if television or radio), interview, survey or letter; and the page number or exact address of the Web site.

When you are thinking of publishing your research, libraries usually offer many different style guides for writing citations. In the meantime, just make sure you have all your citations written down and safely kept with all of your research. It is often easiest to have the citation on the same page as the research to avoid looking all over for it.

Level III
The Seven Steps to Social Action:
Taking It to the Next Level

Level IV
The How-To Guide:
The Global Citizen's Toolbox

Level V
Sources And Resources,
End Notes

Any single source will not provide you with all the information you require, because you need to consider various perspectives. Even if the first one seems totally reliable, it is important to consult a number of different sources and cross-check the information to determine where it agrees and where it conflicts. Considering the issue from different points of view will help you to cultivate a broad perspective, and learn to distinguish fact, opinion, and propaganda in what you read and hear.

This advice may seem like common sense, but many social action groups have been destroyed by their critics because they have not considered the other side of the issue, or have acquired false or unverified information. It's a lot of work, but it's worth the effort to be thorough in your research. You will be far more effective at finding the real solutions if you understand the realities, inside and out.

"ONCE SOCIAL CHANGE BEGINS, IT CANNOT BE REVERSED. YOU CANNOT UNEDUCATE THE PERSON WHO HAS LEARNED TO READ. YOU CANNOT HUMILIATE THE PERSON WHO FEELS PRIDE. YOU CANNOT OPPRESS THE PEOPLE WHO ARE NOT AFRAID ANYMORE."

—Cesar Chávez
(1927-1993)
Labor leader

TAKE MORE ACTION! How To Change The World

HOME	LEVEL I	LEVEL II
Preface, Contents	Global Citizenship: Around the World, Across the Street	Becoming Global Citizens: A Question of Choice

PROFILE

Cheryl Perera: Child Rights Activist

Cheryl Perera had always known that she wanted to help people, but was not sure how. When she discovered that Sri Lanka, her family's home country, was one of the world's worst locations for conditions of child labor, she was left feeling highly disturbed, and was motivated to learn more.

Her research eventually led to her actually travelling to Sri Lanka to investigate some of the sites of child labor. A few days after arriving, Cheryl and a family member visited a number of quarries that used dynamite. Her research had not prepared her for the sight of children perched on high ladders, chipping limestone with hammers and rolling heavy stones into carts. Children as young as five were working dangerously close to the blasts, covered in white dust. Cheryl captured these scenes on video, and became more determined than ever to take action.

In the following weeks, Cheryl worked with local human rights organizations to compile a list of recommended actions to address child labor, prostitution and domestic servitude, which they presented to the President's advisor. Their suggestions included allocating more of the national budget to child protection, appointing labor inspectors, and considering the input of child victims themselves when developing programs that affect them. Because of her first-hand knowledge, Cheryl was able to understand and communicate the hardships faced by these children.

Cheryl later participated with local authorities to expose and apprehend paedophiles. She began a campaign that mobilized youth across Canada to encourage Air Canada to screen an in-flight video warning against child sex tourism. The campaign was a huge success, and the video was screened on both international and domestic flights with a viewership of over 400,000 passengers per month.

She founded OneChild, a youth empowerment organization dedicated to ending the global children sex trade, with chapters across Canada and the United States. She led OneChild team members to the Philippines to meet and rehabilitate with child prostitutes. OneChild is raising funds to construct a rehabilitation center in the Philippines to provide shelter, formal/non-formal education, counseling, therapy, vocational training and legal assistance for victims.

Cheryl now sits on the Senate Committee Against the Commercial Sexual Exploitation of Children, chaired by Senator Romeo Dallaire. She has received many awards, including World of Children Founder's Award, the BR!CK Award, the Flare Volunteer Award and many others. She has been named one of "Canada's Top 20 Under 20" and one of "Canada's Most Powerful Women."

As OneChild's main spokesperson, Cheryl regularly addresses schools, governments and other groups on the child sex trade and ways to take action—to date, she has spoken to over 25,000 individuals, and continues to keep working on behalf of children all over the world.

LEVEL III
The Seven Steps to Social Action:
Taking It to the Next Level

LEVEL IV
The How-To Guide:
The Global Citizen's Toolbox

LEVEL V
Sources And Resources,
End Notes

- Why was research so crucial in inspiring Cheryl to take action on the issue of the exploitation of children? In your opinion, why is sharing the story of what she witnessed in Sri Lanka effective in motivating others to act?

- What are the obstacles and risks that one might encounter in trying to visit sites such as factories to document an exploitative practice such as child labor?

- Make a list of precautions to take when attempting to gather research in this manner. What other ways are there to obtain this type of first-hand testimony?

TAKE MORE ACTION! How To Change The World

| **Home** | **Level I** | **Level II** |
| Preface, Contents | Global Citizenship:
Around the World, Across the Street | Becoming Global Citizens:
A Question of Choice |

Finding the root causes of your issue

In order to find a solution to any social issue, you need to evaluate its root causes. It is important to dig deep and find out why the problem exists and why it has yet to be solved.

Unfortunately, people often react to social issues by focusing on solutions before exploring the causes of the problem. This approach only covers up the problem and often makes it far worse.

For example, the typical approach to overfilling garbage dumps is often to ship the garbage to another city (or even another country!), to dump it into an abandoned mineshaft or to burn it in large, polluting incinerators. These methods do not consider how we could reduce the appalling amount of garbage we produce or how to convince people to reuse and recycle.

As another example, let's take the issue of child labor. Many young people ask Free The Children which companies to boycott to put an end to child labor. They do not realize, however, that only a small percentage of child labor is in the export industry (in which children manufacture goods to be sold in other countries). Boycotts thus only touch the surface of the problem and are not always the best solution. There are many other root causes of exploitative child labor that must be addressed.

LeveL III > The Seven Steps To Social Action: Step Two: Research The Reality

| **LeveL III**
The Seven Steps to Social Action:
Taking It to the Next Level | **LeveL IV**
The How-To Guide:
The Global Citizen's Toolbox | **LeveL V**
Sources And Resources,
End Notes |

Root Causes of Child Labor

Poverty	Exploitation of children and poor people; homelessness; migration from rural areas; high interest rate on loans
Education	Illiteracy; lack of schools and qualified teachers and supplies; poor school programs
Discrimination	Based on sex, religion, ethnic background, traditions
Economic and political realities	National budgets with few social programs,unfair trade policies; high interest rates on debts; conflicts and war
Globalization	Free-flowing capital; jobs moving to cheapest markets; exploitation of workers in poor countries; corporations escaping taxes, with loss of revenue for social programs
Sweatshop labor	Adults who are not paid a living wage for their work must force their children to work in the informal sector (on the streets, as domestic servants, in agriculture) to help the family survive

An effective solution to child labor is one that addresses each of these root causes and considers the perspectives of all stakeholders (individuals who are involved directly and indirectly in the issue). Only solutions that address all perspectives and stakeholders can result in positive change that is meaningful and lasting.

TAKE MORE ACTION! How To Change The World

HOME	LEVEL I	LEVEL II
Preface, Contents	Global Citizenship: Around the World, Across the Street	Becoming Global Citizens: A Question of Choice

LeveL III The Seven Steps to Social Action: Taking It to the Next Level	**LeveL IV** The How-To Guide: The Global Citizen's Toolbox	**LeveL V** Sources And Resources, End Notes

Here is a list of some of the stakeholders in the issue of child labor, and actions that they can take to create positive change:

• National governments can ratify and enforce the International Labour Organization's Convention 182 on the worst forms of child labor. They can pass and enforce legislation that guarantees all workers a livable wage and invest more money in education programs.

• International governments can increase aid to developing countries, especially for education programs, and eliminate unfair trade policies and high interest rates on debts.

• Corporations can pay taxes and give back to countries where they are getting cheap labor, in the form of programs for children. If all companies paid their adult workers a livable wage and provided good working conditions, children would not be forced to work.

• Parents earning a livable wage or who are provided with an alternative source of income would be able to send their children to school.

• Non-Governmental Organizations (NGOs) or foreign aid can help families to develop income-generating projects and schools for their children, including informal education centers for children who work part-time.

• Child laborers who become literate and aware of their rights when provided with an education can break the cycle of poverty and exploitation. Older child laborers can take a stand against exploitation and organize for fair working conditions, with hours adapted so that they have time for education and leisure.

• Young people around the world can continue to speak out against the exploitation of children and the right of all children to go to school and to grow up in a safe and healthy environment.

When doing your research and seeking out organizations that focus on your issue, you may want to ask them how their proposed solutions address root causes and the perspectives of all stakeholders involved. This will allow you to evaluate the effectiveness of their projects and campaigns, and guide you as you begin to develop your own.

TAKE MORE ACTION! How To Change The World

HOme	LeveL I	LeveL II
Preface, Contents	Global Citizenship: Around the World, Across the Street	Becoming Global Citizens: A Question of Choice

Take Action!

Find one page of facts, several key statistics, and two stories for your issue. Write them down (don't forget citations!). Use this information to try to convince one friend or family member to get involved in your issue.

Brainstorm all the root causes of your chosen issue (see page 113). You may need to do some significant research before being able to compile a full list.

Research all the potential stakeholders in your chosen issue and evaluate their role in creating the change you wish to see.

"BY WORKING TOGETHER, THE TINY ANTS CARRY THE ELEPHANT."

—Vietnamese proverb

LeVeL III > The Seven Steps To Social Action: Step Two: Research The Reality

LeVeL III	**LeVeL IV**	**LeVeL V**
The Seven Steps to Social Action: Taking It to the Next Level	The How-To Guide: The Global Citizen's Toolbox	Sources And Resources, End Notes

When researching a complex issue, it's a good idea to work as a team. Divide up different aspects of the issue, and then share what you have learned with one another.

TAKE MORE ACTION! How To Change The World

HOME	LEVEL I	LEVEL II
Preface, Contents	Global Citizenship: Around the World, Across the Street	Becoming Global Citizens: A Question of Choice

STEP THREE: BUILD YOUR DREAM TEAM

As one global citizen, you can certainly make a difference. You can research an issue and make a powerful presentation about it on your own. You can pick up litter in the local park. You can write letter after letter to a public official to pressure for a change in policy.

But imagine what can be done if your entire class got involved and devoted all their time and energy to writing letters as well. What if all the students in your school, and every other school in your community, in your province, across Canada, combined their efforts? Imagine the mountain of letters that would make, and how much harder it would be for officials to ignore the message they contained.

You're probably thinking, "That's impossible!" But it's not. In fact, it's the way Free The Children got started. From a small group of a few young people in Thornhill, Ontario (Canada), the organization has grown into a worldwide network, having involved over one million youth in its projects.

The key to social action is teamwork. It's simple: When you are surrounded by people who are committed to your cause, you can accomplish a lot more. Team members, each with their own gifts, help to make the effort more powerful and meaningful. They encourage and support one another, and remind you of why you first became involved. Many of the great movements for social change were born when individuals discovered a shared sense of what was important to them and what their common purpose could be. In fact, without this shared process, there can be no real movements. How effective would the march on Washington for civil rights that Dr. Martin Luther King, Jr., led in 1963 have been with only one lone man strolling down the street?

So: you have your issue and your research. Can you find a hundred people to join your cause, full-time, right away? Probably not, but never fear! Dozens of members at all meetings may be too many to effectively make decisions and move forward. Try the simple strategy that follows to first build a solid Core Group and find a legion of helpers.

TAKE MORE ACTION! How To Change The World

HOME	LEVEL I	LEVEL II
Preface, Contents	Global Citizenship: Around the World, Across the Street	Becoming Global Citizens: A Question of Choice

First, we begin with *you*. You are passionate and understand the problem well, and you need help.

Next, we add your Core Group: You'll only need three to five people to plan and co-ordinate most of your further research and actions. They must all be very passionate, committed to the cause, and ready to work together on the Dream Team as a high priority in their lives. Look first to your best friends and people involved in your extra-curricular activities—they are likely to share many of your values and thoughts. You could also check out the other social action groups in your school or community such as the student council, leadership council, and other school associations.

It may remain difficult to get others as involved as you are. So ask yourself:

- Who else is most affected by this problem?
- Who is committed to solving it?
- Where can I go to find these people?
- Who is already an activist?
- What specific skills or knowledge am I missing that others can contribute?

You have a whole range of people to consider as potential members of your Core Group. Choose wisely—you will have to trust and depend on these individuals to help you succeed!

Finally, we add the minga. You will find many people who want to help, but who are too busy with sports, band, drama or homework to dedicate a lot of time, but they can offer an hour a week, or one day every month. These are still very valuable members of your Dream Team. They all have talents, ideas, and energy to share, so sign them up and give them a role to play!

Make a list of your Minga Team, with the following info:

- **Name**
- **Contact (phone, e-mail)**
- **Availability**
- **Skill, gift or specific contribution/task such as:**
  - **Phone calls**
  - **Donations**
  - **Posters**
  - **Event participation (car washer, cookie baker)**
  - **Ticket sales**
  - **Running an information booth at lunch or in the mall**
  - **Petition circulation**
  - **Letter writing**
  - **Research**
  - **Minute taking (for meetings)**

TAKE MORE ACTION! How To Change The World

HOME	LEVEL I	LEVEL II
Preface, Contents	Global Citizenship: Around the World, Across the Street	Becoming Global Citizens: A Question of Choice

The Minga

Many indigenous societies in Central and South America accomplish their biggest projects—like constructing houses or schools, planting large plots of crops or making clothes and crafts—by holding a *minga*. Everyone leaves his or her own work to come together for one day to work as a whole community. Everyone performs a specific task, and the project is completed in no time!

Mingas are awesome ways to get big things done quickly, but they are also amazing experiences that promote unity, friendship, and solidarity among community members. These indigenous societies are among the most tightly knit, mutually supportive communities in the world—because of the minga!

There you have all the ingredients for your Dream Team—the Core Group meets regularly, plans and co-ordinates actions, and then delegates tasks to the Minga Team for the big actions, whose members carry out the actions all together. Delegating effectively is key to your success, but the secret to organizing your Dream Team is creating a sense of ownership and responsibility for the issue among all members. Your teammates must be as passionate about the issue as you are!

LeveL III
The Seven Steps to Social Action:
Taking It to the Next Level

LeveL IV
The How-To Guide:
The Global Citizen's Toolbox

LeveL V
Sources And Resources,
End Notes

To keep them inspired:
- Always ask for input—appreciate it and implement it.
- Delegate important tasks—not just the easy or unglamorous ones.
- Tap into people's gifts—encourage team members to contribute their special talents and skills.
- Make decisions as a team—try to achieve a consensus (general agreement) whenever possible.
- Make your passion contagious—regularly remind your team of why you are all involved and what the issue is really about. Make your idealism and positive vibes shine!

TIP

For more information on working effectively with others, see the Connecting with People section of the How-To Guide. Also, consult the Getting the Word Out Through the Media section of the How-To Guide for ideas on how to raise awareness of the issue, which will draw more people to the cause.

"ONE MAN CAN BE A CRUCIAL INGREDIENT ON A TEAM, BUT ONE MAN CANNOT MAKE A TEAM."

—Kareem Abdul-Jabbar
(b. 1947)
Professional basketball player

 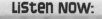

TAKE MORE ACTION! How To Change The World

HOME	LEVEL I	LEVEL II
Preface, Contents	Global Citizenship: Around the World, Across the Street	Becoming Global Citizens: A Question of Choice

TROUBLESHOOTING

What Happens if No One Wants to Join?

If you are unsure of how to ask people to join your cause, try speaking in front of your class or school—that's what Craig Kielburger did! You would be surprised how many people will join just by seeing how passionate you are. Tell your audience exactly what you want: "Join my group," or "Come to our meeting Thursday at 3:15."

Don't give up! Some people may need to watch you take action for a while before they come around, but once you have your first few members, the floodgates will open! You can also try speaking to people individually—find out what their skills are and tell them how those skills would be a valuable asset to your team. If you're still having trouble starting a new group, you can always join an existing one and bring your energy and ideas to them. As a new member, you can take initiative and recruit others to the organization, putting your leadership skills to great use.

Embracing a diverse community

The key to building a strong group is **inclusion**. When organizing a group of people who are dedicated to your cause, remember that **diversity** is an essential and enriching force, not an obstacle. Someone who has had a different experience may see situations in another light and challenge you to broaden your perspective. When you welcome more diverse voices, their shared purpose will break down traditional boundaries between people, spur new ideas, and build a united effort that promotes peace and solidarity at the same time.

TIP

Seek out adults in your community to join your team as advisors and mentors. They may have valuable knowledge, experience and skills to contribute to the cause. Try to find individuals who will be supportive of the youth-led nature of your team. These might be parents, teachers, members of other organizations with a similar mandate or professionals with specific skills who share your passion for the issue.

Level III		**Level IV**		**Level V**
The Seven Steps to Social Action: Taking It to the Next Level		The How-To Guide: The Global Citizen's Toolbox		Sources And Resources, End Notes

As you build your group, look for members who vary in cultural background, political orientation, knowledge, experience, skills, age, and ways of life. By comparing perspectives, group members discover the attitudes, values, and concerns that others have about the issue that you all seek to confront.

The four types of leaders

As you build your team, you will have to deal with team dynamics and various people's views on leadership. Your members may fall into different roles that are essential to the workings of a well-oiled team. It is important to understand various leadership styles so that you can fill every role that your team needs to be effective and direct members toward roles that best suit their personal teamwork style.

There are four kinds of leaders: *visionaries*, *doers*, *reasoners*, and *bridge-builders*. Each leadership type is critical to the success of any team, and can be compared to the parts of a bicycle:

TAKE MORE ACTION! How To Change The World

HOME	LeVeL I	LeVeL II
Preface, Contents	Global Citizenship: Around the World, Across the Street	Becoming Global Citizens: A Question of Choice

- *Visionaries* are the team's trail guide. They dream and inspire. They develop new ideas and ways of approaching a problem or a task that the team must face. Visionaries are always thinking, brainstorming, suggesting, and painting a picture of where the team should go and what it can accomplish.

- *Doers* are the team's pedals. Their actions set the team in motion. They lead by example, motivating people and maintaining team momentum toward the main goal. Doers are in constant motion, working to push the team's accomplishments forward.

- *Reasoners* are the team's handlebars. They guide and protect the team from harm. They analyze the team's goals and actions, and decide the best possible way to achieve the goals, given the specific conditions and circumstances. Reasoners do a lot of calculating, analyzing, organizing, and budgeting, and they often have to redirect team members who wander off lost in the woods somewhere. Often, the most quiet and thoughtful people in the group are the most gifted reasoners.

- *Bridge-builders* are the team's gears and chain. They make all of the other parts work together and move in the same direction. They resolve conflicts among the other members of the team to ensure that the team stays focused and on target. Bridge-builders engage in a lot of negotiations and problem solving, to make sure that the team works as a cohesive unit.

Every team needs all four kinds of leaders in order to succeed. Ask yourself which role best suits you and makes the most of your gifts and skills, and which role would challenge you to develop new skills.

Level III
The Seven Steps to Social Action:
Taking It to the Next Level

Level IV
The How-To Guide:
The Global Citizen's Toolbox

Level V
Sources And Resources,
End Notes

Types of Leaders			
Type of Leader	**A.K.A.**	**Talents**	**Tasks**
Visionaries	"Idea" people	Imagination Passion Inventiveness Courage to dream	Project proposals and design Mission statements Long-term planning Media relations
Doers	"Hands-on" people	Energy Perseverance Flexibility Artistic skills	Posters and logos Fundraising Manual labor Baking, building, shopping
Reasoners	"Details" people	Organization Logic Math and science skills Street sense	Budgets Logistics Coordinating Reporting to supporters
Bridge-builders	"Unifying" people	Compassion Communication skills Oratory skills Listening skills	Holding team meetings Giving pep talks Managing Mediating

TAKE MORE ACTION! How To Change The World

HOme	LeveL I	LeveL II
Preface, Contents	Global Citizenship: Around the World, Across the Street	Becoming Global Citizens: A Question of Choice

Exercise your leadership skills

Working with others is not always easy. Members of even the most solid groups sometimes disagree over strategies, get jealous of one another's achievements, blame one another for mistakes or clash over different personalities. As a leader, you must do your best to promote the unity of your team by reminding everyone of the purpose that brought all of you together, and ensuring that each individual feels that he or she belongs to the group and has a valuable contribution to make.

To avoid conflict and lay the groundwork for an effective team, it is helpful to work together to develop standards of behavior, or group *norms*, that you all agree to uphold. Such norms might include not interrupting one another in meetings, taking turns to speak, and respecting the opinions and feelings of every member. First, sit down as a group and brainstorm potential norms for everyone to follow, and then have a vote on each idea. Try to make the decisions as unanimous as possible.

TIP

For more information on developing group norms and resolving conflicts within a group, see the Connecting with People section in the How-To Guide.

"THE GREATEST THING YOU CAN DO FOR ANOTHER IS NOT JUST SHARE YOUR RICHES, BUT REVEAL TO THEM THEIR OWN."

—Benjamin Disraeli
(1804-1881)
English Statesman, former Prime Minister of Great Britain

LeveL III	**LeveL IV**	**LeveL V**
The Seven Steps to Social Action: Taking It to the Next Level	The How-To Guide: The Global Citizen's Toolbox	Sources And Resources, End Notes

Great Ways to Bring Out the Best in Your Group

1. Find out which skills each person possesses, and how he or she would be most interested in helping.
2. Find out who has previous leadership experience, who is eager to acquire further leadership skills, and who would prefer to take on a less prominent role.
3. Empower individual members to take the lead in an area in which they feel they can contribute the most.
4. Make sure that all members are enthusiastic about the role that they will play.
5. Ensure that group members treat one another with respect.
6. Share and celebrate small victories.
7. Keep up regular communication.

TAKE MORE ACTION! How To Change The World

HOME	LEVEL I	LEVEL II
Preface, Contents	Global Citizenship: Around the World, Across the Street	Becoming Global Citizens: A Question of Choice

TROUBLESHOOTING

Showing Your Appreciation

No matter what level of involvement they choose, be sure to show your appreciation for team members, volunteers, and supporters. No effort to make the world a better place can be a true success without the help and support of people who give of themselves and their time.

Here are some ways to make your invaluable volunteers feel appreciated:

- Thank them personally and congratulate them on their achievement.
- Hold a volunteer appreciation lunch, dinner or fun outing.
- Send cards, e-mails, phone calls, pins or T-shirts that say "thank you!"
- Show recognition in project pamphlets, newsletters or banners (or over morning announcements).

Level III > The Seven Steps To Social Action: Step Three: Build Your Dream Team

Level III The Seven Steps to Social Action: Taking It to the Next Level	**Level IV** The How-To Guide: The Global Citizen's Toolbox	**Level V** Sources And Resources, End Notes

Take Action!

What is your preferred leadership style? Describe a time when you played that role very well.

Brainstorm a list of five or six people you could invite to be part of your Core Group for your chosen issue and a list of places/organizations/people that you could approach to recruit your Minga Team.

Now put together your Dream Team! Recruit your Core Group and fill a sign-up sheet with names, contact info, availability and skills of team members.

TAKE MORE ACTION! How To Change The World

HOME	LEVEL I	LEVEL II
Preface, Contents	Global Citizenship: Around the World, Across the Street	Becoming Global Citizens: A Question of Choice

STEP FOUR: MEET AROUND THE ROUND TABLE

King Arthur and Sir Lancelot had the right idea: recruit the best knights from across the land (your Core Group) and sit them down at a table with no corners or head—sit down together as equals. The concept of the circular table leads us to the next step—after you define your issue, conduct your research, and build your team, you need to hold a meeting.

The meeting is:

- where team members get to know one another and learn more about the goals and nature of the team.
- where research and ideas are shared and developed.
- where passion is re-ignited and support is renewed.
- where group members get a chance to give direct input.
- a chance for team members to compare experiences, thoughts, and difficulties of their individual tasks and projects.
- where team decisions can be made.
- a chance to socialize and have fun with your friends afterward.

Of course, you don't actually need a round table to create an environment of equality. As a leader, it is your responsibility to facilitate, or guide, the discussion so that it is focused, productive and respectful of all participants. It is also important to make sure that decisions made during the meeting are understood and supported by the group, that everyone leaves with a task, and that individual commitments are fulfilled, by following up at subsequent meetings. That is the best way to put your ideals into action. A meeting of minds is a catalyst for change. When creative, energetic and determined people join forces, anything is possible.

LeVeL III > The 7 Steps To Social Action: Step Four: Meet Around The Round Table

LeVeL III	LeVeL IV	LeVeL V
The Seven Steps to Social Action: Taking It to the Next Level	The How-To Guide: The Global Citizen's Toolbox	Sources And Resources, End Notes

TROUBLESHOOTING

The First Meeting

You will want to start slowly at your first meeting with your Core Group. Do not expect to generate a whole list of actions to do the following week. Allow your team members to get to know one another and exchange knowledge, ideas and feelings about the issue.

Your first meeting is also a great opportunity to get people fired up and committed to the cause. Inspire them with stories, pictures and information about the issue and how their specific skills, talents and energy can help make a difference.

TIP

Ask around to find meeting times that avoid scheduling conflicts with other activities. Try early-morning or lunchtime meetings, or get together on the weekend! In your invitation, make sure you tell your recruits about the food and the fun, to make the meeting sound more attractive than doing homework or hanging out at the mall.

You can advertise a larger meeting to gather your Minga Team and other supporters. You could post flyers around your school and community, write an article in the school paper, or include a short message over the morning announcements. If you know students who belong to other organizations, you can ask them to announce your meeting at one of their own. Ensure that you first seek permission to post flyers.

Before the meeting

Before every meeting make a draft agenda—a list of activities you will do and issues you need to discuss during the meeting. You will probably amend it (change the order, or add or subtract items) at the beginning of the meeting based on what participants want to do and discuss. As your team begins to meet regularly, rotate the role of agenda-making among the members of your Core Group. This gives each person the chance to learn how to plan an effective meeting. See below for tips.

Making an Agenda: The Menu of the Meeting

Agendas are very useful for making sure that your meeting stays on track, accomplishes your goals and does not go on too long. An agenda is not complicated; it's just an ordered list of activities to do and topics to discuss. Each point on the list is an agenda "item." Assign time limits to each item according to how much time you have for the meeting overall. The meeting should range from one to two hours, if you have some fun activities and break-out groups to keep people's interest.

Distribute the draft agenda to people at the beginning of the meeting for their approval.

Somebody may want to add a topic to discuss, or change a time limit. After the draft agenda has been amended, ask for approval of the agenda by a show of hands. This act means that people accept the agenda and pledge to follow it as the meeting moves along.

The main points on the agenda will be a discussion of your issue and suggested planning actions. Some other items to include should be the following:

- Amendments to and approval of the agenda
- Icebreakers and introductions
- Questions about the highlights of the last meeting
- Updates from members since the last meeting
- Snack and bathroom breaks (these are always longer than you think they will be—overestimate the time limit on this one and you will be just fine!)
- Work time—make posters, share research, practice speeches, plan upcoming events or other activities you can do outside of official meeting space
- Discussion of date, time, place, and roles for the next meeting
- Post-meeting fun!

TAKE MORE ACTION! How To Change The World

Home	**Level I**	**Level II**
Preface, Contents	Global Citizenship: Around the World, Across the Street	Becoming Global Citizens: A Question of Choice

Sample Agenda

AGENDA

Youth Helping Youth Club
Aspiring Heights Secondary School
Meeting Agenda—December 9th, Laiah's house
Facilitator: Kelsey

1. Greetings (by Laiah) (2 min.)
2. Amendments and approval of agenda (3 min.)
3. Icebreaker (by Lauren) (5 min.)
4. Minutes from last meeting (2 min.)
5. Updates from members on their tasks (5 min.)
6. Discussion about kids in poverty in Canada (33 min.)
    Research (from Nisha and Tim)
    Brainstorm solutions
    Action ideas
7. Break! (Smoothies made by Mike!) (10 min.)
8. Break-Out Groups (30 min.)
    Logo drawing
    Poster making for car wash next Saturday
    Research crew (magazines brought by Elizabeth and Mohammed)
    Banner for car wash
9. Reminder of tasks for car wash next Saturday (by Kelly) (5 min.)
10. Next meeting—date, time, place, roles (5 min.)
11. Meeting adjourns (ends)
12. Pizza!

Post-Meeting Fun! Hike Mount Miguel and Swim (by Ari and Amanda)

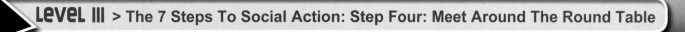
Level III > The 7 Steps To Social Action: Step Four: Meet Around The Round Table

Level III	**Level IV**	**Level V**
The Seven Steps to Social Action: Taking It to the Next Level	The How-To Guide: The Global Citizen's Toolbox	Sources And Resources, End Notes

Choose a facilitator from your Core Group for the meeting (sometimes known as "moderator" or "chairperson," but the word "facilitator" implies more equality and less control by one person). This person will be responsible for ensuring that group members participate, treat one another respectfully and follow the agenda. In the event of a conflict, facilitators cannot take sides, but must instead attempt to bring the group to a consensus, in which everyone's opinions and needs are included. This can be a challenging role, as facilitators sometimes have to remain silent about their own views for the sake of reaching an agreement.

Rotate the responsibility of facilitating among the members of your Core Group for each meeting. This gives everyone a leadership experience.

Making Meetings Fun

Put the fun back into meeting! Ask someone to prepare an icebreaker (a get-to-know-you game or energizer) to establish a fun, relaxed tone. One icebreaker is the Human Knot. The group forms a circle. Then every member reaches into the circle with their right hand and grabs someone else's right hand. Then they reach in with their left hand to grab someone else's left hand. The goal is to untangle the group without letting go of hands until the circle is formed again. Because it is a little messy and a lot of fun, the Human Knot breaks the ice for your team.

Make sure you have a fun activity planned for after the meeting, too. A bike ride, pizza and a movie, mini-putt or bowling are all fantastic ideas to maintain group unity, and to give you something to look forward to after your hard, world-changing work is done!

Ask someone to assume responsibility for recording the minutes of the meeting. The minutes serve as a record of what was discussed at the meeting. They help to clarify the reasons for which decisions were made, inform absent members about what went on, and remind participants of their tasks and responsibilities. Make sure that the individual you assign has read the box on minutes on page 153 to know how to take effective notes, and is available to type up the minutes after the meeting and send them out to everyone by e-mail.

TAKE MORE ACTION! How To Change The World

| **HOME** Preface, Contents | **LEVEL I** Global Citizenship: Around the World, Across the Street | **LEVEL II** Becoming Global Citizens: A Question of Choice |

Greet people as they enter and take a few minutes to answer any questions that they might have. Pass around a sign-up sheet and ask people to write down their names, contact information, availability and the gifts and skills they can contribute to the team.

During the meeting

Here are some suggestions for holding an effective meeting:

- Thank everyone for coming. Keep your opening remarks short and to the point. Remember that people will be looking to you for a sense of how they should act, so relax and be yourself.
- Distribute or display your draft agenda, and invite amendments before asking for final approval.
- Discuss the issue. Your first few meetings will address your goals and starting points (see Step Five, page 146) and, after that, you will focus on continuing research and action planning.
- As a group, set specific tasks for individuals to accomplish by the next meeting. Delegate all tasks and make sure everyone knows what their jobs are and when they have to be done.
- Set a firm date, time, and location for the next meeting.

Whether you are meeting in a small or large group, your discussions can be a catalyst for change. Great things can happen when young people work together.

LeveL III
The Seven Steps to Social Action:
Taking It to the Next Level

LeveL IV
The How-To Guide:
The Global Citizen's Toolbox

LeveL V
Sources And Resources,
End Notes

TROUBLESHOOTING

Tips for New Facilitators

Translated from Latin, "facilitator" means "one who makes things work." At your meeting, create a comfortable environment in which people can share, explore new ideas, and have fun. Use the following guidelines.

1. Establish a "safe" space of respect.
   Ask for input on group norms.
   Manage disputes by trying to find consensus.

2. Guide the discussion.
   Ask open-ended questions (those that don't result in just yes or no) to encourage debate.
   Intervene when people go off track and remind them of the central topic.

3. Summarize and clarify.
   Foster understanding by repeating softly spoken or confusing comments and questions.
   Summarize discussion into major points to help build consensus.

4. Involve everyone.
   Choose people who have not spoken over people who have spoken a lot.
   Ask, "Does anyone who hasn't spoken yet want to say something?"
   Try a "go-around," in which everybody gets a turn to speak about a certain topic.
   This lets them know that their contributions are valuable to the discussion.

TAKE MORE ACTION! How To Change The World

HOME	LEVEL I	LEVEL II
Preface, Contents	Global Citizenship: Around the World, Across the Street	Becoming Global Citizens: A Question of Choice

PROFILE

Kathryn Kinley: Youth Violence Activist

Some of Kathryn Kinley's greatest accomplishments emerged from one of the most challenging periods of her life.

When Kathryn was 16, she was violently assaulted by a group of girls her own age in her small Winnipeg community. Her sense of trust and security were shattered. While she was recovering in hospital, some of her friends found out who was responsible for attacking her and offered to retaliate against the group, but Kathryn refused. She knew that lashing out would not make her feel better or safer. It would only lead to more wounds and leave unanswered the only question that she really had: What had made people her own age want to hurt her, and how could she prevent it from happening to others?

Slowly, Kathryn gathered the courage to take more meaningful action to change the growing culture of violence among youth. She was soon accepted onto Team Youth, a pilot project consisting of a small group of motivated teens who conduct workshops and discussion groups at high schools, with the goal of identifying and finding solutions to the issues surrounding youth violence in Manitoba.

To begin a session, Team Youth facilitators first explain that their purpose is to ensure that every student's voice is heard, then lay out the ground rules to be followed during the workshop, such as the need to show respect for the views of others. In order to put new participants at ease, Team Youth members often share some of their own stories.

Discussing her attack was not always easy for Kathryn, but opening up to educate others has helped her to heal and to create something positive from a terrible experience. Combining the insights of students from diverse communities and backgrounds has also resulted in some eye-opening discussions. Working together, participants have been able to identify issues such as racism, poverty, boredom, stereotypes, and a lack of expectations as factors contributing to problems among their age group. Team Youth sees education and awareness as a major part of the solution, along with bringing their concerns to the government.

Kathryn is also a member of the Manitoba Youth Parliament, working to influence provincial policy concerning youth issues. Her activities have given her the satisfaction of tackling the issue at the root, in the hopes that fewer people will have to encounter the pain and fear of violence first-hand. Speaking out about the issue has helped her to regain the confidence that she had lost in the attack, and to transform one of her most difficult experiences into a moment of leadership, growth, and social change.

Level III > The Seven Steps To Social Action: Profile: Kathryn Kinley

Level III	**Level IV**	**Level V**
The Seven Steps to Social Action: Taking It to the Next Level	The How-To Guide: The Global Citizen's Toolbox	Sources And Resources, End Notes

- How were the Team Youth meetings helpful to Kathryn and her peers in discovering the root causes of youth violence in their communities?

- Try to imagine yourself in a position similar to Kathryn's. How could your group make you feel comfortable talking about a difficult experience that relates to your issue? How could they turn it into an empowering experience for both you and the team?

- Brainstorm a list of group norms or ground rules to make your meetings more effective and encourage everyone (especially quiet people) to participate freely and to share their different perspectives.

TAKE MORE ACTION! How To Change The World

HOME	LeveL I	LeveL II
Preface, Contents	Global Citizenship: Around the World, Across the Street	Becoming Global Citizens: A Question of Choice

Recording Minutes of the Meeting

The minutes for your meeting should include the following:

- The name of your group
- The date, time, and place of the meeting
- Who is present
- Who has sent their regrets
- Who is missing
- The agenda for the meeting
- What time the meeting started
- A short summary of what was discussed with respect to each agenda item, and points made by individual members
- Statement of decisions made
- Tasks delegated for next meeting
- Date, time, and place for next meeting and the roles assigned
- Time the meeting was ended

Evaluating what happened at the meeting

Take some time at the end of the meeting to talk about the meeting itself. Ask your Core Group to consider the following questions:

- What went right and what went wrong, and why?
- Did we meet the goals we set for ourselves?
- Did we address all the points on the agenda?
- Was the discussion on track or unfocused?
- Did we make an effort to help everyone feel comfortable and participate?
- Did group members listen effectively and build on one another's ideas?
- Are we all committed to the decisions that we made?
- Does everyone feel empowered to take on his or her responsibilities?
- Did we have fun?
- What should we do differently next time?

Level III
The Seven Steps to Social Action:
Taking It to the Next Level

Level IV
The How-To Guide:
The Global Citizen's Toolbox

Level V
Sources And Resources,
End Notes

You're not off the hook just yet. After the meeting, don't forget to:

- Call or e-mail first-time participants and thank them for coming.
- To all group members, distribute or e-mail a copy of the minutes to remind them of tasks they agreed to complete before the next meeting.
- Follow up with some people individually, especially those who may need encouragement to see their tasks through. Inform the group that you will be checking in with people in case anyone needs any help. Be sure to assess progress on actions during subsequent meetings. Make yourself available.

TAKE MORE ACTION! How To Change The World

HOME	**LeVeL I**	**LeVeL II**
Preface, Contents	Global Citizenship: Around the World, Across the Street	Becoming Global Citizens: A Question of Choice

Take Action!

Write a draft agenda for a meeting that you could have on your chosen issue. Brainstorm five great icebreakers and team-building activities, and three potential post-meeting activities you would try at a meeting. Share your list with a group of three or four others. Add the ideas you like to your list.

Hold a meeting on your chosen issue. It could be at school or at your home on the weekend. Don't forget the agenda, the minute taker, the food and the fun!

SOLUTION AHEAD

INCREASE SPEED

LeveL III > The Seven Steps To Social Action: Step Five: Set A Mission

LeveL III	**LeveL IV**	**LeveL V**
The Seven Steps to Social Action: Taking It to the Next Level	The How-To Guide: The Global Citizen's Toolbox	Sources And Resources, End Notes

STEP FIVE: SET A MISSION

You are now passionate about an issue that you understand very well. You have a Dream Team, and you are ready to hold effective meetings. It is time, then, to focus on a critical question: What do you want to do? Most of this step will be part of the main discussion at your first few meetings.

In order to turn your dreams into reality, you have to decide what your dreams are. You have to put all of your passion, research and teamwork into charting a path that you can follow to fulfill your mission.

Mission: possible

But what is our mission? Good question! Your mission is your ultimate objective. Again, close your eyes and picture your dream world. What does it look like? What has to be changed to achieve it? That is your mission. It could be to eradicate poverty or AIDS in Africa. It could be to ensure that no animal is ever abused again. It could be to stop the bullying that happens regularly at your school. At Free The Children, our mission is to end the exploitation of children around the world.

Remember: Your mission does not have to be huge. But it can be! For example, if your mission is to have recycling in every school in the world, your concrete goal could be to have a recycling program at your school. If your mission is to provide an education to every child in the world, your concrete goal could be to raise enough money to build one school in a developing country. Your mission does not have to be something that your group will do alone—you can be part of a larger movement. But it has to be what you picture your perfect world to be. The key to mission setting is dreaming.

TIP

Your mission may be smaller. It may be to put an end to the bullying that occurs regularly at your school. But you don't really want to try to solve the bullying that happens at all the other schools in your community. That's okay! Any change for good is a step in the right direction.

TAKE MORE ACTION! How To Change The World

HOME	LeveL I	LeveL II
Preface, Contents	Global Citizenship: Around the World, Across the Street	Becoming Global Citizens: A Question of Choice

Mission statements

Once you have defined your mission in your mind, clarify it and make it stronger by creating a mission statement, also known as your group's mandate. This statement will be an inspirational reminder of the dream that you are all working toward.

For example, the mission statement of a youth organization working on the issue of substance abuse might be:

Safe Choices is a national youth empowerment network dedicated to preventing substance abuse and promoting positive decisions among youth through education, intervention, and advocacy initiatives.

As a team, write out your mission statement in no more than thirty powerful and uplifting words. Have each member post it where he or she can see it—on the mirror, desktop or Web site. Read it aloud at the beginning of a meeting to keep you and your team fired up about your issue every day!

Goals: scoring one at a time

Goal setting teaches you to translate your dreams into incremental steps that lead you steadily to your destination. Your goals then become benchmarks that you can use to measure your progress, and reasons to celebrate the small victories on the road to eventual triumph. Your next step is to break the mission down into three sets of major goals: awareness raising, fundraising and political change. As an example, let's look at the mission of ending child labor. That's how we started out!

Awareness-raising major goals include actions and attitudes that you want the general public to adopt once they are informed about the issue.
Fundraising major goals include what you hope to achieve by giving monetary donations to those in need.

Political change major goals include the end result in changed laws and policies achieved through your pressure campaigns aimed at governments and businesses.

"IT MAY BE THOSE WHO DO MOST, DREAM MOST."

—Stephen Leacock
(1869-1944)
Humorist, economist

TIP

*The **How-To Section** of this book has information on the skills you will want to put to use here. See the sections on **Getting the Word Out Through the Media, Connecting With People, Working With Money, and Plugging Into the Political System** to help you reach these goals.*

These are some daunting major goals staring at you. What are some ways you can realistically hope to achieve them? Your task now is to set concrete goals with tangible results, to help you reach each of your major goals. After that, you will need to come up with different actions that you can take in your school and community to fulfill those concrete goals (there are some fun ideas in Step Six!). Depending on the size of your Dream Team, you can tackle several concrete goals at a time. You can also always add new goals, so start with just a few. For examples, look back to the list of goals for child labor on page 116.

"THE WAY TO ACHIEVE A DIFFICULT THING WAS TO SET IT IN MOTION."

—Kate O'Brien
(1897-1974)
Author, journalist

LeVeL III
The Seven Steps to Social Action:
Taking It to the Next Level

LeVeL IV
The How-To Guide:
The Global Citizen's Toolbox

LeVeL V
Sources And Resources,
End Notes

Taking the time to formulate your goals may sound tedious, but your critics and supporters will always ask how you know that your group is achieving its goals. When your stated goals as an organization are clear, you will be able to indicate the status of your progress toward them (like those money thermometers people use to track their fundraising efforts). You will know where you have succeeded so far, and what still needs to be done. In this way, goal setting can provide legitimacy for you in the public sphere, as it allows for both you and others to measure your impact.

TIP

If you are taking action as a group, the group as a whole must decide upon the goals. You need the support of every member to succeed. Make sure you celebrate when you succeed in meeting one of your goals. This will give you a feeling of accomplishment and keep you energized and moving toward your mission!

TAKE MORE ACTION! How To Change The World

HOME	LEVEL I	LEVEL II
Preface, Contents	Global Citizenship: Around the World, Across the Street	Becoming Global Citizens: A Question of Choice

Creating your identity

When deciding how to present your group to the world, the first thing to do is to choose a name for your organization. Avoid choosing a generic name. "Student Action Group" just does not work. Brainstorm with your group to come up with a personalized and original name. A name should not be too long, although you can always use an acronym (a word formed from the initial letters of a series of words). Choose something catchy and different that will stick in people's minds and that they will not tend to confuse with the names of other groups.

Some well-known examples are:

Oxfam
Amnesty International
Peace Corps
Greenpeace
Doctors Without Borders (Médecins Sans Frontières)

Free The Children
children helping children through education

To be effective, a logo must capture the essence of your group's mission.

The Free The Children logo depicts children embracing the world. This represents the organization's youth-driven spirit and its international identity.

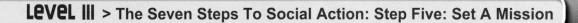

Level III The Seven Steps to Social Action: Taking It to the Next Level	**Level IV** The How-To Guide: The Global Citizen's Toolbox	**Level V** Sources And Resources, End Notes

TIP

Get down to a list of three or four possible names for your organization, then test them out on your friends to see which ones get the most enthusiasm.

Just as major corporations do, social justice groups need their logos too! Design a logo with lots of color that embodies your message in some way. If it is eye-catching and creative, people will always recognize it.

As you define your group's mandate, name, and logo, it is important to keep certain key components of this identity consistent, such as words, colors and visuals, when using different media to raise awareness of your issue. This allows the public to come to associate these elements with your organization, and to make your group more prominent in their minds. This process refers to an important marketing concept known as branding. The most important aspect of branding is to associate your organization with a specific cause and a set of core values that people will immediately think of when they come across your publicity.

Successful branding examples among social action groups include:

- Amnesty International's candle logo and letter-writing campaigns to free political prisoners
- World Vision's television ads for their child sponsorship program and their 30 Hour Famine
- Free The Children's "children helping children" and schoolbuilding campaign

In the Getting the Word Out Through the Media section of this book, you will learn more about how to take your branding effort to the public.

Take Action!

Create a powerful mission statement for your chosen issue. Make it inspiring and post it where you can see it every day.

Create a goals chart for your chosen issue. Start with the mission and major goals. Be creative when brainstorming concrete goals. Present your chart to a partner for review.

Choose a name and design a logo for the social action group that you envision. Present it to two classmates and ask for their feedback.

TAKE MORE ACTION! How To Change The World

HOME	LeVeL I	LeVeL II
Preface, Contents	Global Citizenship: Around the World, Across the Street	Becoming Global Citizens: A Question of Choice

"A SHIP IN THE HARBOR IS SAFE, BUT THAT'S NOT WHAT SHIPS ARE BUILT FOR."

—William Greenough Thayer Shedd
(1820-1894)
Theologian, author, educator

Terry Fox's initial goal was to collect $1 for every person living in Canada, about 24 million people at the time.
To date, the Terry Fox Run has raised well over $300 million for cancer research.

Level III
The Seven Steps to Social Action:
Taking It to the Next Level

Level IV
The How-To Guide:
The Global Citizen's Toolbox

Level V
Sources And Resources,
End Notes

STEP SIX: TAKE ACTION!

In 1977, a young man from Winnipeg named Terry Fox learned that he had bone cancer and was forced to have his right leg amputated six inches above the knee. While recovering in hospital, Terry was so overcome by the suffering of other cancer patients that he decided to run across Canada to raise money for cancer research. He was determined to do something so that others after him would one day have a cure. After 18 months of training, Terry started his run in St. John's, Newfoundland, on April 12, 1980. It was difficult to attract attention at first, and for a long time, Terry ran alone. He ran 42 kilometers a day through Canada's Atlantic provinces, Québec, and Ontario, and slowly public enthusiasm for his cause began to grow.

His action raised awareness and a great deal of money for cancer research, and created hope and inspiration for others who suffered from the disease. After 143 days, Terry was forced to stop running because cancer had spread to his lungs. He died on June 28, 1981, at the age of 22. Terry Fox set the bar on human courage, strength and heart higher than ever before, and millions of Canadians and others around the world have followed his lead.

Many people reach a certain stage in social involvement and stop. Well-intended and well-informed efforts to make a difference often get wasted because of a lack of action. Actions bring your research, teamwork and planning together in a way that informs the public about your campaign, strengthens the voice of your group, and implements concrete change.

A well-planned action is a demonstration of your passion and power. It says that you are committed to change and are willing to do more than just talk. Actions are what separate the complainers from the world-changers. Which one are *you*? What will *your* action be?

TAKE MORE ACTION! How To Change The World

| **Home**
Preface, Contents | **Level I**
Global Citizenship:
Around the World, Across the Street | **Level II**
Becoming Global Citizens:
A Question of Choice |

There are lots of crazy ideas out there, and many traditional ones too, for actions that you can take on your own, at school and in your community to effect real change. Actions can include petitions, letter-writing campaigns, fundraisers, demonstrations, presentations, speeches, vigils, workshops, volunteering in your community or overseas, pressure campaigns, civil disobedience, litter pick-ups, concerts, and sitting up in a tree for two years. They can also include small actions that your group can pass on to others. Some examples are:

- give compliments
- bring litter-free lunches
- buy non-sweatshop clothing
- ride your bike to get to places
- reduce the amount of water you use
- buy rechargeable batteries and bulk groceries
- bring cloth bags on shopping trips
- buy fair trade products
- e-mail greeting cards
- reuse the other side of paper
- buy organic and local food
- do something nice for one person every day

How's *that* for choice?

TROUBLESHOOTING

The Secret to a Successful Action Plan

When making an action plan, start small and get bigger and bigger. When you begin with easy, everyday actions like smiling or carrying a reusable water bottle, your group members are instantly empowered because they have changed the world! The more you do, the better you feel, until the actions become so big that no one can believe how huge your impact has become!

When you are so ready to take action that you are about to explode, you need a plan of action! Think back to your goal chart: What actions can you take to fulfill your concrete goals? Make sure you relate every action back to a major goal—either awareness raising, fundraising or a political change goal—so that you and your team can see the "big picture" as you work! Some actions may fulfill several goals at the same time!

LEVEL III	**LEVEL IV**	**LEVEL V**
The Seven Steps to Social Action: Taking It to the Next Level	The How-To Guide: The Global Citizen's Toolbox	Sources And Resources, End Notes

Two powerful questions to spark your brainstorming are:
- What is a simple, inexpensive way of getting your message across?
- What has never been done before?

A successful action:
- Reflects the values of your group
- Makes good use of all the diverse gifts and skills available
- Is well planned and researched
- Includes activities that build up team spirit and solidarity
- Is valued and supported by all group members
- Establishes the group's credibility as a knowledgeable, passionate force on the landscape of life (or just as a serious, smart, and determined team)
- Enlarges your membership and base of support

An effective plan of action begins with a sound knowledge of where you are and where you want to go.

TAKE MORE ACTION! How To Change The World

| **HOME** Preface, Contents | **LEVEL I** Global Citizenship: Around the World, Across the Street | **LEVEL II** Becoming Global Citizens: A Question of Choice |

Action Ideas

You can adapt some of these actions to your issue, or use this list as a springboard to create your own action ideas for your cause!

- Invite an activist to speak to your class or school to educate your peers about a common issue of concern.
- Publish a school newspaper to raise awareness about social issues and to offer a youthful perspective on current events.
- Arrange a debate at your school between advocates on two sides of a contentious issue, or between political candidates during election time, so they can respond to youth concerns and help your peers become more informed.
- Take a Vow of Silence for a week. Ask people to sponsor you with pledges for every day that you go without speaking. Donate the money you raise to a charity.
- Organize a Stand Up for Human Rights Day at your school, during which students literally spend the entire day standing up to show their support for human rights everywhere.
- Organize a Living Simply Day at your school to raise awareness of the social and environmental impacts of our culture of consumerism every October 10th. Or you can have one every week or month!
- Start a peer mediation program at your school in which students are trained to act as a neutral third party in student disagreements, to help find solutions that all parties can agree on.
- If your school has a graduation prom, organize a post-dance safe grad party offering fun, alcohol-free and drug-free activities (such as live bands, movies, etc.)
- Volunteer as a peer tutor to help students who are having academic problems in school.
- Ask your principal if, once a month, a block of class time can be devoted to cleaning up the school grounds and picking up litter in a local park.
- If your school does not recycle, ask your principal about installing recycling bins for paper, bottles, and cans. If your school does, organize a recycle and reuse campaign that encourages litter-free lunches!
- Involve your school or community in a Car-Free Day.
- Ask your principal to replace junk food in the school cafeteria and vending machines with healthy alternatives.
- Organize a Global Food Fair at your school that invites students to sample new dishes and learn about other cultures at the same time.
- Welcome new students to your school. Match newcomers with peer welcome buddies to show them around.

- If you know of a vacant lot or other outdoor space that is not being used in your community, seek permission to turn it into an organic community garden that your group could upkeep. Consider donating some of the produce to a homeless shelter or food bank.
- Whether your talent is art or computers, share it by teaching a workshop at a homeless shelter, a middle school or a seniors' center.
- Organize "street runs" to take food, warm clothes, and friendship to the homeless on your city streets and brighten their day. In smaller communities, work with existing community groups that provide these services.
- Organize a TV-free weekend featuring outdoor activities in your schoolyard or local park. Make it a fundraiser for a local charity.
- Help alleviate hunger in your community by organizing a Halloween For Hunger campaign to collect non-perishable food items for food banks.
- Hold a 24-hour hunger strike in which you raise awareness and money through donors and sponsors to help starving children in poor communities around the world.

By starting out with small actions, you may find yourself one day tackling much bigger goals such as building a school in a developing country.

TAKE MORE ACTION! How To Change The World

HOME	LEVEL I	LEVEL II
Preface, Contents	Global Citizenship: Around the World, Across the Street	Becoming Global Citizens: A Question of Choice

Actions that a group should avoid

The best way to guard against the wrong path is to choose actions that represent the values of your group and appeal to your collective sense of what is right. Actions that go against the values you are promoting undermine your purpose and credibility. If you are looking for justice, you must be fair; if you want to gain people's respect, you should do so respectfully.

Try to ensure that everyone on the team supports the action. If someone in the group disagrees, be sure to consider his or her reasoning and let it weigh into the group's final decision. No action you take should be violent, destructive or unsafe in any way. Everything you do should contribute toward your ultimate goal: making the world a better place.

Evaluate your action

Once you have acted, it is important to review and evaluate both the project and your teamwork. Gather for a group debriefing session and ask questions that encourage constructive criticism, so that you can learn from the experience and become more effective activists. To know if you have made a difference, for example, you have to find out the following:

- How many people heard you and your group speak, visited a display or walked away with a flyer? How many people signed up to join? (This is called "quantitative" or quantity, number-based evaluation.)
- How did people react to the information presented or to your action? Did you get a lot of community support? (This is called "qualitative"' or quality, word-based evaluation.)
- Did the action put pressure on a decision maker? How do you know? What was the person's reaction (in words and actions)?
- Did the action contribute to your goal?
-

To be able to answer these questions, it is important to plan ahead. Before taking your action, set aside some group time to develop monitoring and evaluation plans that will allow you to measure your success in quantity and in quality to show you and your supporters your accomplishments—and your efforts to be even better! Monitoring materials to use during your action can include feedback forms, surveys and tallies. Before a speech, leave sheets of paper on chairs so that audience members can make comments—both positive and constructive. Assign team members or volunteers to be responsible for designing the feedback forms, distributing and collecting them, and compiling the information and evaluating it afterward.

LeveL III > The Seven Steps To Social Action: Step Six: Take Action!

LeveL III
The Seven Steps to Social Action:
Taking It to the Next Level

LeveL IV
The How-To Guide:
The Global Citizen's Toolbox

LeveL V
Sources And Resources,
End Notes

"PUT SIMPLY IT IS THIS; NO ACTION IS EVER
LOST—NOTHING WE DO IS WITHOUT RESULT."

—Robertson Davies
(1913-1996)
Author

TAKE MORE ACTION! How To Change The World

HOME	LEVEL I	LEVEL II
Preface, Contents	Global Citizenship: Around the World, Across the Street	Becoming Global Citizens: A Question of Choice

A feedback form may look like this:

Sample Feedback Form

Youth Helping Youth Big Event

Thank you for attending our event today. Please take a few moments to provide us with some feedback!

What did you enjoy about this event?

_____
_____

What could be improved next time?

_____
_____

Contact Information (to keep you up-to-date about future events):
Name: _____
Address: _____
Phone #: _____ E-mail: _____
School: _____ Grade: _____

Feel free to elaborate on the reverse side. Please consider writing a short testimonial for our funders and supporters.

Thank you for supporting Youth Helping Youth! See you next time!

It is important that you seek out and receive feedback from participants and outside observers, as their opinions and ideas can help you to improve your planning for the future. Also, you can show the testimonials to your sponsors so that they know how well you are doing. In the end, the measure of your success will be your ability to answer these two questions: Is the world a better place because of your action? Do you feel better as a global citizen because of it?

"THE FUTURE BELONGS TO THOSE WHO BELIEVE IN THE BEAUTY OF THEIR DREAMS."

—Eleanor Roosevelt
(1884-1952)
Diplomat and First Lady of the United States

Changing the world is not easy. In fact, it is downright hard. It looks like it might take forever, because it will require a great deal of continual dedication, energy and effort. However, by starting with small, daily actions and working your way up to bigger campaigns, you can do it! You can change the world. Those five golden words sound idealistic. But they are magic words, because if you genuinely, wholeheartedly believe them—like Julia Butterfly Hill did, and Nellie McClung did, and Nelson Mandela did, and Mother Teresa did, and Terry Fox did, and the members of Free The Children around the world do believe—they are true. If you do not believe them, they are not true. It is as simple as that.

Believe. That's where a better world begins.

TAKE MORE ACTION! How To Change The World

HOME	LeveL I	LeveL II
Preface, Contents	Global Citizenship: Around the World, Across the Street	Becoming Global Citizens: A Question of Choice

PROFILE

Schools Taking Action

Check out what students across North America are doing to take on urgent global issues. Their actions may motivate you to pursue similar initiatives or inspire you to create your own unique approach. How would actions like these work in *your* school?

Level III > The Seven Steps To Social Action: Step Six: Take Action!

Level III	**Level IV**	**Level V**
The Seven Steps to Social Action: Taking It to the Next Level	The How-To Guide: The Global Citizen's Toolbox	Sources And Resources, End Notes

Kingwood High School (Kingwood, Texas)

The students of Kingwood High School have come together in an outpouring of energy and excitement in a number of ingenious fundraisers. They've rallied together for car washes, garage sales, sales of custom-designed T-shirts and a "Battle of the Bands" that showcased the school's many talented students. These actions have brought newfound unity to a student body of over 4,000, getting new kids involved and keeping the spirit alive in graduating students with the "Kiss the Seniors Goodbye" campaign, where students raise money by delivering Hershey's Kisses to their graduating friends. More importantly, classroom presentations and special movie screenings have shown students the effects of their good work, which this year raised enough money to build a school in war-torn Sierra Leone.

Maidstone High School (Maidstone, Saskatchewan)

Student leaders attended a leadership conference where they learned about the negative impact of globalization on the world's children. Upon returning to their school, they wanted to mobilize the entire student body to take action. The students began by launching a school-wide information campaign. They designed posters and banners with statistics on child labor and sexual exploitation, which were then hung throughout the school. They also organized a Dance For Life event to raise funds for Canadian charities working to provide education to children in developing countries.

TAKE MORE ACTION! How To Change The World

HOME	LeveL I	LeveL II
Preface, Contents	Global Citizenship: Around the World, Across the Street	Becoming Global Citizens: A Question of Choice

Neil Reid High School (Clinton Township, Michigan)

Neil Reid High School is a unique school focusing on students with special needs and disabilities. Despite their own personal challenges, these students are reaching out to help their peers in Sri Lanka. They set out the ambitious goal of raising enough money to build a one-room schoolhouse in the Ampara District of Sri Lanka, an area that has struggled to rebound from the 2004 tsunami, which struck this region particularly hard. The students of Neil Reid High School raised hundreds of dollars by selling tickets to watch the hometown football team, the Detroit Lions, play in Ford Field. They showed how they can overcome their personal challenges by inviting families and friends to take part in an afternoon walk-a-thon and picnic to raise awareness and inspire others to chip in. Together, they've empowered themselves to make positive change and brought education to the young people who need help most.

Point Grey Secondary School (Vancouver, British Columbia)

Students founded an organization dedicated to taking action on global issues and supporting charitable organizations working for peace. The group launched one exciting project after the next, beginning with a series of workshops on child labor at local elementary schools, and a documentary film festival to raise awareness of global issues. Next, they held a two-day conference focused on war-affected children, with guest speakers from the Red Cross, and an "amputee for a day" activity, in which participants carried a crutch and could not use a limb, to understand the plight of war-affected children. The group also organized a fundraising Keep the Beat music marathon for an organization called War Child, including a freestyling contest, a drumming circle, a local DJ and a barbecue. Another creative event included slam poets and Capoeira (Brazilian martial art/dance)!

Thornhill Secondary School (Thornhill, Ontario)

A group of students founded the Power and Diversity Club to promote cultural understanding among the student body. One of their most exciting actions was organizing a fashion show called "360 Degrees Around the World," featuring music and traditional fashions from Paris, India, Hong Kong, Iran and Africa. To make this an inclusive and successful event, the club ensured that there was equal participation of students of all cultural backgrounds and body types. For the International Week Against Racism, they designed and distributed T-shirts with positive social messages such as: "There is only one race—the human race," and "Laundry is the only thing that should be separated by color."

LeVeL III
The Seven Steps to Social Action:
Taking It to the Next Level

LeVeL IV
The How-To Guide:
The Global Citizen's Toolbox

LeVeL V
Sources And Resources,
End Notes

Take Action!

   Brainstorm ten simple, everyday actions you can take on your chosen issue or on any other issue that can make a difference. Choose three and commit to doing them, starting today.
   Come up with one action for each of your major goals in the goal chart for your chosen issue: (1) raise awareness, (2) raise funds, and (3) political change. Choose one and describe step-by-step how you will implement the action—whom will you get to help, where will you start, what materials and preparation will you need?
   Carry out your one action on your chosen issue. Don't forget to celebrate when you succeed!

TAKE MORE ACTION! How To Change The World

HOME	LEVEL I	LEVEL II
Preface, Contents	Global Citizenship: Around the World, Across the Street	Becoming Global Citizens: A Question of Choice

STEP SEVEN: BRING IN THE FUN!

The most amazing, fantastic and electrifying thing about taking action is that, in order to truly succeed, you must have fun! Without it, you will succumb to despair during those inevitable moments of your campaign when you feel overwhelmed, discouraged or even bored. This is natural; your dream world will not arrive overnight, spontaneously showing up at your front door one day. Being an active global citizen will often mean taking risks, going against what is popular, and putting yourself on the line. You will encounter opposition along the way. But with the power of fun, your world-changing voyage will become an adventure! Remember: having fun does not mean that you are not committed to the issue. It means that your dedication fulfils you, makes you feel good about yourself, and motivates you to do more.

When Free The Children was first founded, a radio talk show host in Toronto publicly announced that young people were interested in malls and video games, and that it was abnormal for us to be speaking out about social issues. The only thing youth are interested in is having fun, he said. However, with our determination, our research, our passionate Level 3 spirit, we have proved people like him wrong. We have changed the world. And we've had the time of our lives!

Here's how to set the fun-o-meter on high:

- Celebrate your victories, big and small—have a superhero costume party, watch a ball game on TV or enjoy a big tub of ice cream together.

- Let your meetings build friendships as well as action plans—have a fun break with a team-building exercise like building a human pyramid or breaking the Guinness World Record for shoe towers!

- Let go of your inhibitions and try new, fun ideas that sound crazy at first—the more you can truly be yourself and break away from the confines of "cool," the more people will pay attention!

To stay positive, remember your passion booster—that picture, ring or poem you keep handy to remind you of your mission, and rekindle your commitment to act. Make sure you surround yourself with teammates who inspire and encourage one another. Everyone needs the support and friendship of those who share the same vision and goals. Remind each other why you first became involved, and refuse to compromise the values that brought you together. Make a regular habit out of affirmation, either spontaneously or as part of a meeting. Constantly provide a barrage of compliments and appreciation for one another. When you hang around with people who believe in you, your belief in yourself will never let you down.

Celebrate your victories in different and fun ways.

TAKE MORE ACTION! How To Change The World

HOME	LeveL I	LeveL II
Preface, Contents	Global Citizenship: Around the World, Across the Street	Becoming Global Citizens: A Question of Choice

And finally, look to role models to remind you of what is possible. From Stephen Lewis and Terry Fox to local activists, your family and teachers, people have overcome huge obstacles to make this world the beautiful place that it is. We have come a long way thanks to the tireless efforts of millions before us. But there is more work to do. Our legacy begins *now*.

Take Action!

Think of five ways that you could celebrate an accomplishment that is small, but still deserves to be celebrated.

Think of five amazing ways that you could celebrate a major accomplishment.

"DON'T BE AFRAID OF OPPOSITION.
REMEMBER A KITE RISES AGAINST,
NOT WITH, THE WIND."

—Hamilton Mabie
(1845-1916)
Author, editor, critic

TAKE MORE ACTION! How To Change The World

HOME	LEVEL I	LEVEL II
Preface, Contents	Global Citizenship: Around the World, Across the Street	Becoming Global Citizens: A Question of Choice

PROFILE

Rachel Herold: A Responsibility to Take Action

"We have the power and responsibility to do something," says Rachel Herold of Scarsdale, NY. "We can make a difference."

At a young age, Rachel had already learned about poverty issues through her older sister, who had been actively involved in fundraising activities of her own. Rachel saw that the best way to make a lasting impact for families in impoverished regions such as sub-Saharan Africa is not to simply send money or donations, but to probe deeper to explore the root causes of poverty. She could see that providing education resources and long-term sources of income were much more effective ways of helping people. Even where schools exist, extreme poverty often forces children to work instead of attend classes. Rachel saw how families that achieve ways of supporting themselves are better equipped to tackle the many challenges of survival in these troubled areas.

Rachel also recognized the many privileges she and her classmates enjoyed in North America, such as education and health care, which millions of children around the world do not. But rather than feeling guilty over her good fortune, she took it as a source of power—and, most importantly, the need to use that power to help others.

Rachel transformed this power into action, rallying her students by leading the Scarsdale High School Youth in Action Group as Education Coordinator and then President, doing everything within her power to educate her classmates and spearhead projects to help impoverished children.

The Scarsdale group held two carnivals for local youth to raise funds for Free The Children's alternative income projects in the developing world. Their activities featured creative activities such as musical twister, tennis ball bowling, an animal bean bag toss, and "pin the tail on the goat." A dinner dance, a silent auction and the powerful Vow of Silence campaign—in which kids in North America recognize those millions of young people worldwide who lack a voice in standing up for their rights—raised thousands of dollars to help children in Kenya receive an education.

The group's work helped to empower Kenyan women with the provision of milking animals and sewing machines. Through such supplies, women are able to earn a sustainable income to support their families, thereby enabling children to attend school instead of work. With this much-needed support, these communities are taking the first steps toward breaking free of the cycle of poverty.

As she moves on to Cornell University, Rachel passes the reins of leading the Scarsdale group to her successors. Furthering a lifetime of social action, she continues to promote development

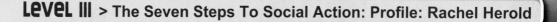

LeveL III	**LeveL IV**	**LeveL V**
The Seven Steps to Social Action: Taking It to the Next Level	The How-To Guide: The Global Citizen's Toolbox	Sources And Resources, End Notes

projects and spread awareness through social issue-based workshops with local middle schools, working to spark the passions of the next generation of global citizens.

Rachel Herold saw that with great power comes great responsibility—and she hasn't looked back since.

- What kinds of challenges might someone in an average North American community face in drawing their peers' attention to problems in faraway countries? How can these challenges be met?

- How can young people engage cynical people to overcome apathy and ignorance in helping others? Is it through triggering their sense of guilt, or appealing to their inner compassion?

- Imagine that you were truly inspired to take a similar action in your school. What kind of reactions would you expect to hear from your friends and classmates? How would they affect your decision to continue? What would give you the energy to keep trying?

TAKE MORE ACTION! How To Change The World

HOME	LEVEL I	LEVEL II
Preface, Contents	Global Citizenship: Around the World, Across the Street	Becoming Global Citizens: A Question of Choice

THE HOW-TO GUIDE:
THE GLOBAL CITIZEN'S TOOLBOX

TAKE MORE ACTION! How To Change The World

HOME Preface, Contents	**LEVEL I** Global Citizenship: Around the World, Across the Street	**LEVEL II** Becoming Global Citizens: A Question of Choice

UNLOCKING YOUR TOOLBOX

The tools in that old banged-up toolbox in your basement can fix leaky faucets and build wood cabinets. But the Global Citizen's Toolbox contains the knowledge and skills to fix world hunger and build a stronger community! It is covered with inspirational quotations and images of a better world, and bursting with Level 3 energy. Once you unlock the power within it, you will develop the ability to do the following:

• Cultivate a network of supporters and allies, find creative solutions to resolve conflicts, and negotiate among different ideas and perspectives
• Make your message convincing and unforgettable, taking it to the larger public through the media, the Internet, artistic expression, and public speaking.
• Exercise your right to political participation and work for real political change by interacting with government
• Make direct change by raising money and materials for your projects and people in need
• Assert your power as a consumer by making and encouraging ethical shopping choices on a daily basis

As you explore these different skills and move ahead into new areas of action, remember the values from which your purpose first emerged. Your task is to use the tools within this How-To Guide to articulate your values, to build them into the world as a concrete reality. When used with the Seven Steps to Social Action, these skills will unlock your power to create a better world.

"BEHOLD THE TURTLE. HE ONLY MAKES PROGRESS WHEN HE STICKS HIS NECK OUT."

—James Bryant Conant
(1893-1978)
Chemist, diplomat

TAKE MORE ACTION! How To Change The World

HOME	LEVEL I	LEVEL II
Preface, Contents	Global Citizenship: Around the World, Across the Street	Becoming Global Citizens: A Question of Choice

CONNECTING WITH PEOPLE

When you are passionate about a social issue and want to draw more people to your cause, you have to create legitimacy for both your voice and your message. As young people, however, making your presence felt among new networks of people can often be a challenge. Because your words will invite greater scrutiny than those of adults will, you must work even harder to establish credibility for yourself and your issue.

LEVEL IV > The How To Guide: Connecting With People

| **LEVEL III**
The Seven Steps to Social Action:
Taking It to the Next Level | **LEVEL IV**
The How-To Guide:
The Global Citizen's Toolbox | **LEVEL V**
Sources And Resources,
End Notes |

First impressions: no second chances!

Interpersonal communication begins with your first contact, even before you open your mouth. They say you don't get a second chance to make a first impression, so when meeting people in a setting where you will be able to discuss your issue, follow these tips to make them take a second look and say, "Who is this wonderful, bright young person?"

- Dress appropriately to feel confident about your physical appearance when you are speaking to people in a professional setting.
- If it's culturally appropriate, offer a firm handshake when meeting a new person. Look the person in the eye when you say hello.
- Try to remember people's names. This shows them that they are important to you and that you are interested in learning more about them. An effective memory technique is to repeat the name right away out loud, while nodding and smiling as a way to verify what the person said, or in a sentence like, "Nice to meet you, Maura."
- Find a place for your hands that is comfortable before you enter a social situation. Try not to cross your arms or put your hands in your pockets; otherwise, find out how you feel most comfortable so that you are not worrying about your hands and fidgeting while talking to people.
- Smile, relax, and be yourself. Many people believe that a professional setting requires a reserved attitude, but we say that's not what will make them remember you! Put people at ease by showing your human side. That said, remember to address people with respect.
- Encourage people to talk about themselves. Try to get to know the individuals, not only their issues.

Assertive listening

Although leaders are often thought of as individuals who are skilled at projecting their own ideas, it is also true that good leaders know how to listen. They know that listening is an opportunity to learn and to understand the perspectives and opinions of others. Listening is also a form of outgoing communication. Your listening habits can strongly influence the way people feel about themselves, about you, and about the relationship between you. Assertive listening makes the speaker feel valued, respect you and enjoy your company. The power of your listening skills to make or break your relationship with any person—friends, family or world-changing colleague—cannot be underestimated.

 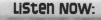

TAKE MORE ACTION! How To Change The World

HOME Preface, Contents	LEVEL I Global Citizenship: Around the World, Across the Street	LEVEL II Becoming Global Citizens: A Question of Choice

- When you are listening to someone, take genuine interest in what he or she is saying. You will learn something.
- Avoid distractions by consciously establishing a space where the only people around that matter are you and the speaker. Concentrate on what the speaker is saying and truly hear him or her.
- Look the speaker in the eyes.
- Nod when you agree with points being made; this lets the speaker know that you are listening.
- Keep an open stance (uncross your arms and legs and be comfortable and relaxed) and an open mind.
- Affirm that the speaker's feelings are valid and try to empathize with his or her emotions. Use words such as: "Yes," "Interesting," and "Please continue." Your facial expressions, a smile or a look of concern, can reflect your empathy as well.
- Ask open-ended questions (not those that result in just "yes" or "no") that encourage the individual to continue speaking.

Take Action!

- Practise your firm handshake with a partner.
- Brainstorm five powerful questions you can ask someone you have just met. Try asking them with a partner and practise listening assertively to the response. Ask one powerful question to someone you meet or run into today, and listen! You will learn something totally new!
- Choose a day this week to be The Assertive Listener. See if you can just listen all day without speaking (except to validate feelings or ask open-ended questions).

"THE LOVE OF OUR NEIGHBOR IN ALL ITS FULLNESS SIMPLY MEANS BEING ABLE TO SAY TO HIM, 'WHAT ARE YOU GOING THROUGH?'"

—Simone Weil
(1909-1943)
Philosopher, mystic, author

Level III
The Seven Steps to Social Action:
Taking It to the Next Level

Level IV
The How-To Guide:
The Global Citizen's Toolbox

Level V
Sources And Resources,
End Notes

Even when in a group, listening carefully is crucial so that you can ask appropriate questions and obtain the information you need.

TAKE MORE ACTION! How To Change The World

HOME	LEVEL I	LEVEL II
Preface, Contents	Global Citizenship: Around the World, Across the Street	Becoming Global Citizens: A Question of Choice

The art of networking

Your success as a socially involved global citizen can be greatly enhanced by building up a network of supporters who can help you to achieve your goals. To do this effectively, you will identify the talents and resources that will further your cause, and find out who in your community can help you tap into them. Learning how to introduce yourself to people, express your interests, and build relationships that you can draw upon in the future is an essential skill known as networking. Making one "contact" can lead to a few more, and from there dozens more, until you have supporters all over the place ready to assist you in fulfilling your mission!

The following tips will help you in a formal atmosphere, such as a school board meeting or a fundraiser, but also in keeping in touch with the new, fascinating people you meet as you continue to explore your issue.

LeveL III
The Seven Steps to Social Action:
Taking It to the Next Level

LeveL IV
The How-To Guide:
The Global Citizen's Toolbox

LeveL V
Sources And Resources,
End Notes

- Before going to an event, mentally prepare a thirty-second speech that explains who you are, what you do, and why you are doing it. Your goal is to engage the person you are talking to with your confidence, creativity, and conviction.
- Create a business card containing your contact information and your organization's logo. Carry several of them with you at all times and exchange cards at the end of a conversation. This is your key to establishing contact in the future.
- At the end of the day, make notes on the back of the cards you have collected: date and nature of the meeting, the content of your conversation, how that person offered to or could help your cause, and personal notes to remember about the person for future conversations.
- When you have met with someone at an event or a meeting, it is a good idea to follow up with an e-mail to say thanks for the person's time, and to give a reminder of you and your organization.
- Add new contacts to your mailing list to keep them informed of your projects and successes.
- Personalized touches, such as holiday greetings and thank-you notes, are key to maintaining your communication with people who may be able to open doors to other networks, expanding your network in the process.

TAKE MORE ACTION! How To Change The World

HOME	LEVEL I	LEVEL II
Preface, Contents	Global Citizenship: Around the World, Across the Street	Becoming Global Citizens: A Question of Choice

Conflict mediation

When you are involved in social issues, conflicts (with team members and also with people who oppose your ideas) are inevitable. As an effective leader, your goal is to come up with ways to avoid conflicts and also ways to deal with them when they arise. One of the best ways to prevent conflicts is to develop group norms that will serve as your team's ground rules and determine how you work together and interact with other organizations.

TIP

Conflicts, if addressed early, can be healthy. They offer a chance to express opposing viewpoints. Provide a regular time during meetings for your group members to air grievances (in a calm, collected manner) before they become problems.

Group norms might include such guidelines as the following:

- Be reliable. If you say that you are going to complete a task, do so.
- Be considerate of other people's time. Be punctual when attending meetings.
- Show respect for the ideas and feelings of others.
- Express your needs and feelings, not your frustrations or resentment.
- If you have a conflict with an individual, approach him or her directly. Do not gossip behind the person's back.

When all team members have a say in the development of group norms, they will be more likely to uphold them. Any violations of group norms are offences to the group, not solely to the individual involved. If conflict arises within your group, here are some techniques to help you mediate it:

"SHOUTING HAS NEVER MADE ME UNDERSTAND ANYTHING."

—Susan Sontag
(1933-2004)
Author, critic, filmmaker

TAKE MORE ACTION! How To Change The World

HOME	LEVEL I	LEVEL II
Preface, Contents	Global Citizenship: Around the World, Across the Street	Becoming Global Citizens: A Question of Choice

If *you* are in a conflict:

- Be proactive and address the conflict immediately. Letting it build up can create resentment, hurt, and anger.
- Seek clarification by using your assertive listening skills. Show that you want to understand the other individual, and this person will be open to understanding you. Plus, exchanging perspectives can clear up minor misunderstandings before they escalate.
- Voice the other person's position and ask him or her to voice yours to make sure that you both understand each other's view. Make corrections if you feel there is a misunderstanding.
- Express your feelings and needs, using "I-statements" such as "I feel," "I believe," "It is important (to me) that," and "I need"—instead of firing accusations and blame.
- Transfer responsibility by asking if the person has any constructive solutions to the problem that would be mutually beneficial. When both parties are engaged in the problem solving process, a win-win situation can often be achieved.

If you are mediating a conflict between *others*:

When two individuals or groups of people (called "parties") are having a conflict, you can act as a "third-party mediator." You essentially step in and facilitate a discussion or negotiation between the conflicting parties by clarifying the problem, encouraging them to understand each other's perspective, and helping them come to a mutually satisfactory solution. This process often involves asking probing questions to isolate the conflict in terms of what each party feels and needs (not just what they see or want). As a mediator, your role is to do the following:

- Redefine the conflict from a competition between two sides to a mutual problem that can only be solved co-operatively. Make "winning" include the satisfaction of everyone's needs, not just those of one party.
- Encourage honest and open communication of perspectives and needs in order to identify the true source of the problem.
- Keep the dialogue on track, and keep people engaged.
- Focus on the solution, not the problem. While anger and frustration do need to be communicated and acknowledged, it is not useful to dwell on these emotions.
- Encourage people to come up with solutions on their own that are beneficial to both parties.
- Create a set of ground rules that will ensure that similar problems do not arise in the future.

TAKE MORE ACTION! How To Change The World

HOME	LEVEL I	LEVEL II
Preface, Contents	Global Citizenship: Around the World, Across the Street	Becoming Global Citizens: A Question of Choice

PROFILE

Dalal Al-Waheidi: Peace Activist

When Dalal Al-Waheidi was seventeen and living with her family in the Gaza Strip, she gained acceptance to the Red Cross Nordic United World College in Norway, which brought together students from over eighty countries in the spirit of leadership and solidarity. As she faced the task of representing the Palestinian identity and culture to the international student body, Dalal felt both honored and anxious. She wondered whether other students would be open-minded enough to see beyond the stereotyped media image of aggressive Palestinian youth and actually listen to her views. When she learned that Israeli students also attended the college, Dalal realized that she would have to deal with her own prejudices as well.

It took Dalal a long time, during her first year at the college, to move beyond her perception of Israeli youth as the "other," or as people to be feared. But as the students slowly began to discover one another, shared meals and social events led to deeper conversations and moments of understanding. These connections were growing at a time when the Palestinian-Israeli peace process was reaching a new moment of crisis. Concerned about their future, Dalal and her fellow students decided that they had to set a positive example for the politicians who could not seem to agree. They had to prove that, despite their differences, Palestinians and Israelis could work together for peace.

Putting this ideal into action, however, was not always easy, and arguments flared up over such basic issues as whether the group's name would be in Arabic or Hebrew. But despite their frustrations, the team members committed themselves to solving problems through open dialogue and respect for everyone's views. As one of their actions, they prepared petitions out of cloth, and asked people in the street to write peace messages. Together, Dalal and an Israeli student presented one of these petitions to the President of the Palestinian Council, Yasser Arafat. They also sent one to Yitzhak Rabin, the Israeli Prime Minster at the time, and to King Hussein of Jordan. The action symbolized the students' commitment to pursuing peaceful partnerships, and challenged their leaders and the rest of the world to do the same.

Dalal had come to see her Israeli friends not in political terms, but as individuals who shared similar interests and laughed at the same jokes that she did. She learned that if they could form relationships based on trust, empathy, and sharing, all Israelis and Palestinians—or both sides of any conflict— could do the same. Dalal had cultivated a new vision of peace, one in which the voices and actions of youth possessed the strength to uplift the spirit of every movement for peace, and to create a more compassionate world.

LeveL III The Seven Steps to Social Action: Taking It to the Next Level	**LeveL IV** The How-To Guide: The Global Citizen's Toolbox	**LeveL V** Sources And Resources, End Notes

- Why did Dalal and her Israeli schoolmates decide to work together on an action plan for peace? What was the message they sought to promote?

- What would have been the result if Dalal had decided to work with only Palestinian students, and the Israeli students had also formed their own separate group? What would have been their message then? How effective would it have been?

- What skills are involved in working with individuals who represent the opposing side of a conflict? Why is it important to understand their perspective?

TAKE MORE ACTION! How To Change The World

HOME	LEVEL I	LEVEL II
Preface, Contents	Global Citizenship: Around the World, Across the Street	Becoming Global Citizens: A Question of Choice

Take Action!

Design your own business card based on a group you could start on your chosen issue.

Prepare a 30-second speech in which you explain who you are, the issue on which you are working, and why you were moved to take action. Try your speech out on a classmate and see if you can spark interest in supporting the cause.

Think back to a time when you had a conflict with another person. How did you handle it? How did it turn out? How would you deal with it differently using the skills outlined in this section?

GETTING THE WORD OUT THROUGH THE MEDIA

One-on-one contact is key to making a difference, but it's a slow route. The "media" (referring to anyone who works with TV, radio, newspapers, the Web or magazines) often get a bad rap for being biased and sensational, but they hold tremendous power to do a lot of good for your group and your issue. A successful organization's impact is achieved through publicity (news and media coverage of your events) rather than advertising (paid marketing). As such, the media are a valuable resource, a crucial link to free publicity and support for your cause. They get their message across to hundreds, thousands, even millions of people at a time. Instead of just watching the news every night, why not be the news?

Working effectively with the media allows you to:
- Spread your message
- Familiarize the public with your group
- Recruit new support (and people, to give time and money)
- Advertise a campaign or event

News does not just happen—you have to make it happen! Your group should have a team of people in charge of media strategy and tasks. Now instead of you having to go out there to the world to make a difference, the media can bring the world to you!

LeveL IV > The How To Guide: Getting The Word Out Through The Media

LeveL III	**LeveL IV**	**LeveL V**
The Seven Steps to Social Action: Taking It to the Next Level	The How-To Guide: The Global Citizen's Toolbox	Sources And Resources, End Notes

TAKE MORE ACTION! How To Change The World

| HOME
Preface, Contents | LEVEL I
Global Citizenship:
Around the World, Across the Street | LEVEL II
Becoming Global Citizens:
A Question of Choice |

Branding your message

When using different media to take your message to the public, it is important to keep the central aspects of this message consistent, such as words, colors, and visuals. This is where branding comes into play (see page 151). It helps your organization stand out in the public eye. Two key components of a successful branding effort include your group's name and logo, which we discussed in Step Five of the Seven Steps to Social Action. A third key component is your "sound bite."

Sound bites

Sound bites are short, catchy sentences or slogans that communicate your message to the public. They give your audience words to associate with your group, your mission, and your values. To really drive your message home, repeat your sound bite often, during speeches, interviews, and when you are networking. You can also include it in posters, flyers, and at the end of letters to the editor, to political officials, and to supporters. Good sound bites are what journalists will insert into news stories. For instance, the Me to We slogan is a sound bite: "Think we. Pass it on."

Here are some effective sound bites pertaining to specific social issues:

Sample Sound Bites	
Topic	**Sound Bite**
Poverty	"The world can't wait." —*Make Poverty History*
Peace	"Give peace a chance." —*John Lennon*
Trade justice	"Make Trade Fair." —*Oxfam International*
HIV/AIDS	"HIV doesn't discriminate…people do." —*Australia National AIDS Campaign*
Environment	"For a living planet" —*World Wildlife Fund*

TAKE MORE ACTION! How To Change The World

| HOME
Preface, Contents | LEVEL I
Global Citizenship:
Around the World, Across the Street | LEVEL II
Becoming Global Citizens:
A Question of Choice |

The challenge of creating a sound bite lies in compressing all your detailed information into a single statement; you want to say something that captures your message powerfully in as few words as possible.

How to create an effective sound bite

Focus on a key idea. What is the most important thing you want your audience to remember? Try to develop a catchy phrase that will stick in a person's mind. A good sound bite might be a play on words, a catchy slogan or a short acronym.

- Write down your sound bite, then say it out loud to see how it sounds. Play around with the sentence structure and the order of the words. Does it flow well? Is it easy to say? Take out any unnecessary words.
- Keep it brief, preferably under ten seconds.
- A sound bite should be simple, clear, precise and easy to understand without any background details.
- A sound bite should be powerful and quotable.
- Test your sound bite on a group of students for their reaction.
- Work on your sound bites before dealing with the media.

Take Action!

Sound bites permeate our society. See how many common sayings you can list that have originated as sound bites, and where they came from. They can be from government, business or social action groups.

Create a sound bite for your chosen issue. Test it out on a partner and watch the reaction. Refine it until it is perfect!

LeveL IV > The How To Guide: Getting The Word Out Through The Media

LeveL III
The Seven Steps to Social Action:
Taking It to the Next Level

LeveL IV
The How-To Guide:
The Global Citizen's Toolbox

LeveL V
Sources And Resources,
End Notes

"THE MEDIUM IS THE MESSAGE. ANY UNDERSTANDING OF SOCIAL AND CULTURAL CHANGE
IS IMPOSSIBLE WITHOUT A KNOWLEDGE OF THE WAY MEDIA WORK AS ENVIRONMENTS."

—Herbert Marshall McLuhan
(1911-1980)
Media philosopher

TAKE MORE ACTION! How To Change The World

HOME	LEVEL I	LEVEL II
Preface, Contents	Global Citizenship: Around the World, Across the Street	Becoming Global Citizens: A Question of Choice

"LEADERS ARE INDISPENSA
BUT TO PRODUCE A MAJOR SC
CHANGE MANY ORDINARY PE
MUST ALSO BE INVOLVED."

—Anne Firor Scott
(b. 1921)
Educator, author

LeveL III
The Seven Steps to Social Action:
Taking It to the Next Level

LeveL IV
The How-To Guide:
The Global Citizen's Toolbox

LeveL V
Sources And Resources,
End Notes

Where your publicity efforts begin

Your publicity efforts will start locally on a small scale—at your school or in your community (local TV and radio, weekly local newspapers)—and work their way up to the bigger media outlets like national TV and newspapers. Small-scale efforts require the imaginative use of a variety of media tools such as posters, flyers, pamphlets, and newsletters. You can use them to spread information about your cause and organization, and to publicize any upcoming events. Plus, they are reasonably easy and inexpensive to make.

Colorful, eye-catching posters can potentially reach a large number of people. The downside to this approach, however, is that they may be covered up or go unnoticed on a crowded bulletin board. Banners are even more effective because of their size, although they require a little more planning, materials, and money. The printing companies that print local daily newspapers may be willing to give you banner-size paper for free. Images on banners and posters must communicate your message in a single glance. You want to capture the public's attention, so be creative. Do not forget to include the name of your organization and contact information.

When posters or banners are not appropriate, consider distributing flyers, pamphlets or newsletters. Their advantage is that they give passersby something to keep as a reminder (i.e., for an upcoming event), while information on a poster may be more easily forgotten. Good places for distribution include high-traffic areas in your school, at extra-curricular activities, in food or entertainment districts or in mailboxes. You could also get permission to leave a supply of them at the information desks of libraries or community centers. Don't trespass—get permission first!

TIP

Don't waste paper! Use recycled paper and the back of used paper. Put a "Recycle me or pass me to a friend" note on your flyers to make sure they don't immediately end up in the blue box.

TAKE MORE ACTION!

How To Change The World

HOME	LeveL I	LeveL II
Preface, Contents	Global Citizenship: Around the World, Across the Street	Becoming Global Citizens: A Question of Choice

LeveL IV > The How To Guide: Getting The Word Out Through The Media

LeveL III	**LeveL IV**	**LeveL V**
The Seven Steps to Social Action: Taking It to the Next Level	The How-To Guide: The Global Citizen's Toolbox	Sources And Resources, End Notes

Creating a media list

First, you will want to make a comprehensive list of the media outlets and individual journalists in your community who may be interested in your cause. To start, think about the media that your family and friends tune in to. What do you read or watch? Make a note of these newspapers and programs. Some cities also publish media guides—check if yours has one by contacting the local chamber of commerce or city hall. If you contact other local groups who have a similar cause, or your local Member of Congress or Parliament, they may let you borrow their list of media outlets if you convince them that your issue is important.

Weighing Your Chances With the Media		
Media	**Your Probability of Being Covered**	**The Range of People you Can Reach**
Network and cable television news stations	Unlikely	Extensive
Talk and popular radio stations	Unlikely	Fairly extensive
Local daily or weekly newspapers	Likely	Fairly extensive
College or high school newspapers	Very likely	Limited
Neighborhood newsletters	Extremely likely	Limited
Church or religious news bulletins	Extremely likely	Limited
Community-based Internet sites or message boards	Very likely	Limited

TAKE MORE ACTION! How To Change The World

HOME	LeveL I	LeveL II
Preface, Contents	Global Citizenship: Around the World, Across the Street	Becoming Global Citizens: A Question of Choice

TIP

Ask to meet with the editor of your community newspaper or the program manager of your community cable station to discuss your cause (or be bold and aim for the big players too—the worst they can do is say no!). Their support can be invaluable—if they are your friends, you can get media coverage more often!

To get the best coverage, it is important to take advantage of a variety of media outlets and to tailor the information you provide to suit their different interests and needs. Along with the mainstream news outlets, be sure to contact community publications, which are distributed in your area or are related to a specific language or cultural group. You can also check out alternative magazines, which are smaller and independently owned, and are often run by non-profit or arts organizations. Look for the ones that are free in coffee shops and health food stores! These, too, are widely read, and are more likely to cover smaller events and focus on social issues. For each entry on your list, collect the outlet name, contact names, phone and fax numbers, street address, e-mail address, Web site, television channel, format (live, taped, etc.) and deadlines. An organized, detailed list will simplify your future communications. Keep this information in a file or database and update it as necessary.

TIP

Stories about youth making a difference are often covered by media (especially local media) just because it's youth taking action—stress in your communication with the media that you are youth—it sells!

TAKE MORE ACTION! How To Change The World

HOME	LEVEL I	LEVEL II
Preface, Contents	Global Citizenship: Around the World, Across the Street	Becoming Global Citizens: A Question of Choice

Let Them Know You're Here!

Here are some great ways to communicate your message to the media.

News release: a brief news article that announces your group's upcoming event, fundraiser or information session, and encourages the media to profile it.

Public service announcement (PSA): a short (free) advertisement or commercial broadcast on local radio and television stations, and printed in newspapers, that is used to announce events or to pronounce your message; for instance, the "Say No To Drugs" campaign.

Letter to the editor: a letter written to be published on the editorial page of a newspaper, which is a forum where readers can express their opinions and concerns.

Op-ed: an article written for the opinion page, opposite the editorial page. It has the same purpose as a letter to the editor, but can be longer.

Take Action!

Draft a list of the various media outlets in your community suitable for your group on your chosen issue.

As a class, compile a list of contacts by calling each media outlet and finding out all the necessary information for a comprehensive media list.

Brainstorm ways to make your chosen issue newsworthy—what elements of appeal can you use to catch the media's attention?

Holding a media event

When holding fundraising or awareness-raising events, invite the press and get your message out to more people. How do you get them there? Send them a news release with the details of your event. On the day of your event, assign one or two people to be responsible for speaking with journalists.

Be sure they are informed, capable, and prepared (meaning that they have practised a lot with mock interviews). Your media liaison person will give journalists press kits, show them around, offer them refreshments, and help to arrange interviews. This person helps to control the message that gets out and directs reporters to the most articulate members of your group.

When dealing with the media, you want to be polite, assertive, and calm—and not sound urgent or lecturing. It is important to maintain a professional relationship with journalists.

LeveL IV > The How To Guide: Getting The Word Out Through The Media

LeveL III	**LeveL IV**	**LeveL V**
The Seven Steps to Social Action: Taking It to the Next Level	The How-To Guide: The Global Citizen's Toolbox	Sources And Resources, End Notes

...of Experience!

Writing an Effective News Release

- Start with a catchy headline. This is your "hook"!

- Include the 5 "W"s—who, what, where, when, why—and how of your event and, of course, your sound bite.

- Write your news release in the neutral third person ("he" or "she," not "I").

- Fax or e-mail your news release to the media outlet three times: (1) one or two weeks before your event; (2) two or three days before your event; and 3) 24 hours before your event. Your news release may be updated if you have any new information.

- Keep your audience in mind. Who is the audience of the media you are sending your release to? You may have to present your story with a different slant to appeal to different kinds of media.

- Send a follow-up news release describing the event. Include testimonials from participants about how great the event was. Often, journalists will not have time to come to your event, but if you send photos and details immediately afterward, they can still write an article.

TAKE MORE ACTION! How To Change The World

HOME	LeveL I	LeveL II
Preface, Contents	Global Citizenship: Around the World, Across the Street	Becoming Global Citizens: A Question of Choice

Sample News Release

To make your news release easy to read, keep it neat and use a standardized format that journalists are used to. Keep the length within one or two pages.

The body of the text should be centered on the page. Use 1-inch margins on both sides.

Headline/Title:

Local Youth Gather to Debate Globalization

Contact Information:
Stephen Lawson
225 Pinegrove Avenue
St. Catharines, ON L9N 6Y1
Tel: 555-555-5555
Fax: 555-777-8888
slawson@e-mail.com

Date of the News Release:
October 23, 20—

Opening paragraph(s), in which you clearly state your purpose or main point, and answer the 5 Ws.

Hundreds of youth, conscious of their role as global citizens and their right and responsibility in helping to create a more just and sustainable world, will gather together to discuss the pressing realities of an increasingly globalized society, and the role they can play in shaping a better world for all.

LeveL IV > The How To Guide: Getting The Word Out Through The Media

LeveL III	LeveL IV	LeveL V
The Seven Steps to Social Action: Taking It to the Next Level	The How-To Guide: The Global Citizen's Toolbox	Sources And Resources, End Notes

On October 26, from 9 A.M.-3 P.M. at Pierre Trudeau Secondary School (2 Kennedy Road) in St. Catharines, three hundred young people from surrounding municipalities will come together to discuss the challenges and opportunities posed by globalization.

2 to 3 short paragraphs to expand on your story using details about your organization, the goal of your event, and any other newsworthy information.

This event will be inaugurated by Craig Kielburger, founder and chair of Free The Children. It aims to give young people a space to think critically about the issues facing humanity in an era of increasing globalization. Several key issues will be examined through a dynamic and interactive series of lectures and workshops. These include: education, war-affected children, poverty, and the girl child. A workshop devoted to leadership skills will encourage youth to take steps to bring about positive change. Each young person involved will also develop an action plan, committing themselves to undertaking concrete actions in their schools and communities.

Free The Children is an international network of children helping children through representation, leadership, and action. Since its founding in 1995, it has grown into the world's largest youth empowerment organization, with over a million youth involved in programs in 35 countries. Unlike any other children's charity in the world, Free The Children is an organization by, of, and for children, and fully embodies the notion that children and young people themselves can be leaders of today in helping to end the poverty and exploitation of children.

If the news release is more than one page, write "more" at the bottom of each page. Indicate the last page with the following symbol:

-30-

TAKE MORE ACTION! How To Change The World

HOME	LEVEL I	LEVEL II
Preface, Contents	Global Citizenship: Around the World, Across the Street	Becoming Global Citizens: A Question of Choice

What's in a press kit?

A press kit allows you to provide the media with detailed documentation about your issue and group. However, you do not want to overload them with too much information, so keep the contents within ten pages. Make sure the press kit is attractive and easy to read. Put each one in a folder, with your group's contact information clearly displayed on the front, and hand them out to journalists at the event.

Each kit should include:
• A copy of your news release
• A copy of the statement to be read by your spokesperson at the event
• A one-page description of your group
• Contact information for your group, particularly the media officer
• Brief biographies of the speaker(s) or people of note, such as local politicians or celebrities attending the event
• Information about the issue: facts and statistics, recent articles or press clippings, letters to the editor with replies, quotations, comments, a list of additional sources, etc.
• Visuals: graphics, charts, diagrams, maps, photographs
• Group newsletters or pamphlets

Hold a news conference at your event

A news conference can be useful if several media outlets want to talk to your spokesperson(s) at one time. It is an opportunity for your group to make announcements or statements at your event, or to launch a new campaign, drive or fundraiser. You have more control over the information flow in this situation than you would have in an interview. Take advantage of this by being well-prepared.

Write a statement (essentially, a speech) that is no longer than two or three typed pages. Have enough copies for all the reporters, to be included with the press kits. Speaking at a news conference can be intimidating, so practise delivering your statement and answering questions.

TIP

For tips on writing and delivering a speech, and answering questions, see the Public Speaking section later in this How-To Guide.

TAKE MORE ACTION! How To Change The World

HOME	LEVEL I	LEVEL II
Preface, Contents	Global Citizenship: Around the World, Across the Street	Becoming Global Citizens: A Question of Choice

In the interest of deadlines (newspaper articles for the next day are usually due by 6 p.m., and the evening and night news articles are due a couple hours ahead of airing), try to schedule your news conference in the morning.

Your location should be practical and easily accessible by the media. You may also want to consider using a novel setting that provides good photo opportunities and creates the kind of background you want to appear in your publicity (for example, environmental groups may choose a wooded area or a location next to a polluting factory). Make sure your location will be able to accommodate lighting and sound equipment. The usual format of a news conference is to have an announcer introduce your spokesperson(s) before they deliver the statement. Together, the introduction and statement might last about 20 minutes, followed by 10 minutes of questions. When there seem to be no more questions, close the conference and thank the press for attending.

Showtime! Interviews at your event or in studio

Preparation is an essential part of giving a good interview. Here are some tips to help you feel confident on the day of the event.

Be informed. Do your research and reading from reliable sources, and be able to back up your points with accurate information. Familiarize yourself with both sides of your issue. This allows you to anticipate what kinds of arguments you might come up against and be more prepared to defend your position. Memorize important statistics and their sources in advance.

Establish goals. Make the interview work for you by always bringing the discussion back to your objective—what you want the audience to hear. Decide beforehand on three important points you want to make and stick to them. One of them should be the what, when, and where of your next event—take advantage of the free advertising! Any question can be turned to bring you back to your objective.

Know your audience. For your message to be understood, you must consider who your target audience is. Watch, read or listen to various media sources in advance to get an idea of how to tailor your message accordingly. Keep subtle differences in mind; for example, morning and evening programs will attract different audiences. You should know whether you are addressing the general public, the government, corporate executives or your peers.

Understand the interview type. Is it live or recorded? Will they edit it later or include it in its entirety? How long will the interview clip be in the end? The answers to these questions will determine how long your answers should be, whether you can try again if you mess up, and how much emphasis to put on your sound bite.

Practise. Have a friend videotape you while another pretends to be the interviewer and asks potential questions. Then watch the tape carefully for things to improve. Keep practising that sound bite until you are whispering it in your sleep and your family starts saying, "We know! We know!"

Practising with a partner allows you to hear yourself speak
and also to receive feedback on your presentation.

TAKE MORE ACTION! How To Change The World

HOME	LEVEL I	LEVEL II
Preface, Contents	Global Citizenship: Around the World, Across the Street	Becoming Global Citizens: A Question of Choice

TIP

Before the interview, you might ask the journalist to ask a specific question, or to mention your Web site. It is also common to show visuals, such as photographs, posters or books, at the end of a broadcast, so bring such items along with you, and give them to the reporter before the interview. Do not be afraid to make requests.

Take Action!

Write a news release about an event that you could hold in relation to your issue. Show it to two friends and ask if it would convince them to come, if they were journalists.

Watch an interview on the TV news and critique the interviewee's style. What did he or she do well? What could the person have done better? Exchange your thoughts with a partner.

Brainstorm a list of possible questions that you could be asked in an interview on your chosen topic. Come up with the answers and practise a mock interview with a partner.

Letters to the editor: make your opinion heard!

The editorial page is a highly read section of your local newspaper or magazine that gives the public a forum to express their concerns. Writing a letter to the editor is the easiest and most likely way of making your voice heard. The letter can reach a large number of people and motivate others who may feel the same way about your issue. The editorial page in a magazine is usually found in the first pages, while in a newspaper, it is most often in the last pages.

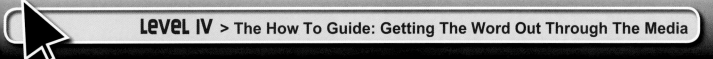

TIP

Newspapers are more likely to publish your letter if you have been directly affected by a current issue, can offer insight or an interesting opinion on it, or if you strongly disagree with something that was published.

TAKE MORE ACTION! How To Change The World

HOME	LEVEL I	LEVEL II
Preface, Contents	Global Citizenship: Around the World, Across the Street	Becoming Global Citizens: A Question of Choice

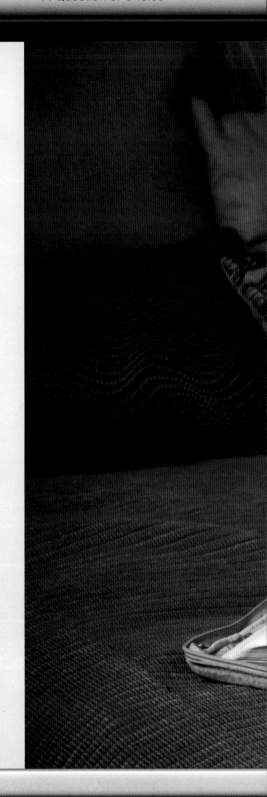

Here are some points to keep in mind when writing a letter to the editor:

- Before writing, read examples of the types of letters that are printed to find the guidelines that your letter should follow regarding length, format, and deadlines.
- Begin your letter by introducing yourself and specifying your purpose in writing.
- If you are referring to a particular newspaper article, cite the date, title, writer, and subject in your letter.
- You can include your personal side of the story; describe your experiences or those of your group.
- Suggest solutions—what major decision makers should do, but, more importantly, actions that individuals can take to make a difference.
- Keep your letter simple and the paragraphs short. Be aware that your letter may be edited or shortened prior to publication.
- Do not forget to add your complete contact information, including your full name and daytime and evening phone numbers. Sign a letter or a fax by hand.
- Sending your letter by e-mail allows you to react promptly to a recent article, and timely letters are more likely to be published. Be sure to include your letter in the main body of an e-mail text, not as an attachment, which will not be opened due to viruses.
- Mark your e-mail, fax or envelope 'Attention: The Editor.'

You may have to send a number of letters before one gets published. Be patient and keep trying!

TAKE MORE ACTION! How To Change The World

HOME	LEVEL I	LEVEL II
Preface, Contents	Global Citizenship: Around the World, Across the Street	Becoming Global Citizens: A Question of Choice

Sample Letter to the Editor

Excerpts from a letter to the editor by Craig Kielburger, published in *The Toronto Star,* November 13, 2000.

It's Time 16-Year-Olds Were Given The Right To Vote

Recently, a special Studio 2 TVO broadcast examined the issue of globalization with representatives from government, business, unions and the media. A young woman from the audience raised her hand to ask a question.

"Where are you from?" asked host Steve Paikin.

"I'm from B.C.," she replied.

"Did you ever vote for the NDPs? he inquired.

"I'm not old enough to vote," she answered.

"And your question?"

"I was wondering if John Crosbie can comment on what his opinion is on the way in which the WTO has integrated developing nations into the platform of globalizing trade and if the panel could comment on the ramifications that it has had for these countries."

Like this young woman, tens of thousands of intelligent 16- and 17- year-old Canadians, who are deeply interested in issues such as poverty, homelessness, debt reduction, education and globalization, will be denied the right to have a voice through their vote in the upcoming elections. Section 50 of the Canada Elections Act states that only Canadian citizens who have attained the age of 18 on or before the day of the elections are allowed to vote.

Level III The Seven Steps to Social Action: Taking It to the Next Level	**Level IV** The How-To Guide: The Global Citizen's Toolbox	**Level V** Sources And Resources, End Notes

NAME
NOM

I submit that most individuals at age 16 do have the maturity and intelligence required to vote. Many 16-year-olds have part-time jobs and pay taxes. All pay PST and GST. Should they not also have a say as to how their tax dollars are spent?

Consider how little discussion there has been in this federal election on child poverty, education, and other youth-related issues. Canada was one of the first of 194 countries of the world to ratify the United Nations' Convention on the Rights of the Child that gives children (under the age of 18) the right to participate in finding solutions to issues that affected them and their peers. Empowering 16-year-olds with the vote would open the door to new respect for young people's opinions and an era of equality for all generations.

Lowering the voting age to 16 is not a novel idea. Brazil has recently given the right to vote at all levels of government to 16-year-olds in that country. France, England and Australia are also contemplating lowering the voting age.

Last month, I attended meetings with world leaders at the State of the World Forum in New York City and talked to the Japanese minister of finance about youth issues during a trip to Japan. On Nov. 27, however, I shall be denied the right to cast my vote for the individual I believe should lead my own country. Why? Because I am 17 years old.

The time has come for Canadians to take a serious look at lowering the voting age to 16.

TAKE MORE ACTION! How To Change The World

HOME	LeveL I	LeveL II
Preface, Contents	Global Citizenship: Around the World, Across the Street	Becoming Global Citizens: A Question of Choice

Internet activism

The Internet has limitless possibilities for enhancing your outreach activities. Almost everyone can access the Net, whether at home, school, the library or an Internet café. It is fast, cheap, and wide-reaching, putting local and global contacts at your fingertips. All you need to get started is a computer with Internet access and e-mail software.

E-mail

E-mail can be an efficient way to be in contact with the media and supporters of your group. You can take advantage of this medium in several ways:

- **Mailing list:** E-mail accounts let you put together a mailing list, so you can send a message to hundreds of recipients at once. You should e-mail relevant groups only, however, and do not subscribe individuals to your mailing list without their permission.
- **E-newsletters:** Send them to friends, journalists, and other people interested in your cause (such as those who may have signed up at an information table). You can also distribute them to e-mail discussion lists, blogs and newsgroups on the Internet.
- **Online action alert**: This is an urgent e-mail to be passed on through friends and forwards. It can rapidly and easily spread the word about an upcoming event or let others know about an urgent news issue, unfair legislation, etc. Make sure people will open your alert by including an attention-grabbing subject line.
- **Social networking**: Your message can also be distributed through such sites as MySpace, Facebook, Flickr or other networking services.

Web sites

A Web site is the way to make your group and its issue known. It is easy to access, and if it is done well, it gives your group immeasurable publicity (many social action sites get thousands of hits a day), provides information, and facilitates communication between you and potential supporters. It is a valuable tool if it is designed well and kept up-to-date, which can be a big commitment. Your group should designate someone to take care of this task, and to answer inquiries and messages.

The Volunteer Now Web site was created to help students become socially involved and meet their 40-hour community service requirement. The youth-friendly design of the homepage suggests that the site is creative and easy for students to use.

LEVEL III	**LEVEL IV**	**LEVEL V**
The Seven Steps to Social Action: Taking It to the Next Level	The How-To Guide: The Global Citizen's Toolbox	Sources And Resources, End Notes

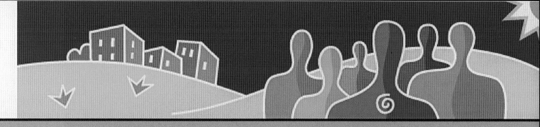

look no further...

HOME - ABOUT US - SITE MAP - CONTACT US

Current Volunteer Opportunities

TAKE ACTION

VOLUNTEER NOW

- WELCOME ○
- VOLUNTEER NOW! ○
- TAKE ACTION ○
- INSPIRATION ○
- PARTNERS ○
- CONTACT US ○

welcome volunteers

Welcome to **volunteernow.ca**, a unique web site dedicated to helping students from the Toronto District School Board become socially involved and meet and exceed their 40-hour community service requirement.

This web site is being powered by Leaders Today, an international organization that seeks to motivate young people to become active in their communities and around the world.

Leaders Today was founded by Marc and Craig Kielburger, who are also the authors of *Take Action! A Guide To Active Citizenship*, which is the in-school educational resource accompanying this site.

The goal of volunteernow.ca is to provide YOU with the skills and tools to volunteer and change the world. This site includes the following:

- Information about the 40 hour volunteer requirement.
- Organizations in your area that need volunteers.
- Details about how to create your own volunteer project.
- Overview of social issues and projects that need your help.

TAKE MORE ACTION! How To Change The World

| **HOME**
Preface, Contents | **LEVEL I**
Global Citizenship:
Around the World, Across the Street | **LEVEL II**
Becoming Global Citizens:
A Question of Choice |

Making your own Web site can be an intimidating task. Here are some guidelines for the computer novice:

Web Site Tips For Rookies	
Tip	**Here's How**
Make your text Web-friendly.	Convert the text you want to use into HTML, the main language of the World Wide Web. There are a number of online tutorials and HTML editing applications that can teach you how to do this.
Make your Web site easy to navigate.	Organize the information using headings, highlighting the most important aspects of the site. Subdivide the categories on a menu or sidebar, and include a site map.
Make it easy for people to find your Web site.	Register the URL with major search engines, such as Google, Yahoo and Windows Live Search. Carefully chosen meta tags help search engines to locate your site in a keyword search. They are HTML tags that supply information about the page but do not appear in its display.
Provide feedback for regular visitors to your site.	An FAQ (Frequently Asked Questions) page can be revised regularly to respond to repeat questions received through e-mail.
Make the information easy to read.	Be sure the writing is edited and polished, and that the text is legible, in terms of color and size.

	LeveL IV		**LeveL V**
LeveL III The Seven Steps to Social Action: Taking It to the Next Level	The How-To Guide: The Global Citizen's Toolbox		Sources And Resources, End Notes

Identify your group clearly.	**Include your group name, complete contact information and mission statement or slogan.**
Encourage people to visit your Web site often.	**Update your site frequently with fresh information, with the most current news displayed on the front page, but maintain the same structure.**
Make the Web site attractive and exciting, but ensure the information is easy to access.	**Use colorful graphics and pictures. Include videos to download or view using YouTube. Try designing a Flash intro (under 100 kb with a skip option). Avoid slowing things down with an excess of visuals, however. Your site should load in under 10 seconds on a typical Internet connection.**

Take Action!

Look for a few prominent, reputable e-newsletters on your chosen issue. You can search for these on the Web sites of social justice organizations, and subscribe to them to get regular updates on the issue and new campaigns.

Create an online action alert for your chosen issue. Send it out to the people on your mailing list (your friends, family, and other interested individuals.)

Examine some of your favourite Web sites. Which features are most effective? What makes them work well? How could you incorporate similar aspects into your own Web site? Create a home page for a Web site on your chosen issue. Share it with your friends, classmates, and one organization that works on your issue—they may ask to link it to their site!

TAKE MORE ACTION! How To Change The World

Home	**Level I**	**Level II**
Preface, Contents	Global Citizenship: Around the World, Across the Street	Becoming Global Citizens: A Question of Choice

Art as media

There is no single way to make your voice heard. The world is filled with avenues for self-expression. While every group needs members who can give great speeches and interviews, a steady supply of imagination and creativity is equally essential.

This is where art becomes a valuable tool for communication. Theatre, visual arts, music and poetry all have the power to raise awareness, to speak the truth, to move an audience, and to inspire action and change. They can lend a visible, positive presence to your group and the issues for which you stand.

"A TRULY GOOD BOOK TEACHES ME BETTER THAN TO READ IT. I MUST SOON LAY IT DOWN, AND COMMENCE LIVING ON ITS HINT. WHAT I BEGAN BY READING, I MUST FINISH BY ACTING."

—Henry David Thoreau
(1817-1862)
Author, Philosopher

LeVeL III
The Seven Steps to Social Action:
Taking It to the Next Level

LeVeL IV
The How-To Guide:
The Global Citizen's Toolbox

LeVeL V
Sources And Resources,
End Notes

Visual arts

When you reflect on everything you know about your issue, can you envision shaping all your information and feelings into an image? Many social activists express their thoughts and ideals about issues through such works as paintings, sculptures, photographs, and sketches. Community mural projects are also currently gaining popularity across the world as catalysts for rallying people together. These efforts often serve to beautify vacant lots or reclaim a public space, as alternatives to graffiti frequently used by gang members to mark their territory.

TROUBLESHOOTING

Make sure to get permission before starting a big project, such as a mural in your school. Present your principal with a goal, an action plan, and perhaps even a sketch!

Action Ideas

School can be the ideal place to display a mural. Ask permission from your principal to cover a section of a wall (in the gym or cafeteria, or other high-traffic area) with heavy white paper, and then gather a group to put their ideas about a chosen issue into a series of powerful images.

You can organize an art exhibit of paintings, drawings or photographs by individual artists, linked by the common themes of your issue. Place the exhibit in a location where lots of people will see it, like your school hallways, or during events such as pep rallies and fairs.

Use art and design skills to make all of your posters, banners, and pamphlets more eye-catching and inspiring.

TAKE MORE ACTION! How To Change The World

HOME	LEVEL I	LEVEL II
Preface, Contents	Global Citizenship: Around the World, Across the Street	Becoming Global Citizens: A Question of Choice

Street theatre

Street theatre is untraditional drama that can be performed both inside and outside (in a public park, for example). It is more interactive than a typical play. Because there is no stage, the audience and performers are on the same level. Street theatre is meant to be available to a broad audience, including those who might not be able to afford the price of a theatre ticket. By presenting larger issues through individual characters, dramatic presentations make complex and distant political issues more personal.

Action Ideas

Create a funny play or skit to deliver a controversial message in a light-hearted way. Incorporate dance, masks, costumes, songs, or puppetry into your performance.

Follow your performance with a question-and-answer session, so that the actors and audience can discuss reactions to the play and exchange ideas.

Hold a "sweatshop fashion show" in your school auditorium. Get the story behind clothing made through exploitative practices: research where it was made, under what conditions, and what wages the workers were paid compared with the retail price of the item. As each model comes out, give the audience the details on the outfit.

Poetry and prose

Writers have always used poetry and prose to express revolutionary ideas, critique society, and challenge conventional thought. Many use their fictional characters and stories to reflect on cultural or historical issues, or to voice an opinion. Think of some of the writing you may have read at school or on your own. Such works as the poem "In Flanders Fields," or the book *Anne Frank: The Diary of a Young Girl* force us to consider the consequences of social issues in emotional, human terms. Stories have the power to draw readers in and help them to relate to people and perspectives that they normally would not connect with in everyday life.

TAKE MORE ACTION! How To Change The World

HOME	LeveL I	LeveL II
Preface, Contents	Global Citizenship: Around the World, Across the Street	Becoming Global Citizens: A Question of Choice

Action Ideas

If you identify a voice within your issue that needs to be heard, consider writing a piece from this perspective. Be creative. How would an enslaved child laborer feel about her life? How would a stream feel about being polluted?

If there is a current issue in the news that people at your school are concerned about, gather their thoughts in an anthology or chapbook (i.e., a small, handmade book of poems and stories). You can sell copies of the completed book as a fundraiser.

Showcase students' creative voices by organizing a poetry, prose, or spoken word performance. Arrange a program of speakers in advance, or use an open mike format, allowing anyone from the audience to get up and read or perform a piece.

Music

Music has inspired audiences since the beginning of time. It strikes a chord with our beliefs and struggles, and has the power to heal and to move and awaken a crowd. In the 1930s, Billie Holiday's song "Strange Fruit" called attention to the millions of African Americans who had been murdered by lynching in the United States. During the 1960s, popular music became increasingly political, when artists such as Bob Dylan, Bob Marley, and Aretha Franklin sang about civil rights and the importance of social action. John Lennon's "Imagine" inspired a whole generation and beyond to dream of a peaceful future. In the years since then, many bands and musicians have expressed an indignant call for profound political, economic, and social change.

Instead of making a positive statement, however, a lot of mainstream music perpetuates social problems—from drugs and misogyny to racism and violence. You can shift the trend by supporting artists who promote social messages, and, more importantly, by memorizing and sharing the lyrics that really move you. Music has the power to work its way into people's minds, hearts, and souls: the very places where change must begin.

Action Ideas

Incorporate social themes into your choice of music. Find musicians in your community with a social conscience and gather a group to go hear them in concert.

Take note of the injustices and issues around you and write a song to express how you feel about them.

Hold a concert to raise funds and social consciousness, or make music the centerpiece for one of your events by assembling a showcase of local musicians to help you promote your cause.

TAKE MORE ACTION! How To Change The World

HOME	LEVEL I	LEVEL II
Preface, Contents	Global Citizenship: Around the World, Across the Street	Becoming Global Citizens: A Question of Choice

PROFILE

Regent Park TV: Media Activists

Young people at Toronto's Regent Park are using modern media technology to share a timeless message.

In 2006, RPTV hit the online airwaves—a network far from the ordinary typical news network.

Regent Park TV is the creation of the Regent Park Focus Youth Media Arts Centre, a community center which produces newspapers, video segments and other media that take on issues important to the region.

With digital audio and video equipment becoming increasingly affordable and accessible, the kids who participate in the program can make polished video segments with little experience. They write, shoot and edit their own short videos and post them online using the hugely popular video sharing site YouTube.

Their videos have covered a diverse array of subject matter, including crime, bullying, police relations, cultural conflicts, teen homelessness and other topics on which they have strong opinions, as well as comedy, music and current affairs segments. The wildly popular program began in the summer of 2006, but is now running every day after school.

Shortly after its launch, RGTV featured coverage in the *Toronto Star*, Canada's highest-circulated newspaper. "This new media is giving the kids a chance to represent themselves," Adonis Huggins, program coordinator with the group, told reporters. "It's the kids who are defining what they want to do. They're really excited about producing."

As Canada's oldest social housing project, Regent Park has long suffered a reputation as a rough neighborhood, with high rates of crime and poverty. "The media tend to cover Regent Park in stereotypical ways," Huggins said. "They focus on crime and poverty. That's not what our community is about. That's a part of it, but that's not what we're about."

The kids get a chance to portray the realities of their community through their own eyes while learning valuable technology skills, as well as media literacy and interviewing techniques. They learn that expressing personal attitudes about their beliefs, culture and community is simply a matter of taking action and bringing their ideas to life.

"It was good," Kody Ellis, 13, told reporters. "I did this instead of going out on the street and getting in trouble."

• Why is a video, story or song sometimes more convincing than a lecture or article? What are the advantages of this approach? What are the limitations?

• In your opinion, what issues would most benefit from a multimedia approach? Why?

• What are other simple but effective ways young people can get their message heard?

TAKE MORE ACTION! How To Change The World

HOME	LeveL I	LeveL II
Preface, Contents	Global Citizenship: Around the World, Across the Street	Becoming Global Citizens: A Question of Choice

Take Action!

Read a classic novel with a social theme. Ask your teacher for suggestions based on your chosen issue.

As a class, organize a competition for the best art project (poster, skit, song, poem, etc.) expressing ideas on a social issue. Display or present the creations in your school and community.

Research the lyrics of a socially active musician from another era. Find out what historical or social context inspired the artist and whether the lyrics contain references to any well-known speeches or spiritual texts.

"TO BE GREAT, ART HAS TO POINT SOMEWHERE."

—Anne Lamott
(b. 1954)
Author

PUBLIC SPEAKING: THE POWER TOOL

Public speaking is a powerful force that can break the silence and raise awareness of difficult issues. Throughout history, speeches have inspired people and rallied them together in challenging times.

- During the bleakest hours of World War II, for example, Winston Churchill made many speeches that inspired the British not to give up hope. His voice helped give people the strength to persevere until the war was over.

- On August 28, 1963, Dr. Martin Luther King, Jr.'s famed "I Have a Dream" speech, delivered on the steps of the Lincoln Memorial in Washington, D.C., galvanized the American Civil Rights Movement and inspired millions to put an end to racial discrimination. In 1992, 12-year-old Severn Suzuki of British Columbia made a dramatic speech at the beginning of the Rio Earth Summit and energized the entire audience to push forward in the movement to address urgent environmental problems.

When you speak with force and expression, you command attention and have the power to move people with your ideas. If you could stand in front of a million people, what would you say?

TAKE MORE ACTION! How To Change The World

HOME	LEVEL I	LEVEL II
Preface, Contents	Global Citizenship: Around the World, Across the Street	Becoming Global Citizens: A Question of Choice

Making your voice heard

Everybody has a message to deliver. Everybody has a vision of an ideal world. We are constantly bombarded with messages about a multitude of issues and, as a result, social advocacy is a challenging yet exhilarating activity. As you advocate for the change you would like to see, your passion and conviction must be strong and influential. How will you make your voice heard above all others?

Fear of public speaking is one of the most common phobias in the world. If you feel a little or a lot nervous when speaking up in front a group of people, or to just one important person, you're not alone. There are many simple, proven techniques, however, that you can practise to overcome nervousness and awkwardness and deliver your message with passion and poise.

TIP

Public Speaking Skills
You can use these skills anywhere, in addition to working on your chosen issue; for example:
- School presentations
- Debates (formal or informal)
- Student council elections
- Media, job, and college interviews
- Trying to convince anyone of anything, anytime, for any reason!

Making an Ordinary Topic Extraordinary

No matter what your topic, no matter what your environment, your overall goal when public speaking is to make your listeners care about your topic. To do that, you must make your ordinary topic extraordinary—something that will turn their heads, something that is so exceptionally critical for them to listen to that they cannot possibly do anything else.

Remember to show your passion, informing your audience that there is a problem, involving them by telling them how that problem affects them, and inspiring them to take action to solve it!

"WHEN THERE IS VIOLENCE AGAINST ANY PERSON IN SOCIETY, BECAUSE HE OR SHE IS DIFFERENT, IT THREATENS US ALL. ONLY BY SPEAKING OUT ARE ANY OF US SAFE."

—Madeleine Kunin
(b. 1933)
Former governor of Vermont, politician

TAKE MORE ACTION! How To Change The World

HOME	LEVEL I	LEVEL II
Preface, Contents	Global Citizenship: Around the World, Across the Street	Becoming Global Citizens: A Question of Choice

Every speech you give is an opportunity to change the world, even in a small way.

LeveL IV > The How To Guide: Public Speaking: The Power Tool

LeveL III	**LeveL IV**	**LeveL V**
The Seven Steps to Social Action: Taking It to the Next Level	The How-To Guide: The Global Citizen's Toolbox	Sources And Resources, End Notes

The goals of a speech

To write a powerful speech that will inform your audience of an issue and persuade them to take action, use the three I's: *Influence*, *Involve*, and *Inspire*.

1. *Influence* them

Go to your research for your key information. Organize your facts, statistics, and stories in a logical order to make a solid argument. To convince your audience of your perspective, use a combination of the three main tools of persuasion:

- Logic: Appeal to rational thinkers by citing hard facts and statistics.
- Values: Overcome logical counter-arguments to your thesis by citing universal values such as equality, freedom of speech, and democracy.
- Emotion: This is the most powerful way of moving your audience, as feelings often overcome logic and values. Use stories and personal anecdotes to appeal to your audience's emotions.

TIP

Don't overuse any of the three persuasion tools, or you may overwhelm your audience with numbers, guilt, or feelings. Find an appropriate balance and you will appeal to every member of the audience in some way.

2. *Involve* them

Show your audience how your topic directly relates to their everyday lives. Make the issue personal for them, and explain to them why and how they should get involved.

- Avoid blaming people or using guilt as your primary emotion. Instead, focus more on telling your audience that they can make a positive difference by acting. Use the word "challenge" a lot: "I challenge you to take action." This is more effective than saying "You have to," or "You should."
- Do not assume that your audience will know what you want them to do; give them specific actions to take and offer them three different levels of involvement to choose from (easy, medium, and hard), so that everyone can get involved, regardless of how influenced they are.

TAKE MORE ACTION! How To Change The World

Home	**Level I**	**Level II**
Preface, Contents	Global Citizenship:	Becoming Global Citizens:
	Around the World, Across the Street	A Question of Choice

Three Levels of Involvement

Easy: something small before you leave the room (signing a petition to improve education around the world, picking up and reading a pamphlet about the issue)

Medium: a significant but easy action to do after you leave, a slight change in daily routine (putting together school supplies for children in need, biking to school or work rather than driving)

Hard: getting fully involved in the issue (fundraising to build a school in a developing country and volunteering overseas to construct the school, buying a hybrid car)

3. *Inspire* them!

Give your audience hope that change is possible, and motivate them to realize that they can be the ones to bring it about. Find success stories of people who have made a difference on your particular topic, as well as powerful quotations from famous people who share your passion.

LEVEL III
The Seven Steps to Social Action:
Taking It to the Next Level

LEVEL IV
The How-To Guide:
The Global Citizen's Toolbox

LEVEL V
Sources And Resources,
End Notes

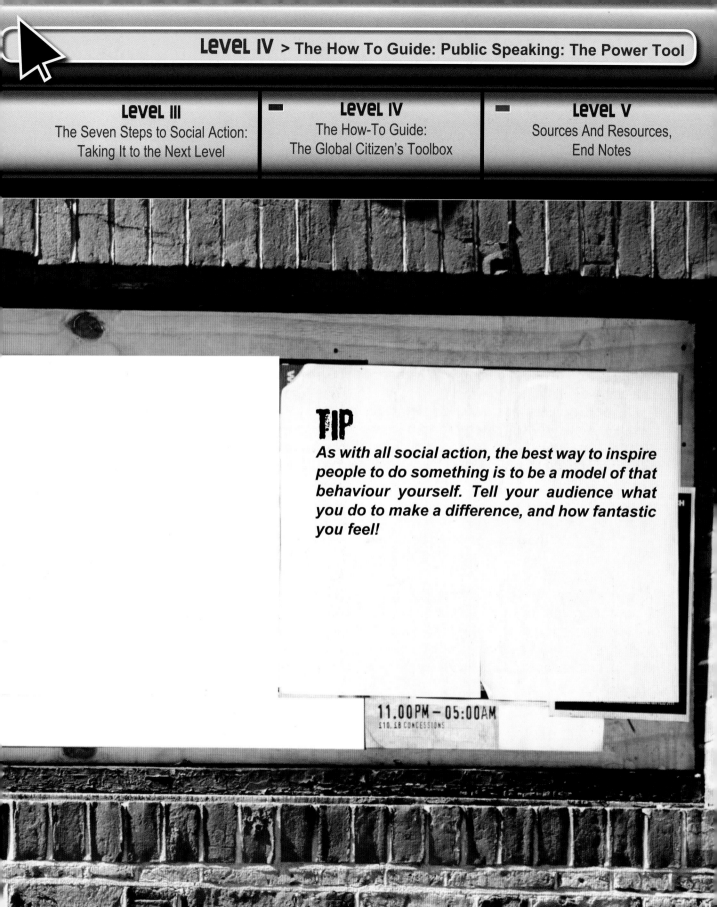

TIP

As with all social action, the best way to inspire people to do something is to be a model of that behaviour yourself. Tell your audience what you do to make a difference, and how fantastic you feel!

11.00PM – 05:00AM
£10. £8 CONCESSIONS

TAKE MORE ACTION! How To Change The World

HOME	LEVEL I	LEVEL II
Preface, Contents	Global Citizenship: Around the World, Across the Street	Becoming Global Citizens: A Question of Choice

Writing a Speech: a Sample Structure

Now that you are ready to write your speech, here is a sample speech structure you can use for any topic. A speech is divided into an **introduction**, a **body**, and a **conclusion**.

Introduction

- *Casual Intro*: Thank the person who introduced you and the group that invited you, and say it's a pleasure to be there and why. Then pause, breathe—and begin.
- *The Hook*: Grab their attention with a startling statistic, fact, or story, or ask them to picture a powerful scenario. You have 10 to 15 seconds to convince your audience that your topic is important and that you are worth listening to. If, for example, your speech is on child labor, you might choose an opener like: "Did you know that there are over 250 million child laborers around the world?" The success of an opening "hook" relies not only on the words you choose, but also on an energetic, emotional delivery.
- *Introduce yourself and your topic*: "My name is _____, and I am here to talk to you about _____, an extremely important issue because..."
- *Present your thesis and a preview of your main points*: The thesis is the central message of your speech. It is not the subject of your speech, but an explicit statement about that subject, often for or against a specific aspect of the subject. A thesis is the one point that you want to be sure your audience remembers. It should, therefore, be a short, clear sentence, as in: "We must take action now to free children from oppressive child labor."
- Next, *provide an overview of your arguments*, in logical order, in one to three sentences: "Child labor is the result of poverty and a lack of political will to do something about it. But there are many things that we can do as a global society to change that, in our everyday actions, and as citizens, consumers, and youth activists."

Body

Facts and stats: Here is where your first "I" comes in—**influence** them. Make your arguments in logical order and appeal to your listeners' values and emotions. Cite facts and statistics that prove your thesis. Describe how the problem started. Explain in detail why the problem is so serious and why society allows it to continue. Make sure to always relate each major argument back to your thesis:

LeveL III
The Seven Steps to Social Action:
Taking It to the Next Level

LeveL IV
The How-To Guide:
The Global Citizen's Toolbox

LeveL V
Sources And Resources,
End Notes

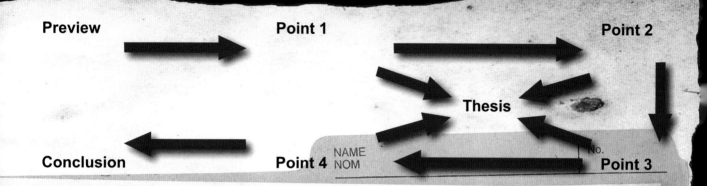

Preview → **Point 1** → **Point 2**

Thesis

Conclusion ← **Point 4** **Point 3**

- *Tell a story*: Make sure it contains several powerful elements such as suspense, sadness, inspiration, humor, or action. Express your personal feelings about the situation and why you are committed and involved. Practise telling your story to friends or mentors and take note of their reactions and advice to make it ultimately effective.
- *List three actions*: The second "I": involve them. For example: "There are three things that you can do to help this situation. I challenge you to try at least one." For each (easy, medium, and hard), explain what to do and how it will make a difference.

Conclusion
- *Summarize your thesis and main points again*: Quickly state your thesis in one sentence, and your main points in one or two sentences.
- *Summarize three actions*: In one sentence: To make a difference, you can do the following: restate your easy, medium, and hard actions.
- *Thank-You*: You are not finished yet. Prepare your audience for one last, powerful, inspirational note: "I'd like to thank you for your time, and I will leave you with one final thought…"
- *Inspire them*: The third "I": Finish with a quotation, your vision of a perfect world, or an inspirational pep talk that will send a tingle throughout your audience. They will remember it as they are taking action and changing the world, just as you said!

Then sit back and wait for the applause. Can you hear it?

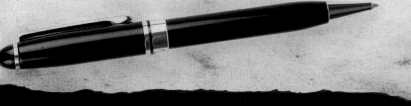

TAKE MORE ACTION! How To Change The World

| HOME Preface, Contents | LEVEL I Global Citizenship: Around the World, Across the Street | LEVEL II Becoming Global Citizens: A Question of Choice |

Take Action!

1. For your chosen issue brainstorm how you will **Influence**, **Involve**, and **Inspire** your audience.
2. Come up with three sample actions that you can ask the audience to take (easy, medium and hard).
3. Write a speech on your chosen issue. Keep it short for now: three to five minutes.

The four keys to delivering an outstanding speech

There have been many scientific studies done about the impact of a speech on an audience. Audience members are often surveyed after a speech to find out what aspects of it influenced them the most. And, as strange as it may seem, most report that the speaker's appearance or presentation makes a greater impression than his or her words.

When you are in front of an audience, how you deliver your speech is often more important than what you say! An influential, involving and inspiring speech must be delivered with passion and with the following four crucial factors in mind: stance, eye contact, voice and gestures. Follow these guidelines as you step out before an audience for a delivery that will move them to action.

1. Stance

Stand with your legs shoulder's width apart, knees slightly bent and your arms at your sides. To avoid fidgeting, pretend that you are holding a pen horizontally in front of you, just below your belly button. Keep your chin up and your nose in line with your belly button (this way, when you pivot to see people on both sides of the room, you move from your waist instead of your neck). This is your Ready Position. It may feel uncomfortable because it leaves you open, and therefore vulnerable, to your audience.

The more open you are, however, the more approachable, secure and compelling you will seem as you speak. It also means that your hands are not in your pockets, fiddling with rings or keys, behind your back, or clasped in front.

TAKE MORE ACTION! How To Change The World

| HOME
Preface, Contents | LEVEL I
Global Citizenship:
Around the World, Across the Street | LEVEL II
Becoming Global Citizens:
A Question of Choice |

2. Eye contact

Eye contact is the key to your audience's heart. It is the best way to make your listeners know what you want them to know, and feel what you want them to feel. Direct eye contact builds a rapport between you and individual members of the audience and conveys the feeling: "The speaker cares about me."

Eye contact also enables you to survey your audience to determine how they are responding to the speech. If you notice that some people have lost interest, you can take steps to adjust your speech to win them back. When you see, on the other hand, that your audience is fully engaged, it will give you a wonderful boost of confidence.

3. Voice

Your voice is what can make your audience want to go out and change the world immediately after your speech. When people hear the passion in your voice, they will become passionate about your issue. Your voice should be articulate and expressive. To be articulate is to pronounce your words clearly, pausing at appropriate moments. To be expressive is to fill your voice with emotion. At all times, it is crucial to speak loud enough for your whole audience to hear you. Most speakers, unfortunately, do not.

4. Gestures

To emphasize certain points in your speech, co-ordinate your words with specific gestures. Follow these simple guidelines:
- Your gestures must be deliberate and visible. Decide ahead of time what specific points you want to emphasize with gestures, and follow through confidently. Again, you will likely feel awkward at first with calculated gestures; however, once you have used them a few times, they will seem very natural to you and to your audience. They are also highly effective in demonstrating your passion and intensity.
- Do not be afraid to let your facial expressions reflect your emotions and passion. Let the feeling flow. Just be careful to avoid exaggeration.

Effective Gestures for Public Speaking	
Sentence	Gesture
• "I..." • "Speaking to you" • "Three points to share with you" • "Passionate about" • "Come together"	• Point to yourself • Open hand toward audience • Hold three fingers up • Clench fist • Bring hands together

TAKE MORE ACTION! How To Change The World

HOME	LEVEL I	LEVEL II
Preface, Contents	Global Citizenship: Around the World, Across the Street	Becoming Global Citizens: A Question of Choice

On nervousness

Nervousness is inevitable—even we at Free The Children and Me to We, although we've presented hundreds of speeches, get nervous at the start of every speech we give. What will happen if our listeners don't laugh at the first joke? What if they are not interested? What if the projector breaks down?

The key is to channel that nervous energy into passionate energy. If you believe in yourself (giving yourself a pep talk before going on helps!) and in your message, your chances of success are far greater. Little things such as practicing your speech in front of a mirror or a friend can help melt away nervousness. Here are a few other tips that may come in handy.

- Know the room and your position: the size of the room, where your visual aids can be set up, whether you will be sitting or standing, behind a lectern or not, with a microphone or without.
- Be familiar with the sound system, i.e., how far your mouth should be from the microphone.
- Know the audience: size, age range, profession, interests, VIPs to mention.
- Know the process: who will introduce you, who will speak before and after you, whether or not there will be questions.
- Set a tone with your first words. A loud, clear and friendly "Good morning" will give

"IF ONE IS GOING TO CHANGE THINGS, ONE HAS TO MAKE A FUSS AND CATCH THE EYE OF THE WORLD."

—Elizabeth Janeway
(1913-2005)
Author, critic, journalist

LeveL IV > The How To Guide: Public Speaking: The Power Tool

LeveL III	**LeveL IV**	**LeveL V**
The Seven Steps to Social Action: Taking It to the Next Level	The How-To Guide: The Global Citizen's Toolbox	Sources And Resources, End Notes

you a moment to collect yourself. Don't forget the casual introduction to set you and your audience at ease.
- Have a glass or bottle of water available. This is quite acceptable in most settings, and invaluable when your mouth runs dry.
- Realize that your audience wants you to succeed.

Take Action!

1. Look up the full text of Martin Luther King, Jr.'s "I Have a Dream" speech of 1963. Identify the different parts in the speech structure. Count how many times the central message or sound bite is repeated, as well as the number of times King uses the words "I have a dream," and "free." What is the effect?
2. Practise your written speech in front of the mirror at home. Focus on stance, variance, use of pauses and gestures.
3. Say your speech to a partner (or in groups of three or four), first without interruptions. Ask for feedback—first on what was good, then on what can be improved. Next, have one member of your group stop you whenever he or she has advice.

TAKE MORE ACTION! How To Change The World

HOME	LEVEL I	LEVEL II
Preface, Contents	Global Citizenship: Around the World, Across the Street	Becoming Global Citizens: A Question of Choice

Using visual aids

Visual aids enable the audience to more effectively grasp the message you are trying to convey. Studies by educational researchers suggest that approximately 83 percent of human learning occurs visually. Use PowerPoint or a similar program to create a slide show of pictures that link directly to your stories. Pictures enable your audience to actually see what you are talking about, to better visualize your stories as you tell them and to take away a more vivid attachment to your issue.

TROUBLESHOOTING

Inform people that you will need the lights turned down at a specific time for the presentation. If they are ready, you will avoid having to scramble. Also, if you cannot reach the controls to switch the slides, have a volunteer do it for you. Work out a signal (a nod or eye contact) to indicate when to switch, and ask him or her to be totally focused on you and ready to switch at any time, to make your presentation run smoothly. Do not read from your slides.

Use short video clips, if relevant, to add to the visualization of your stories and diversify your means of communication with your audience. Young people crave video—they will love you for it!

Creating a great slide show presentation

You can use PowerPoint or a similar program for pictures alone, if you wish, but if you choose to use it for informational purposes, follow these helpful guidelines:

- Start with a title slide in big print.
- Include only one piece of information on each slide. The only text on the slides should be in point form or brief sentences.
- Avoid placing text directly over images, as this makes it difficult to read.
- Use a consistent background or format for every slide.
- Do not use bright or neon colors.
- Do not overdo the slide transitions and animations.
- Use only relevant graphics and pictures, and use them sparingly: not more than 2 or 3 per slide.
- Focus on content rather than design.
- Go over your speech in its entirety to rehearse the slide changes. Mark them clearly them on your speech notes.
- Ensure that you have properly tested the software program, projector and computer you will be using for your presentation beforehand. Be sure all systems and software are compatible.
- Technical difficulties are inevitable. Make sure that you have a backup plan so you can continue smoothly if they arise.

LEVEL IV > The How To Guide: Public Speaking: The Power Tool

| **LEVEL III**
The Seven Steps to Social Action:
Taking It to the Next Level | **LEVEL IV**
The How-To Guide:
The Global Citizen's Toolbox | **LEVEL V**
Sources And Resources,
End Notes |

YOU CAN MAKE AN AUDIENCE SEE NEARLY ANYTHING, IF YOU YOURSELF BELIEVE IN IT.

—Mary Renault
(1905-1983)
Author

TAKE MORE ACTION! How To Change The World

HOME	LEVEL I	LEVEL II
Preface, Contents	Global Citizenship: Around the World, Across the Street	Becoming Global Citizens: A Question of Choice

Questions and answers

Effectively handling questions and answers can strengthen your overall presentation, giving you extra time to make your case. This is your time to show you really know your stuff.

Tips for a Great Q & A Session

1. **Practise answers before the presentation.**
   Think of the questions that your audience is likely to ask. Outlining and rehearsing your answers ahead of time will add to your self-confidence and credibility.

2. **Repeat the question.**
   The rest of the audience may not have heard the question, so repeat it for their benefit. Rephrasing the question also ensures that you understood it correctly, and gives you time to consider how to best phrase your answer.

3. **Control the question.**
   If an audience member asks a difficult or hostile question, do not panic. Acknowledge the question politely and positively, and then offer your point of view. Showing respect will often defuse hostility, and at least maintain your credibility for being open to criticism. If the person continues to be hostile, offer to discuss the issue one-on-one after the presentation.

4. **Admit when you do not know the answer.**
   Do not make up an answer. Tell the questioner that it is an excellent question and that you will do further research and get back to him or her.

5. **There are no dumb questions.**
   If someone asks a question that some would consider silly or ignorant, treat it as a normal question and answer it—the person who asked it doesn't think it's silly.

6. **Have questions ready.**
   If there is a lag in the Q & A session, do not stand there in silence. Have some questions on hand to offer to your audience. You could start with: "A question I often get is…" This will get the ball rolling.

Take Action!

1. Design a PowerPoint or other slide show presentation to go along with the speech on your chosen issue.
2. Brainstorm questions you may be asked in a Q & A session after your speech. Research and practise the answers.
3. Do your entire presentation—speech, visual aids and Q & A—for the class.

TAKE MORE ACTION! How To Change The World

HOME	LEVEL I	LEVEL II
Preface, Contents	Global Citizenship: Around the World, Across the Street	Becoming Global Citizens: A Question of Choice

PLUGGING INTO THE POLITICAL SYSTEM

Politics play a big part in your everyday life. Public policy affects your schools, hospitals, parks, the funding of your community programs and the way your country interacts with the rest of the world. Understanding politics and connecting with the government is an important aspect of social action. Adults make up and control the government for the most part, but this does not mean that there is no place for the voices of youth. It is the duty of political leaders to represent the whole population: This includes you. Your active participation is key.

But I don't get to vote! What am I supposed to do? Good question—lots! Voting is only one way to become involved with the government. There are a number of other ways to participate in the system and make your opinions count. The first step is to become informed. Do some research on the structure and workings of your federal, provincial and municipal political systems. Find out who is responsible for which issues and how legislation is passed. Attending public meetings, acting as a representative on a community youth council, volunteering in a political campaign, or

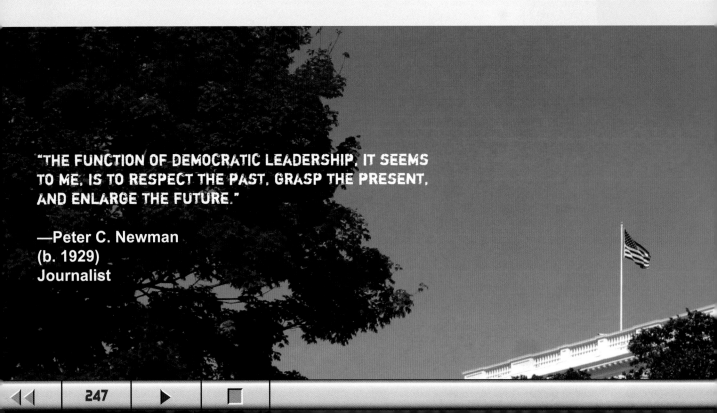

"THE FUNCTION OF DEMOCRATIC LEADERSHIP, IT SEEMS TO ME, IS TO RESPECT THE PAST, GRASP THE PRESENT, AND ENLARGE THE FUTURE."

—Peter C. Newman
(b. 1929)
Journalist

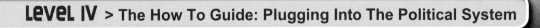

| **LeVeL III**
The Seven Steps to Social Action:
Taking It to the Next Level | **LeVeL IV**
The How-To Guide:
The Global Citizen's Toolbox | **LeVeL V**
Sources And Resources,
End Notes |

helping to register voters at the polls are all ways to be a politically active citizen.

All members of society have a right to communicate with legislators, influence their decisions and impact the way the government invests in social programs. How do you do this? Through the art of lobbying.

What is lobbying?

Lobbying is attempting to influence legislation or political decisions. You may try to convince the government to support your point of view either in person, in writing, or through the media. Lobbying means asking an elected official for active support, requesting that he or she do something specific in the interests or on behalf of the people whom he or she was chosen to represent. It can be as easy as meeting with the official to share your passionate concerns for an issue—and don't forget, it's that person's job to listen to you!

TAKE MORE ACTION! How To Change The World

HOME	LEVEL I	LEVEL II
Preface, Contents	Global Citizenship: Around the World, Across the Street	Becoming Global Citizens: A Question of Choice

Lobbying may be an appropriate action to take in situations such as the following:

- The government is considering a Bill that affects your issue, whether to help it or to make it worse, and you want your representative to vote a certain way.
- New legislation could solve a particular problem that you care about, and you want your representative to try to make it happen.
- You wish to gain the government's help with your campaign, either with resources, advice, legislation, or other government action like starting programs to help your issue or persuading other countries' governments to take action on your issue.

Whom should I lobby?

You can lobby officials from any level of government, from the civil service to Members of Parliament or Congress to Cabinet Ministers and Senators—even the President or Prime Minister. First identify whether your issue is a federal, provincial, or municipal responsibility.

"THERE'S NO QUESTION IN MY MIND BUT THAT RIGHTS ARE NEVER WON UNLESS PEOPLE ARE WILLING TO FIGHT FOR THEM."

—Eleanor Smeal
(b. 1930)
Women's rights leader

LeveL IV > The How To Guide: Plugging Into The Political System

LeveL III	**LeveL IV**	**LeveL V**
The Seven Steps to Social Action: Taking It to the Next Level	The How-To Guide: The Global Citizen's Toolbox	Sources And Resources, End Notes

In order to find out whom to contact, you will have to determine the responsible government ministry or Cabinet agency, department within that ministry or agency and the individual(s) within that department.

The following chart shows how some of the key responsibilities are distributed:

Government Responsibilities		
Federal	**Provincial**	**Municipal**
Agriculture Census and statistics Citizenship Criminal law Environment Foreign affairs Immigration Indian affairs Military and defense Penitentiaries Sea coast and inland fisheries Trade and commerce Transportation	Agriculture Education Hospitals Immigration Labor and trade unions Local matters (e.g., highway regulation) Natural Resources Provincial property and civil rights Timber and wood Trade and commerce	By-laws for the municipality Garbage collection Licensing Parks and recreation for the municipality Public libraries Recycling programs Zoning

- The Blue Pages section of the phone book lists government departments at all levels (check under House of Commons, Congress, Legislature or City/Town Hall for names, phone numbers and office addresses of your representatives), or you can research at the library or on the Internet. Ask your teacher or family for the name of your congressional district in the United States or "riding" in Canada (federal and provincial), or for the "ward" (municipal)—that is how you will know which representative is yours.
- You do not have to wait for an emergency to touch base with your representatives. You may wish to contact them when you do not know where they stand on an issue, or when you

TAKE MORE ACTION! How To Change The World

HOME Preface, Contents	LEVEL I Global Citizenship: Around the World, Across the Street	LEVEL II Becoming Global Citizens: A Question of Choice

agree with what they are doing. Their office staff keeps track of how many telephone calls and letters they receive on both sides of an issue and then informs the representative what their constituents (the people they represent in their riding or electoral district) think. Add one "vote" to the side you are on! Your voice can make a difference, particularly at the local and provincial level.

Remember that because many people choose to remain silent, one voice can be taken to represent many, especially if you can show that others support your position. Get your friends to write in as well, and you'll have a landslide!

TIP

How do you know what your representative has done recently, or what issues are currently big in your area? Most of them send reports that explain what they have been doing for you (called "householders" in Canada) to every home in their riding. Read up on it, and contact your representative's office with your thoughts!

"WATER CONTINUALLY DROPPING WILL WEAR HARD ROCKS HOLLOW."

—Plutarch
(CE 46-c. 119)
Biographer, author

LeVeL IV > The How To Guide: Plugging Into The Political System

| **LeVeL III**
The Seven Steps to Social Action:
Taking It to the Next Level | **LeVeL IV**
The How-To Guide:
The Global Citizen's Toolbox | **LeVeL V**
Sources And Resources,
End Notes |

Lobbying tips

There are several ways to make contact with political figures. These include letters, petitions and meetings with legislators. Here are some tips that you can use no matter which lobbying method you choose:

- **Get the title right:** Make sure the official's name is preceded by the proper title or honorific. Examples of titles that you may need to use include *The Right Honorable* (for the Prime Minister and Governor General of Canada), *The Honorable* (for a premier, cabinet ministers, a member of the House of Commons, a senator, or members of parliament in Canada), *The Honorable* (for the President of the United States, governors, cabinet members, mayors and many appointed governmental heads in the United States; note the spelling difference!) and *Your Worship* (for mayors and judges in Canada).
- **Do your research:** Being well-informed enables you to support your arguments with evidence, answer questions and defend your position. Verify your research sources to ensure that you are providing legislators with accurate, up-to-date information. Know of any laws or bills that relate to your issue and be able to identify other organizations or non-governmental organizations (NGOs) that support you.

TAKE MORE ACTION! How To Change The World

HOME	LEVEL I	LEVEL II
Preface, Contents	Global Citizenship: Around the World, Across the Street	Becoming Global Citizens: A Question of Choice

- ***Know your legislator:*** In order to persuade your legislators of something, you will want to know where they already stand. Read their speeches (check government Web sites or read their reports) to find out what issues they care about and what their ideals are. The best way? Ask them! Write a letter or set up a meeting to discuss their position on whatever issues you want!

- ***Use appropriate language:*** Remain courteous and open-minded, even when you disagree with someone. Communicate your message tactfully about controversial or sensitive topics; your goal is to engage the legislator's interest. Avoid being overemotional or making unreasonable demands.

- ***Make the issue personal:*** Show the human side of your issue by drawing attention to people's stories and experiences. Discuss the consequences of the problem on the people your legislator represents. It can be useful to bring forth a spokesperson who has been personally affected by the issue.

- ***Be considerate:*** Your representatives are used to being pulled and pushed in every direction. Show that you understand that they are under a lot of pressure, but that this issue is very important to you. They will appreciate the understanding, and will be more likely to take your interests personally.

- ***Be confident:*** Lobbying can be intimidating, but remind yourself that you have done your research and know your topic well. You have a right to express your opinion, and by speaking out for something you feel strongly about, you may be able to affect politics in ways that will improve the lives of others.

Level IV > The How To Guide: Plugging Into The Political System

Level III	**Level IV**	**Level V**
The Seven Steps to Social Action: Taking It to the Next Level	The How-To Guide: The Global Citizen's Toolbox	Sources And Resources, End Notes

Take Action!

1. Watch an hour of CPAC (Canadian Parliamentary Access Channel) or C-SPAN (Cable-Satellite Public Affairs Network). Even if the government is not in session, these networks often have excellent coverage of the major political issues of the day and what various members of Parliament and Congress do. Write a summary of what you saw.

2. Find out who your representatives are in federal, provincial and municipal government. Get their contact information and office address. Ask your family to keep their next mailing so you can read through it and see what the representatives stand for. See if you can obtain the latest US Congressional Record or "Hansard" (the minutes of Canada's Parliament and Legislatures, organized by day) and look for your representative's latest speech. What was it about? What was his or her position? Discuss the speech in class.

3. Find out which level of government, and which legislators you should contact with concerns about your issue. Get their contact information and try to find some of their speeches to get a preview of their position on various issues.

TAKE MORE ACTION! How To Change The World

| **HOME**
Preface, Contents | **LeveL I**
Global Citizenship:
Around the World, Across the Street | **LeveL II**
Becoming Global Citizens:
A Question of Choice |

Writing letters to government officials

Your first stop to lobbying success is writing a letter to government officials. Ask directly about the official's view or stance on the situation. Include a question in your letter that is too specific to be answered in a general form-letter reply. You may want to follow up your letter with a phone call one week later to make sure it was received. If you do not receive a response within a reasonable amount of time (normally, six to eight weeks), follow up with a phone call or another letter.

If you are writing to oppose or disagree with something, say so, and explain why. Mention any alternatives or solutions you or your group has to suggest.

Writing a petition to the federal government

To be successful, your lobbying efforts must show not only how you feel, but also that others support your point of view. Legislators are more likely to take actions that represent the unified interests of a community of citizens. A petition can be an effective tool for gathering support and proving your strength in numbers. You can petition your government to reject legislation by referendum, amend your constitution or introduce new laws. The most important guideline in filing a petition is knowing what level or branch of government corresponds most directly to your specific issue. The table on page 250 can help you determine to whom you should direct your petition.

If you wish to petition the federal government, there are specific rules and guidelines that you must follow. At the provincial and state levels, legislatures vary in their procedures, so check with your MPP (Member of Provincial Parliament) or MLA (Member of the Legislative Assembly) in Canada, or your House Representative or Senator in the United States.

**Think of how much more effective a petition
with hundreds of signatures can be than one lone voice.**

TAKE MORE ACTION!
How To Change The World

HOME	LEVEL I	LEVEL II
Preface, Contents	Global Citizenship: Around the World, Across the Street	Becoming Global Citizens: A Question of Choice

- A petition to the House of Commons must be submitted orally or to the Clerk of Petitions by your Member of Parliament (MP). Once it is presented, the government will send a response to the MP within 45 days. Similarly, a petition to a U.S. state government should be filed with the secretary of state (or equivalent office in your state) before it will be considered for voting in Congress.

- It is recommended that, before collecting signatures, you submit a draft petition to your MP or Member of Congress and ask whether he or she would agree to present it (which does not necessarily mean he or she supports it). Make sure the petition is worded precisely and will not change after being filed.

- Petitions can be handwritten, printed, typed, or photocopied on letter-sized or legal-sized paper measuring 21.5 cm x 28 cm (8.5" x 11") or 21.5 cm x 35.5 cm (8.5" x 14").

- At the top of your petition, indicate clearly to whom it is being sent, stating their full title.

- The petition should address a single issue for which the given level of government is responsible. Explain your issue briefly and include any essential information supporters would have to know. Use respectful, rational language.

- A petition cannot simply state your opinion or complaint; it must contain a clear request—called a prayer—or action you want the government to take.

- Do not attach any additional documents to a petition.

LeveL III
The Seven Steps to Social Action:
Taking It to the Next Level

LeveL IV
The How-To Guide:
The Global Citizen's Toolbox

LeveL V
Sources And Resources,
End Notes

• Circulate your petition widely in public areas to collect as
many signatures as possible.
Contact your local representative to know how many
names are required—set a target and get your message
out to meet your goal.

• Petitioners' names must be signed as well as printed
directly on the sheet. They may give a full home address
or simply a city and province. No additional marks
should appear anywhere on the petition pages.

• Signatures can begin on the first page and continue
for as many pages as necessary.

• Each subsequent page of the petition should
indicate the topic of the petition. For example,
you may write at the top of each page something
along the lines of, "Petition asking
Congress/Parliament to take immediate action
to end child poverty."

TAKE MORE ACTION! How To Change The World

HOMe	LeVeL I	LeVeL II
Preface, Contents	Global Citizenship: Around the World, Across the Street	Becoming Global Citizens: A Question of Choice

Sample Petition to the House of Commons (Canada)

A PETITION REGARDING (sum up your issue in a phrase) *CHILD POVERTY TO THE HOUSE OF COMMONS IN PARLIAMENT ASSEMBLED*

(Identify in general who the petitioners are):

We, the undersigned citizens of Canada (or residents of the province/ city/ town of, etc.), draw the attention of the House to the following:

THAT (state the purpose of your petition) *child poverty deprives its victims of their rightful opportunity to develop, learn and grow in a secure and nurturing environment, and prevents them from achieving their full potential as human beings and citizens, and therefore must be immediately remedied by all means necessary;*

THAT (back up your statement with facts or information) *1 in 6 Canadian children live below the poverty line and have inadequate access to food, shelter, quality education and quality of life.*

THEREFORE, (outline the prayer, or the request you are making of the federal government) *your petitioners call upon Parliament to protect our children by investing federal funds and working with provinces to provide adequate food, health and shelter to Canada's poor children, and to raise the capacity of schools in poor areas to educate their students to be equal to that of schools in more wealthy areas.*

SIGNATURE   PRINTED NAME   ADDRESS
           (full home address, or city and province)

_____

_____

_____

LeveL III
The Seven Steps to Social Action:
Taking It to the Next Level

LeveL IV
The How-To Guide:
The Global Citizen's Toolbox

LeveL V
Sources And Resources,
End Notes

Sample Petition to the House of Representatives (US)

A PETITION REGARDING (sum up your issue in a phrase) *CHILD POVERTY*
TO THE (government entity being petitioned) *U.S. HOUSE OF REPRESENTATIVES ASSEMBLED*

(Identify in general who the petitioners are):

We, the undersigned citizens of the United States of America (or state/city/town of, etc.), draw the attention of the House to the following:

THAT (state the purpose of your petition) *child poverty deprives its victims of their rightful opportunity to develop, learn and grow in a secure and nurturing environment, and prevents them from achieving their full potential as human beings and citizens, and therefore must be immediately remedied by all means necessary;*

THAT (back up your statement with facts or information) *one in five children in the United States (or other statistic) live below the poverty line and have inadequate access to food, shelter, quality education and quality of life.*

THEREFORE, (outline the prayer, or the request you are making of the federal government) *your petitioners call upon Congress to protect our children by investing federal funds and working with states to provide adequate food, health and shelter to poor children, and to raise the capacity of schools in poor areas to educate their students to be equal to that of schools in more wealthy areas.*

SIGNATURE   PRINTED NAME   ADDRESS
(full home address, or city and state/province)

_____

_____

_____

TAKE MORE ACTION! How To Change The World

Home	**Level I**	**Level II**
Preface, Contents	Global Citizenship: Around the World, Across the Street	Becoming Global Citizens: A Question of Choice

"IF ENOUGH PEOPLE THINK OF A THING AND WORK HARD ENOUGH AT IT, I GUESS IT'S PRETTY NEARLY BOUND TO HAPPEN, WIND AND WEATHER PERMITTING."

—Laura Ingalls Wilder
(1867-1957)
Author

Level III	**Level IV**	**Level V**
The Seven Steps to Social Action: Taking It to the Next Level	The How-To Guide: The Global Citizen's Toolbox	Sources And Resources, End Notes

Meeting with legislators

You can meet with your representative to discuss an issue that you have raised in letters or petitions, or to discuss his or her views on another issue of your choice. Know your goal; you are unlikely to get a commitment to help right away, but make sure that the representative is very clear about what you want, and assure him or her that you will follow up. Use the following tips when meeting with legislators:

• Thank your legislator for taking the time to meet with you.

• Be able to state your case in about five minutes, which should leave time for questions and discussion.

• Bring an information package to leave with your legislator after the meeting. It should include a one- to two-page fact sheet that summarizes your position and your complete contact information, as well as supporting documents, such as three to five newspaper articles.

• Ask the legislator some personal questions, such as how he or she enjoys the job, why he or she got started, and what he or she really thinks about different issues. Do not chat too much if you have the impression that your time with the legislator is limited.

• Even if your legislator does not agree to support you, it is important to end on a positive note, so thank him or her again as you leave. Follow up with a thank-you letter afterward, including any additional information the person may have requested, along with the responses to any questions that you were unable to answer during the meeting.

TAKE MORE ACTION! How To Change The World

HOME	LEVEL I	LEVEL II
Preface, Contents	Global Citizenship: Around the World, Across the Street	Becoming Global Citizens: A Question of Choice

PROFILE

Jean-Dominic Lévesque-René: Environmental Activist

Jean-Dominic Levesque-René's battle for a cleaner environment began unexpectedly. In 1994, he was watching television when he felt a bump on the side of his neck. His parents took him to the hospital for tests, and soon discovered that he had non-Hodgkin's lymphoma, a form of cancer. Only ten years old, Jean-Dominic was told that he had a 50 percent chance of survival and would be in chemotherapy treatment for 49 weeks. Being hooked up to a machine was lonely and strange, but it gave Jean-Dominic time to think. He began to wonder: *How did I get this cancer?*

LeveL III
The Seven Steps to Social Action:
Taking It to the Next Level

LeveL IV
The How-To Guide:
The Global Citizen's Toolbox

LeveL V
Sources And Resources,
End Notes

More than half of the area of Île-Bizard, the Québec suburb where Jean-Dominic grew up, is covered with golf courses, which use a lot of pesticides to keep the fairways green. After stumbling across a pamphlet linking cancer to pesticide exposure, Jean-Dominic remembered having unexplained nosebleeds and rashes as a child, and noticed that a number of his friends in the cancer ward also came from Île-Bizard. Jean-Dominic decided that others should know about this frightening connection.

He organized a youth demonstration calling for a ban on pesticides and repeatedly brought his request to town hall meetings. He made the news, but when the mayor did not take him seriously, Jean-Dominic did not give up. He could not ignore the evidence he saw around him. He set to work to prove what he believed: that the pesticides being used in his community had caused his cancer.

In 1998, he pushed the researchers at his hospital to conduct a study, and their statistics showed that the cancer rate among children in Île-Bizard was ten times the national rate. Jean-Dominic began organizing letter writing and petition campaigns, and went on to speak to various associations, student groups and government officials. He widened the scope of his crusade, asking for a pesticide ban not just in Île-Bizard, but throughout the country as well. Jean-Dominic found it difficult to be patient when change seemed to come so slowly.

His persistence paid off, though, when after six years, the town council of Île-Bizard finally banned pesticides. In 2003, the Minister of the Environment of Québec presented the new provincial pesticide management code. The code, which is also the strongest law in the world concerning health and the environment, bans the non-essential use of pesticides on Québec lawns and public green spaces, including schools and daycare centers. In addition, the government of Québec has decided to use a non-toxic bacteria alternative to chemical insecticide in preventing the West Nile Virus.

Jean-Dominic's dedication has been recognized with multiple awards, including the YTV Terry Fox Award for Environmental Activism and the Canadian Order for Youth. In 2001, he was elected to the United Nations Environment Programme's Global 500 Youth Environmental Roll of Honor. His crusade was a battle not only for his own life, but also for health and lives of others, especially children.

- What were the different lobbying methods in Jean-Domenic's action plan to ban the use of pesticides?

- To be successful, how would he have had to approach government officials?

- Think of an issue that concerns you and that you would like to solve through political change. What is the first lobbying action that you would take? How would you keep yourself motivated from one action to the next?

TAKE MORE ACTION! How To Change The World

HOME	LEVEL I	LEVEL II
Preface, Contents	Global Citizenship: Around the World, Across the Street	Becoming Global Citizens: A Question of Choice

Speaking out through your ballot

Voting is instrumental to the workings of an effective political system. A democracy cannot be truly and equally representative when people remain silent. Yet, many individuals do not exercise their right to vote. In 2004, a mere 60.5 percent of eligible voters in Canada cast a ballot in their federal election. This included only 21 percent of Canadians in their twenties, suggesting that the trend toward voter apathy is not improving with the next generation. In the United States, voter turnout has declined even further—in the 2004 presidential election, only about 55 percent of eligible voters exercised this right.

Why are young people not voting? Some feel that political parties and leaders do not address issues that represent their interests and values. They feel that leaders are not speaking to them, that politics are irrelevant to their lives, or that their votes do not count. The truth is, however, that feeling alienated by the political system is not a reason to not vote. In fact, there is all the more reason to vote if you disagree with a decision or policy. Remember, not speaking up makes you a bystander. The people who lead your country and make laws now are shaping the world that you are inheriting, so your input to them is crucial.

Educating yourself about politics at an early age allows you to understand what factors will influence your vote when the time comes. Look at the issues and platforms that affect the ideals and actions of political leaders in order to make an informed decision about which parties and people you want to be handling the issues that matter to you.

Take Action!

1. Begin your political participation by writing and then sending a letter to the appropriate legislator (send it to several people if you can!) regarding your chosen issue.
2. Draft a petition according to the guidelines for the level of government that deals with your issue, and invite your family, teachers and friends to sign!
3. Set up a meeting with a local politician to discuss his or her position on your chosen issue, or any other issue that is important to you.

Ballot

VOTE

"PROGRESS LIES NOT IN ENHANCING WHAT IS, BUT IN ADVANCING TOWARD WHAT WILL BE."

—Kahlil Gibran
(1883-1931)
Philosophical essayist, novelist, poet, artist

TAKE MORE ACTION!   How To Change The World

HOME	LEVEL I	LEVEL II
Preface, Contents	Global Citizenship: Around the World, Across the Street	Becoming Global Citizens: A Question of Choice

Level III	**Level IV**	**Level V**
The Seven Steps to Social Action: Taking It to the Next Level	The How-To Guide: The Global Citizen's Toolbox	Sources And Resources, End Notes

Working With Money

As global citizens, you will need money to help you help others and to change the world. When taking on an issue, your group will need to base its actions on a solid understanding of the sources of money within your community and how they can be tapped. Successful fundraising efforts can raise not only money, but also awareness of your issue and commitment to the cause. The proceeds from these initiatives can be used to cover the basic operating costs of your group and your world-changing projects and campaigns.

Create a fundraising plan

When you are fundraising for a major cause, it is a good idea to stagger your fundraising activities and events. A big project, such as building a school overseas, might take a year of fundraising initiatives. Dividing your goal into three to five different initiatives and spreading them out over the year helps to make each one more manageable, and therefore more successful.

Choose at least two major fundraising ideas that will potentially take a good deal of time to plan and will require sponsorship from outside sources, such as a walkathon or a community carnival. Then select at least two to three smaller fundraisers in which you will give people a product or service in return for their donation (for example, a bake sale, car wash, cultural dinner night or chocolate bar sales). Consider ongoing fundraising methods as well, including odd jobs and other employment. Put a different member of your team "in charge" of overseeing the details of each fundraiser—this empowers team members and makes sure everything gets done without overloading one or two people.

For the two major fundraising events, you will probably be asking the same individuals for donations and pledges. To avoid donor fatigue (when people feel overwhelmed by your requests), it is important to leave a considerable amount of time between one major fundraiser and the next. The space of time between them gives you the perfect opportunity to host the few smaller fundraising events that you have selected.

TAKE MORE ACTION! How To Change The World

HOME	LEVEL I	LEVEL II
Preface, Contents	Global Citizenship: Around the World, Across the Street	Becoming Global Citizens: A Question of Choice

Sample Yearly Fundraising Plan

September—Bake sale
October—Walkathon!
November—Planning and debriefing
December—Holiday greeting card sales
January—Open-mike poetry night
February—Valentine-o-grams sales
March—Spaghetti dinner night at Nisha's house
April—Nothing (gearing up for next month)
May—Major: Community carnival!
June—Bake sale
July—Nothing (taking a break)
August—Car wash

Create a budget

A budget is an effective way of organizing your information about sources of funding. It doesn't have to be complicated—some people even get a kick out of it! The following steps and sample budget will help clarify the process.

Step 1: As a group, determine your fundraising goal. If, for example, your concrete goal is to build a school for children in Kenya, you might set your fundraising goal at approximately $8,500, which could potentially cover the labor, materials and administration costs needed to organize the construction.

Step 2: Brainstorm possible ways of reaching this fundraising goal. In the sample fundraising plan above, the students selected many different initiatives, ranging in complexity from bake sales to an open-mike poetry night to a walkathon.

Step 3: Estimate the expenses involved in organizing each of these fundraising initiatives. You may wish to seek the advice of people who have carried out similar campaigns or who are familiar with budgeting for community

Level IV > **The How To Guide: Working With Money**

Level III	**Level IV**	**Level V**
The Seven Steps to Social Action: Taking It to the Next Level	The How-To Guide: The Global Citizen's Toolbox	Sources And Resources, End Notes

efforts. As you estimate costs, try to be as detailed and specific as possible. Because raising a lot of money is often a challenge for youth groups, it is a good idea to plan to keep your expenses as low as possible.

As an example, the expenses involved in an initiative such as a walkathon might include the cost of flyers and posters to advertise the event, pledge forms, bottles of water and town licences to host a post-event party in the park. As you estimate the expenses of these items, consider how many of them can be covered by in-kind donations and make a note of organizations and businesses that can support your cause with their contributions. Record all the projected expenses and in-kind donations in your budget, using the sample walkathon budget as a model.

Step 4: Estimate the projected revenue from the fundraising initiative (the money you expect to bring in). For a walkathon, you would raise money primarily through sponsorship by students and adults. Estimate roughly how much money participants are likely to raise. Record the projected revenue in your budget, listing each different source on a separate line in the budget.

Step 5: Total each column separately: revenue, in-kind donations, and expenses. Then compare the projected fundraising revenue to the projected expenses. Subtracting the expenses from the revenue will determine the net income of your fundraising initiative and will help you to determine how close it will bring you to your ultimate fundraising goal!

TROUBLESHOOTING

Keeping the costs down
- Get facilities donated or work out of someone's home.
- Work on finding in-kind donations—meaning businesses give away what they make, such as supplies (like food, drinks, or CDs); services (like baseball tickets or mini-golf coupons); or things people aren't using any more (like computers, telephones, or filing cabinets).
- Recruit volunteers—remember your Minga Team? This is their time to shine!
- Send your newsletters out by e-mail instead of by post.
- Research long distance telephone plans for the one that suits your needs most economically.
- Find an existing organization on which you can piggyback resources such as mail-outs, telephone calls, office space, media lists, etc.

TAKE MORE ACTION! How To Change The World

HOME	LEVEL I	LEVEL II
Preface, Contents	Global Citizenship: Around the World, Across the Street	Becoming Global Citizens: A Question of Choice

Contingency Funds: Just In Case

Even though you may plan your budget carefully, unforeseen events and circumstances often arise and can result in additional expenses. To compensate for these unexpected costs, it is usually a good idea to factor contingency funds into your budget. Contingency funds should be on a separate line in the budget and can be anywhere from three to five percent of your total expenses.

Once the budget is made, distribute detailed copies to your group members and ask for their opinion and input. They may think of something you forgot, or have a great idea to get something donated! When individual members feel involved with the goals of the group, they are committed to working toward them.

LeveL III	**LeveL IV**	**LeveL V**
The Seven Steps to Social Action: Taking It to the Next Level	The How-To Guide: The Global Citizen's Toolbox	Sources And Resources, End Notes

Take Action!

1. Brainstorm 10 to 20 local businesses that might be willing to make "in-kind" donations to an event held by a social action group, and what they could contribute.
2. Select one action from the goal chart you developed in the Seven Steps to Social Action section (see page 79). Create a draft budget for that action—what would your expenses be? Put a star next to those items you could get donated "in kind." Don't forget the contingency funds!

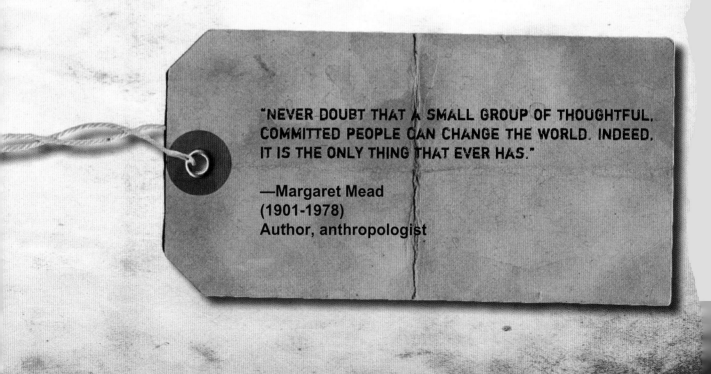

"NEVER DOUBT THAT A SMALL GROUP OF THOUGHTFUL, COMMITTED PEOPLE CAN CHANGE THE WORLD. INDEED, IT IS THE ONLY THING THAT EVER HAS."

—Margaret Mead
(1901-1978)
Author, anthropologist

TAKE MORE ACTION! How To Change The World

Home	**Level I**	**Level II**
Preface, Contents	Global Citizenship: Around the World, Across the Street	Becoming Global Citizens: A Question of Choice

People look around their homes for things that they no longer needed and organize a yard sale to raise money for their cause. You don't have to look very far to find a way to change the world.

LeVeL IV > **The How To Guide: Working With Money**

LeVeL III	**LeVeL IV**	**LeVeL V**
The Seven Steps to Social Action: Taking It to the Next Level	The How-To Guide: The Global Citizen's Toolbox	Sources And Resources, End Notes

Great fundraisers

Look through the following list for fundraising ideas that you would like to try. Or be creative and come up with your own! People get excited when something is new and different. A good fundraiser should boost your spirits as well as your budget.

Remember to get permission to hold an event in your school or community before beginning to organize.

Fundraising Ideas

1. *Raffles:* Request local businesses to donate a variety of items to give away as prizes. Sell tickets and raffle off the items. Each winner receives a prize.
2. *Candy or Card Sales:* Ask businesses to provide merchandise that you can sell, ensuring that at least half of the proceeds go toward your cause. Or, ask an artistic friend to help design a holiday greeting card and have them printed to sell.
3. *Car Wash:* Organize a car wash in the parking lot of your school, place of worship, or public area, and have your group bring supplies from home.
4. *Silent Auction:* Hold a silent auction for donated items, such as a pair of hockey season's tickets or esthetic services.
5. *Guest Speaker:* Invite a guest speaker associated with your cause to your home, school, or community hall and sell tickets to the event.
6. *Bracelets for Freedom:* Make bracelets with colorful thread or beads and sell them for roughly $1 each. They'll go fast!
7. *Tip-A-Teen:* Have your friends volunteer as servers for the day in a deli or a café. Dress up crazy, and liven up the place a little. Ask the deli/café managers if they will donate 10 percent of the day's profits and tips to your group.
8. *Dump the Change:* Every Friday during the school year, staff and students at your school can dump their small change into a jar. At the end of the semester or school year, the change can be put toward your goal.
9. *Dress Down Day or Dress Glam Day:* Students pay $2 to "dress down" at school or to dress as a celebrity.
10. *World Food Fair:* Sell tickets to a banquet featuring dishes from different parts of the world.
11. *Theme Party or Dance:* Ask students to come to the party dressed as a television character or favourite music star, depending on the theme. Charge admission at the door. People can buy ballots to vote for their favourite costume and, at the end of the evening, the winner receives a prize.
12. *Garage Auction:* Have a garage sale, but sell things auction-style. Bring things from home that you do not want anymore, and have the auction during lunch hour.

TAKE MORE ACTION! How To Change The World

| HOME
Preface, Contents | Level I
Global Citizenship:
Around the World, Across the Street | Level II
Becoming Global Citizens:
A Question of Choice |

13. *Talent Show:* You can twist the idea around so that it will be a talent show involving only movie spoofs, or one in which participants sing well-known songs for which you have changed the lyrics. Be creative!

14. *Match Your Money:* When you have reached your fundraising goal, contact community organizations and business groups and ask them to match the money that you raised. Do not forget to write thank-you notes afterward.

15. *Bazaar:* Sell goods and provide services. Your items can include: barbecued food, cookies, muffins, and artwork. You can also teach people how to make bracelets or other crafts. Again, it is all about creativity and making your market different from other conventional markets. This is the key to attracting more people.

16. *Pop-Can Drive:* Have a contest within your school, including teachers, to collect as many cans as possible. Collect money for the cans from a recycling center. You decide how long you want the can drive to run.

17. *Request a Share in the Profits:* Pick a popular event in your city or town (sports/theatre/concert), and ask the organizers, far in advance, about sharing the profits. Suggest that they mention their sponsorship of you in the printed program. This way, they receive recognition, and more people become aware of your cause.

18. *Grocery receipts:* Collect grocery store receipts and ask the store to donate a percentage of the total sales listed on the receipts. Make this agreement with the store manager before you start collecting.

LeVeL IV > The How To Guide: Working With Money

LeVeL III The Seven Steps to Social Action: Taking It to the Next Level	**LeVeL IV** The How-To Guide: The Global Citizen's Toolbox	**LeVeL V** Sources And Resources, End Notes

19. *Day-Old Donations:* Ask a local coffee shop to donate their "day-old" doughnuts. Sell the doughnuts during lunchtime. This idea works with any kind of donated baked goods—check with a local bakery.

20. *Restaurant Fundraiser:* Ask a restaurant to sponsor a fundraising dinner. They may provide food "at cost" or cover the cost of the entire evening. Sell tickets to the general public. This is a great way for a restaurant to promote itself.

21. *Walkathon:* Invite your community to participate in a walk/run through a park in your area (you can plan how long the route will be). Charge participants a sign-up fee (offer a slightly lower cost per family) and have them ask for sponsors to donate to the cause. Ask a grocery store to donate food for a breakfast/brunch to serve participants afterward.

22. *Benefit performance:* Ask a local entertainer (musician/magician/clown) to donate his or her talents for an evening performance. Ask your local hall to donate the space for the performance. Sell tickets and promote the event well in advance.

23. *Sports Contest:* Organize an arm wrestling contest or a basketball free-throw contest. Have people pay a sign-up fee to participate. Hold it in the gym during lunchtime and announce the winner over the PA system.

24. *Banquet:* Many schools have banquets recognizing student athletes. Ask the organizers to share part of the ticket sales. Offer to help with the organizing of the banquet.

25. *Community Party:* You can hold it at someone's house or in a more public place (try to get the space for free). Ask a local caterer or grocery store to provide the food, either free or "at cost." Set up a volleyball net or soccer goal posts and other games. Sell tickets to the general public well before the event so that you know how much food to have on hand.

26. *Second-Hand Sales:* Find businesses in your area that buy used clothing (called consignment shops) and used CDs. Collect the clothing and CDs to sell. Everyone gets to clean out their closets and contribute to your cause at the same time.

27. *War Is Not a Game:* Organize war toy "trade-ins" in your school to make a symbolic statement that says "While we play war, for millions of kids around the world, war is not a game." Get sponsors to donate a set amount for each war toy turned in.

28. *Child Labor for Child Labor:* Perform odd jobs around your neighborhood in return for pledges or donations to help child laborers around the world. These jobs might include neighborhood beautification projects, lawn mowing, snow shovelling, and window cleaning.

29. *Speeches:* Give a speech about your issue at a community event, place of worship, or local service club, and request donations for your cause.

Making the most of your fundraising event

Most people do not realize that it is possible to raise money before, during and after a fundraising event. To make the occasion as productive as possible, consider every moment a valuable fundraising opportunity.

If your fundraiser is a charity softball event, for example, there are many ways, outside of ticket sales, in which you can raise funds. It is important, however, to select only two or three fundraising activities for each time period. Too many gimmicks may appear exploitative and can turn people away from contributing to your cause. Here are some ideas to choose from:

Making the Most of Your Event: Charity Softball	
Timing	**Action**
Before	• Find corporate sponsors • Sell tickets to the game • Collect celebrity memorabilia to auction off • Hold a pre-event reception (night or day before) • Organize valet parking
During	• Raffle off the first pitch/pay for the first pitch • Take pictures with celebrities • Offer celebrity autographs • Wash cars during the game • Sell food and drinks (hot dogs, pop, cotton candy, etc.) • Set up a face-painting booth
After	• Hold a post-event reception • Auction off items used by celebrities during the game • Sell tickets to upcoming events • Give a brief presentation about the cause to encourage more donations

"THE DIFFERENCE BETWEEN THE IMPOSSIBLE AND THE POSSIBLE LIES IN A MAN'S DETERMINATION."

—Tommy Lasorda
(b. 1927)
Professional baseball manager

TAKE MORE ACTION! How To Change The World

HOME	LEVEL I	LEVEL II
Preface, Contents	Global Citizenship: Around the World, Across the Street	Becoming Global Citizens: A Question of Choice

Who to ask for money

Think of all the different groups of people or institutions that can help you fundraise for your project—through pledges, donations and participation in your events. Think big. Start with your family's address book, the Internet and the telephone directory to draw upon all your potential sources of funding. It is always best to start with individuals, businesses and other organizations that share similar values and would likely be sympathetic and supportive of your cause. Aside from your friends and family, this list might include the following:

- Adults at school (teachers, guidance counsellors, principal, coach, parent/teacher council)
- Students at school (classmates, student council members, leadership council, specific teams or clubs)
- People in your community (coaches, neighbors, postal workers, librarians)
- Businesses in your community, especially ones your family frequents
- Local community organizations and service clubs (Rotary Club, Lions Club, Optimists Club, Girl Guides, Scouts, Venturers, YMCA, YWCA)
- Places of worship (church, synagogue, mosque, temple)
- Local government official (who has discretionary funds to grant to groups and organizations)

TIP

Keep in mind that it may be hard for some people to donate a lot of money. Tell them that "every little bit counts." This will encourage them to give whatever they can spare, because they know it will make a difference.

"THE OCEAN IS MADE OF DROPS."

—Mother Teresa
(1910-1997)
Catholic nun, Humanitarian

TAKE MORE ACTION! How To Change The World

HOME	LeveL I	LeveL II
Preface, Contents	Global Citizenship: Around the World, Across the Street	Becoming Global Citizens: A Question of Choice

Looking after your money

Looking after money is as important as raising it. As a responsible social action group, you have to keep track of every single dollar that comes in, and every single one that goes out. You may be able to find a local accountant who would be willing to volunteer to show you how to keep your records properly. If not, here are the basics:

- Set up a bank account in the name of your organization. You will be issued a deposit book and checks, to make sure you keep track of every single transaction in and out.
- Select a treasurer who is talented in math who will be responsible for keeping track of financial transactions and looking after the account.
- Choose signing officers (members who can sign checks). For security and accountability, a check must have two signatures. You may want to have three officers, two of whom must sign each check. That way you can still write checks when one officer is away.
- Provide monthly or quarterly reports to members. These do not have to include everything, just an overview of the revenue (what came in) and the expenses (what went out).

Level III The Seven Steps to Social Action: Taking It to the Next Level	**Level IV** The How-To Guide: The Global Citizen's Toolbox	**Level V** Sources And Resources, End Notes

How to ask for money: what's in it for them?

When you are organizing a fundraising effort, it is easy to imagine that your group and the people it serves are the only ones to benefit. There are many reasons, however, why it is in the interests of others to give. Knowing what these interests are will help you appeal to them more effectively, so that both your cause and its supporters can benefit.

Individuals give for a variety of reasons:
- They are passionate about the issue.
- They want to help even though they are not socially involved themselves.
- They want to see you succeed.
- Registered charities can issue them a tax receipt (a receipt that they submit with their income taxes that allows them to receive a tax deduction).

TROUBLESHOOTING

Know the Answers to Tough Questions!

Individuals want to know that their donation is going directly to a cause and is being spent wisely. To illustrate that you are competent and professional, be able to provide accurate answers to technical and financial questions regarding your campaign and group:
- If you are raising money on behalf of an organization (a food bank, a charity), can they issue a tax receipt? What is involved in that process? Do they have brochures, posters or other materials to help you with your efforts?
- How much of the donor's money will go toward administrative expenses and fundraising? How much will directly benefit people in need?
- Who else is supporting the campaign? (i.e., affiliations with other organizations, other community supporters, corporate sponsors, places of worship)
- How will you follow up? (for example, if people have donated to the building of a school in a developing country, you can send each person a picture of the school and the students once it is built)

TAKE MORE ACTION! How To Change The World

Home	**Level I**	**Level II**
Preface, Contents	Global Citizenship: Around the World, Across the Street	Becoming Global Citizens: A Question of Choice

Asking in person

Here are some guidelines to follow when meeting people for the first time and asking them for money:

- Introduce yourself with a firm handshake and ask for a minute or two of the person's time. If they are not willing to give you this, they are not going to give you any money.
- Explain the cause that you are working for and why you are passionate about it. Try to relate a short personal story about why this issue is so close to your heart.
- State the concrete goal that you are working toward. Show that your goal is worth supporting with money!
- Ask specifically for money. When you do this, you are actually transferring responsibility for the issue from yourself to your potential donor. The amount that you request must equal something specific and concrete. For example: "Would you be willing to donate $10 to the organization in order for us to send a Basic Needs Kit to a child in Sierra Leone?" Examples of phrases that you can use to ask for financial support include:
  - "We are asking 100 people to donate $10 each toward this project. Would you be willing to participate in this way?"
  - "Would you be in a position to support our cause?"
- Thank your donors for their time and tell them that you will follow up with an update about their donation. You will want to contact them again in the future. At this time, it may be appropriate to ask for their business card and to give them yours, if you have one.

TIP

Avoid canvassing door-to-door! There are many better, safer and more effective fundraising ideas.

LeVeL IV > The How To Guide: Working With Money

LeVeL III	**LeVeL IV**	**LeVeL V**
The Seven Steps to Social Action: Taking It to the Next Level	The How-To Guide: The Global Citizen's Toolbox	Sources And Resources, End Notes

"THE PRICE OF SUCCESS IS HARD WORK, DEDICATION TO THE JOB AT HAND, AND THE DETERMINATION THAT WHETHER WE WIN OR LOSE, WE HAVE APPLIED THE BEST OF OURSELVES TO THE TASK AT HAND."

—Vince Lombardi
(1913-1970)
Professional football coach

TAKE MORE ACTION! How To Change The World

Home Preface, Contents	**Level I** Global Citizenship: Around the World, Across the Street	**Level II** Becoming Global Citizens: A Question of Choice

Asking businesses for money: the art of partnerships

Most businesses, even small, local ones, have budgets set aside for donations to local charities. They often feel that it is in their interests to donate to good causes, for the following reasons:

- It improves their public image as a "good corporate citizen."
- It creates loyalty among their consumers.
- In-kind donations give them a chance to show people how fantastic their products are.
- It strengthens the community from which both their employees and customers come.
- They can obtain a tax receipt if you are working with a registered charitable organization.

Sometimes a business will support a cause by donating food "at cost" or free. As a relationship develops, the business may donate money instead.

But it's not so easy! Making partnerships with businesses (especially large corporations) must be handled professionally and cautiously. Money rarely comes without conditions attached; there is often a lot of paperwork and other requirements that you must fulfil first!

Follow these guidelines for dealing with businesses effectively:

- When considering companies for financial support, make sure that the organizations from which you accept money are ones with which you would be proud to be associated. After all, you are promoting them by having them as a partner! For example, if the mission of your group were to eliminate sweatshop labor, asking for the support of a company that is known for its exploitative labor practices would compromise the integrity of your work.

- On the flip side, finding a company that actively demonstrates that it takes its corporate responsibility seriously through ethical practices (environmentally sound, fair wages for its workers, organic food growing, for example) is a jackpot! Tell them you know of their high ethical standards, and that you respect them enough to give them the privilege of being your corporate partner! They will respect you in return for having researched so well and being so dedicated to your principles.

- Make initial contact with your chosen company for details about whom your funding request should be directed to, and then personally address the letter so that it is an individual, and not a division of a company, who receives it.

- As it may take time for larger companies to process funding requests, be sure to ask for donations early, even six months in advance. Follow up no later than one week after sending out your letter, either in person or by telephone.

- Be prepared to provide the representative with specific information about your group, its goals, needs, and other sources of support. Offering to make a powerful multimedia presentation to the organization is an effective way to secure donations.

- Businesses and corporations can provide either monetary or in-kind donations for a specific event or to help cover your group's administrative costs. When requesting a moderate amount of money, such as $500, you can turn to small independent businesses or local branches of large corporations. When requesting larger donations, such as $5,000, contact the corporation's head office, either directly or through the local branch, to make your funding proposal.

TAKE MORE ACTION! How To Change The World

HOME	LEVEL I	LEVEL II
Preface, Contents	Global Citizenship: Around the World, Across the Street	Becoming Global Citizens: A Question of Choice

Writing a fundraising letter

Writing a fundraising letter is a good way of informing local businesses about your group and its mission and how their contributions might be helpful. To be successful, a funding letter must follow a specific format:

Sample Fundraising Letter

[Your full mailing address]:

Noel McCarthy
St Andrew's College School
450 Main Street
Boston, MA 02141
(617) 555-4747

Date
March 19, 20-

[Full mailing address of your contact]:

Ms. Anita Cormier
Fitness World
62 Oakfield Drive
Boston, MA 02122

[Salutation, with the name of your contact]:

Dear Ms. Cormier,

[Introduction: State who you are, information about your group and its mission, highlight previous accomplishments and successes of your group]:

Greetings! My name is Noel McCarthy and I am the Fundraising Co-ordinator for Kids for a Cure.

We are a youth organization whose mission is to help raise awareness of Breast Cancer and donate money for research. As you may know, there are one million new cases of breast cancer annually. Last year, our group succeeded in raising more than $5,000 for the American Cancer Society through a series of fundraising initiatives.

LeveL IV > The How To Guide: Working With Money

LeveL III	LeveL IV	LeveL V
The Seven Steps to Social Action: Taking It to the Next Level	The How-To Guide: The Global Citizen's Toolbox	Sources And Resources, End Notes

[An explanation of the project/event you are planning (who, what, where, when, why), and the type of donation you are seeking]:

This year, we are organizing a fundraising Aerobathon on April 30 from 11 a.m. to 3 p.m., in which 250 students from St. Andrew's College School will be participating. We are seeking the support of Fitness World to donate a six-month membership to its facilities as a raffle prize for this event.

[The type of recognition that the donor can expect to receive from your organization (i.e. advertising, tax receipts, etc.)]:

We would be happy to highlight the name and logo of Fitness World on all the promotional material for the event, as well as offer your company a public vote of thanks for its support during the opening ceremonies of the Aerobathon.

[A mention of other donations that you may require. The representative may have contacts with other businesses that can provide additional goods and services]:

We are also looking for sporting goods to be donated as raffle prizes. If you know of any companies that might be interested in supporting our initiative, please contact me. All the proceeds from this event will go to support the American Cancer Society.

[A statement of thanks for the person's time and attention]:

Thank you in advance for your time and consideration. If you have any questions, please do not hesitate to contact me. I look forward to hearing from you soon.

[Closing: Do not forget your name, your position in your organization and of course, your signature]:

Yours Sincerely,

Noel McCarthy
Fundraising Co-ordinator
Kids for a Cure
St. Andrew's College School

TAKE MORE ACTION! How To Change The World

HOME	LEVEL I	LEVEL II
Preface, Contents	Global Citizenship: Around the World, Across the Street	Becoming Global Citizens: A Question of Choice

TROUBLESHOOTING

Can't or Won't Give Money?

What do you do if people tell you that they are not interested in donating money to your cause? The truth is that some people are more likely to give if you ask them for something other than money. When you encounter people who hesitate to give you money, suggest other ways in which they can be involved:

- Ask a business owner to put up one of your posters in his or her window.
- Suggest in-kind donations.
- Ask people to volunteer their time and/or expertise.

When individuals take action on an issue, no matter how small the action is, they begin to feel as though they are involved, and will quite possibly continue to play that role and move on to higher levels of commitment.

Working with foundations

Picture a group of people who work long, hard hours every day to raise a lot of money—to give to you (and other worthy organizations)! Welcome to the Foundation, friends. There are hundreds of foundations—some of which are offshoots of large corporations or run by wealthy families—whose sole objective is to find worthy social action groups and charities to support financially.

Most foundations have "niches"—specific types of projects or groups or issues to which they donate. There are big ones and little ones, and a number of excellent guidebooks (the American Institute of Philanthropy and the Canadian Centre for Philanthropy both put out great ones) to figure out which foundations are for you! As with companies, make sure the ethical practices of foundations you approach for partnerships are in line with your group's values and ethics. Research the foundation thoroughly to find out its mission, vision, and goals in order to determine if your project fits within its mandate.

When you find one that is compatible with your group, inquire about the application process and specific guidelines for submitting project and grant proposals. Every foundation has a different procedure. Grants can be difficult to come by, so do not expect them to be your main source of funding. However, it may be worth trying because one niche for foundations is youth-based initiatives. Here is an example of one amazing foundation that works with youth:

TAKE MORE ACTION! How To Change The World

HOME	LeveL I	LeveL II
Preface, Contents	Global Citizenship: Around the World, Across the Street	Becoming Global Citizens: A Question of Choice

PROFILE

The Toskan Casale Foundation: A Foundation Working With Youth

When they established MAC Cosmetics in 1985, Julie Toskan-Casale, Victor Casale and Frank Toskan knew that there would be more to their mission than selling make-up. During the company's first years, AIDS was emerging as a reality that no company wanted to discuss or link in any way to their brand. However, the makers of MAC challenged this trend by creating a special lipstick color and donating all the proceeds from its sale to an HIV/AIDS fund. They then encouraged their employees to go out into the community and choose a grassroots organization working on this issue to support financially. For Julie, the success of this fundraising effort was the most fulfilling aspect of her experience with MAC. When they finally sold the company, she wondered what she could do with her time and resources that would be as rewarding.

The Toskan Casale Foundation was thus created in 2000, with the goal of supporting community-based grassroots organizations that reach out to at-risk people and provide them with immediate relief and long-term stability. Julie knew, however, that she did not want to simply sit behind a desk and write out checks. Rather, she wanted to go beyond financial solutions by actively encouraging people to become aware of social problems and to decide for themselves where resources were most needed—and this type of learning, she believed, must begin at an early age.

The Toskan Casale Foundation soon launched the Youth and Philanthropy Initiative (YPI). This program provides high school students who have participated in a Me to We leadership training program with a real experience in philanthropy. Students learn the skills to assess community needs, seek out organizations that are working to meet them, and finally make a recommendation for funding one in particular. Student representatives from various high schools select a local community-based organization helping those in need, research and volunteer with the organization, and then give a presentation about their chosen organization before a panel of their peers and community representatives. After viewing the students' presentations, a decision is made by the panel as to which registered charity will be awarded one of several donations of $5,000, provided by the Toskan Casale Foundation.

Through the YPI, students learn a valuable lesson in social action: that passion and credibility are two sides of the same coin. The Toskan Casale Foundation hopes that the students will develop an interest in the future of the community, searching out areas of need in the world around them and working hard to make a difference.

- What is the Toskan Casale Foundation's reasoning for wanting to support youth initiatives?

- Imagine that you are the director of a foundation. What criteria would a social action group have to fulfil in order to receive a grant from you? What information regarding their mission, goals and actions would you first have to consider? Write a paragraph describing the ideal candidate for a grant.

TAKE MORE ACTION!
How To Change The World

Home	**Level I**	**Level II**
Preface, Contents	Global Citizenship: Around the World, Across the Street	Becoming Global Citizens: A Question of Choice

LeveL IV > The How To Guide: Working With Money

LeveL III	**LeveL IV**	**LeveL V**
The Seven Steps to Social Action: Taking It to the Next Level	The How-To Guide: The Global Citizen's Toolbox	Sources And Resources, End Notes

Appreciating your donors

Always show gratitude for the support you receive, no matter how large or small, and be sure to properly recognize and thank the donor. Letters or thank-you cards work best, because they are something that can be kept by the recipient to remember you the next time. Try a simple telephone call as well—it will be appreciated and make it more likely that the person or organization will support you again! This is an important part of building a sustainable organization and relationship.

Make sure that asking for money is not the only reason you ever contact your donors. Encourage a sense of belonging, membership or connection to the cause by providing supporters with updates on your achievements and project plans. Invite them to your group's events, send them holiday greeting cards, and add their names to your mailing list (with their permission). Regular communication with past donors creates relationships, which is crucial to long-term funding, for a single reason: People like to give money to people they know.

Take Action!

1. Brainstorm ten fundraiser ideas that would work at your school or in your community.
2. Select one fundraiser and list all the steps you would need to make it a reality. What materials do you need? How many volunteers?
   Whose permission should you seek? When and where would it be held?
3. Convince a partner to give you a donation for your chosen issue. Next, convince one of your teachers to donate money to your issue (let them know in advance that this is a simulation).

TAKe MORE ACtiON! How To Change The World

HOME	LeveL I	LeveL II
Preface, Contents	Global Citizenship: Around the World, Across the Street	Becoming Global Citizens: A Question of Choice

VOTING WITH YOUR CHOICES: ETHICAL AND SUSTAINABLE CONSUMPTION

Have you ever voted? If your answer is "no," you are wrong! Unless you have never bought anything or eaten anything or worn any clothes, you have voted—with your choices. Our friend Simon Moll, a young environmentalist activist, says that our wallets are like election ballots in our pockets, because every time we buy something, we vote for that product over its alternatives. Different companies manufacturing the same product can have vastly different impact on workers, communities, and the environment. This means that when you choose to support one company over another by purchasing its products, you are contributing to a certain type of impact. Your every purchase, then, is like a vote, and has the power to elect the businesses and practices that run the corporate world.

As a young person, your vote is even more potent. Teens and youth are the fastest-growing consumer demographic. Marketing companies target you specifically for brand names and designer products. What matters to you and how you spend your money is thus of vital interest to them; their survival depends on it. This is your key source of power. You can choose to send the corporate world a message by modelling your consumer actions on your values. When you make informed and deliberate decisions about which companies and practices your dollars support, you have the ability to effect great change—this change is what we call your "ecological footprint." How big or how small, and what shape of a footprint you leave, is up to you. What kind of world have you voted for today?

TAKE MORE ACTION! How To Change The World

HOME	LEVEL I	LEVEL II
Preface, Contents	Global Citizenship: Around the World, Across the Street	Becoming Global Citizens: A Question of Choice

"PERHAPS IT IS IMPOSSIBLE FOR A PERSON WHO DOES NO GOOD NOT TO DO HARM."

—Harriet Beecher Stowe
(1811-1896)
Author, abolitionist, philanthropist

LeveL IV > The How To Guide: Voting With Your Choices

LeveL III	**LeveL IV**	**LeveL V**
The Seven Steps to Social Action: Taking It to the Next Level	The How-To Guide: The Global Citizen's Toolbox	Sources And Resources, End Notes

Consuming with a conscience

Some of the most important and influential choices we make every day have to do with our consumption of resources (water, energy, food, air, paper and wood) and products (clothes, books, etc.). During the course of a single day, we consume a *lot* of stuff! We all have to consume—there is no question about that. But most of us consume without thinking! That means consuming without asking a number of important questions that allow us to assess the impact that our consumption has on other people and the planet. For example:

- *Do I need this?*
- *Do I have enough of them already, or is there something similar I can reuse or repair?*
- *Is there an alternative that is reusable, more recyclable or uses less packaging?*
- *Do I know where this resource or product comes from?*
- *Do I know who harvested or made it and how much workers got paid for their work?*
- *Do I know where it goes when I have finished with it?*

Sustainable consumption means meeting your needs with minimal negative social and environmental impact while maximizing positive impact.

When we consume anything in public, we implicitly endorse its consumption to others. Professional athletes and other celebrities are paid millions of dollars to endorse certain products, but we actually pay to promote them. They say, "You are what you eat." Well, we say, "What you consume reflects who you are and what you believe in." Does the logo across your chest reflect the values you hold dear as a global citizen? What message are you telling the world when you eat what you eat or drink what you drink? How we live is what we tell the world we believe in. What is the message you give through your consumption?

"FEELING THAT MORALITY HAS NOTHING TO DO WITH THE WAY YOU USE THE RESOURCES OF THE WORLD IS AN IDEA THAT CAN'T PERSIST MUCH LONGER. IF IT DOES, THEN WE WON'T."

—Barbara Kingsolver
(b. 1955)
Author

TAKE MORE ACTION! How To Change The World

HOME	LEVEL I	LEVEL II
Preface, Contents	Global Citizenship: Around the World, Across the Street	Becoming Global Citizens: A Question of Choice

Shop like you mean it

In order to compel corporations to act responsibly, you have to be a communicative consumer—let them know that you are paying attention. It may seem at first that one letter can never influence a major corporation, but never underestimate the power of the pen (or keyboard!) Because most consumers remain silent about the company labor practices used in the production of goods that they purchase, when one voice speaks up, it sounds like a roar. Did you know, for instance, that Wal-Mart will consider a change in policy upon receiving as few as 20 letters from its 70 million customers? If you are concerned about a company's practices, send them a letter detailing the specific issue involved and requesting a socially responsible change in policy.

- Request copies of the mission statements and codes of conduct followed by the company, its subsidiaries and all of its subcontractors. You can find the company's address on the packaging material.
- Ask for assurances that exploitative practices are not used in the production of the company's goods, and that widely respected international teams or human rights groups can freely visit their factories and workshops at any time. Tell them that you are not assuming that their practices are unethical, but rather, that as a global citizen and ethical shopper, you will buy from companies that best satisfy your request for proof that their products are made ethically
- If you are writing to companies whose products you personally use, submit receipts to them, a bit of packaging material, or even cut off labels that clearly identify the product's name. This shows that you have, in fact, purchased these items and will only continue to do so when you are confident that they were made through ethical means.
- Mention that many other people share your views, especially young people, and will support only companies that act ethically. You can do this personally or collect these items at school and submit them to the company as a group project. Ask the same questions about the products that you may be selling at your own part-time job.

TROUBLESHOOTING

Don't Get Sued!

The wording of your letter—especially when cc'd to newspapers and watchdog groups—is extremely important. You can be sued for slander (oral) or libel (written) if you are perceived to be defaming the company (damaging their image through your accusations). Remember you should not accuse them of anything. You are simply concerned because you have not received satisfactory proof that its practices are in line with your personal values. Have a teacher or family member look over your letters before sending to make sure!

TAKE MORE ACTION! How To Change The World

HOME	LEVEL I	LEVEL II
Preface, Contents	Global Citizenship: Around the World, Across the Street	Becoming Global Citizens: A Question of Choice

You can look for information about companies and their reputations on the Internet. There are a number of organizations that are dedicated to this work and publish guides or Web sites on socially conscious shopping. Consult the resources below.

Where to Go for Information on Companies

Multinational Monitor

This tracks the activities and ethical practices of multinational corporations regarding environmental and labor issues. It is available in a print magazine and on the Internet.

Maquila Solidarity Network

Their mailing list sends regular action alerts about urgent workers' rights issues in Mexico, Central America and Asia. You can also find out how to start a "No Sweat" campaign to ensure that uniforms and sports equipment purchased by your school are made through ethical practices, and not sweatshop labor.

The New Internationalist

This magazine features the latest global and social issues that will inspire you to take action. Ask your school librarian to subscribe to it!

Once you are fully informed, make a concerted effort to buy from environmentally and socially responsible companies. This is perhaps your most challenging task: to change your own personal shopping habits and preferences to bring them into line with your values and new knowledge. But believe us—when you wear your ethics, you always look good!

"I SKATE TO WHERE THE PUCK IS GOING TO BE, NOT TO WHERE IT HAS BEEN."

—Wayne Gretzky
(b. 1961)
Professional hockey player

TAKE MORE ACTION! How To Change The World

HOME Preface, Contents	LEVEL I Global Citizenship: Around the World, Across the Street	LEVEL II Becoming Global Citizens: A Question of Choice

"No Sweat" Campaign

Most high schools purchase sports equipment and uniforms for students, sports teams, and bands in bulk. The mission of a "No Sweat" campaign is to help end abusive workplace conditions of workers of brand-name companies, beginning with those that supply your school. Your goal is to raise awareness of sweatshop abuses and to convince your school or school board to adopt a No Sweat Purchasing Policy.

Here are some steps you can take to urge your school to go No Sweat:

- Check the labels to find out which companies make the clothing and sports equipment used in your school and where these items are manufactured. Determine who is responsible for school purchasing decisions, and whom you will need to convince to adopt a No Sweat Policy. Ask coaches and administrators for information.
- Start a petition urging your school and your school board to adopt a No Sweat Purchasing Policy. Hold a school-wide vote on the policy and share the results with the school board and local media.
- Ask teachers to incorporate sweatshop issues into the curriculum and to urge their union to support the campaign or help you set up meetings with sympathetic trustees.
- Me to We: [Responsible Style] is a clothing line that specializes in ethically-manufactured, environmentally friendly apparel, and is perfect for schools or organizations looking for socially responsible options. Best of all, 50 percent of profits go directly toward funding Free The Children projects in developing nations. Check out www.metowestyle.com for more information.

100% Certified Organic Cotto
and Bamboo

50% of profits go to charity partn
Free The Children

Sweatshop-free Manufacturin

TAKE MORE ACTION! How To Change The World

Home	**Level I**	**Level II**
Preface, Contents	Global Citizenship: Around the World, Across the Street	Becoming Global Citizens: A Question of Choice

Be a role model and make your passion contagious!

Inspire others to be socially conscious consumers, supporting only responsible companies with their dollars. The best way to do that is to be loud and proud that you are an ethical consumer! Show them all that you have decided to live your message!

- **Spread the word**: Tell your friends and your family about the new product choices you have made and the reasons for your decision.
- **Get your family to invest ethically**: Encourage your family members to find out what companies they support through their stocks or mutual fund portfolios, and then do some research into their practices. Making ethical investment choices is a direct way of voting for the world you want to see.
- **Wear your message**: Put away those logos and break out the positive! There are plenty of clothes with inspiring social messages on them. Why not design your own and sell them to support your cause?
- **Make a statement**: Give a speech in a class or organize a display about the power consumers have to shape a better world.

No matter what you do to live your message and change the world—whether it's doing your research, starting a social action group, meeting with your MP or making ethical shopping choices, do it because you want to. Making any choices because you feel bad or guilty will make you resent your action, and eventually make you sad and no longer psyched to change the world. Be positive and others will follow!

Take Action!

1. Create a flowchart of five major products that you use every day, showing their origins from raw materials to production to distribution, their costs, selling prices, and where they go when you are done with them. For each step, estimate the ecological footprint.
2. Think of a brand-name product worn or used by a lot of the students at your school. Use the socially conscious shopping resources listed in this section to research the practices of that company. Bring your research to the company's attention in a letter, and request an explanation.
3. What are some of the things that you can change about your own consumer habits to make the world a better place? *Now do it!*

TAKE MORE ACTION! How To Change The World

PART 5: SOURCES AND RESOURCES

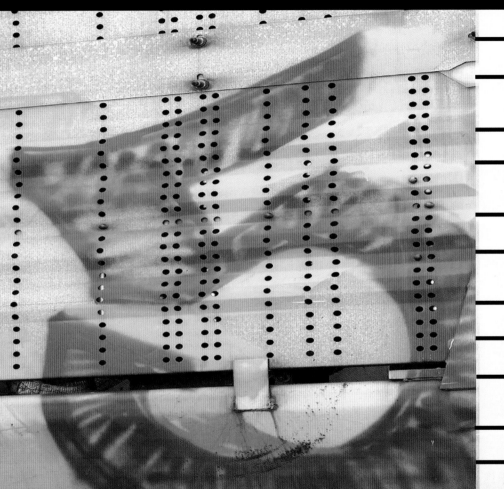

TAKE MORE ACTION! How To Change The World

HOME	LEVEL I	LEVEL II
Preface, Contents	Global Citizenship: Around the World, Across the Street	Becoming Global Citizens: A Question of Choice

Check out the following organizations that are working on a wide range of global issues. Many of these are youth organizations, started by and for young people. They can provide you with solid information on your issue, additional resources, and exciting action ideas.

HIV/AIDS

AIDS Committee of Toronto
399 Church Street, 4th Floor
Toronto, Ontario
Canada M5B 2J6
Tel: 416-340-2437
Fax: 416-340-8224
E-mail: ask@actoronto.org

A Loving Spoonful
1300 Richards Street, Suite 100
Vancouver, British Columbia
Canada V6B 3G6
Tel: 604-682-6325
Fax: 604-682-6327
E-mail: info@alovingspoonful.org

AVERT
4 Brighton Road
Horsham
West Sussex
RH13 5BA
UK
E-mail: info@avert.org

Level V > **Sources and Resources: HIV/AIDS**

Level III	**Level IV**	**Level V**
The Seven Steps to Social Action: Taking It to the Next Level	The How-To Guide: The Global Citizen's Toolbox	Sources And Resources, End Notes

Advocates for Youth
2000 M Street NW, Suite 750
Washington, DC
USA 20036
Tel: 202-419-3420
Fax: 202-419-1448
E-mail: information@advocatesforyouth.org

CARE
151 Ellis Street NE
Atlanta, GA
USA 30303-2440
Tel: 404-681-2552, 1-800-521-CARE
Fax: 404-577-5977
E-mail: info@care.org

Canadian Aboriginal AIDS Network
602-251 Bank Street
Ottawa, Ontario
Canada K2P 1X3
Tel: 613-567-1817
Toll free: 1-888-285-2226
Fax: 613-567-4652
E-mail: info@caan.ca

Canadian AIDS Treatment Information Exchange (CATIE)
555 Richmond Street West, Suite 505
Box 1104
Toronto, Ontario
Canada M5V 3B1
Tel: 416-203-7122
Toll free: 1-800-263-1638
Fax: 416-203-8284
E-mail: info@catie.ca

TAKE MORE ACTION! How To Change The World

HOME	LeveL I	LeveL II
Preface, Contents	Global Citizenship: Around the World, Across the Street	Becoming Global Citizens: A Question of Choice

Canadian Working Group on HIV and Rehabilitation
1240 Bay Street, Suite 600
Toronto, Ontario
Canada M5A 2A7
Tel: 416-513-0440
Fax: 416-595-0094
E-mail: info@hivandrehab.ca

Centre for Disease Control and Prevention
1600 Clifton Rd
Atlanta, GA
USA 30333
Tel: 404-639-3311
E-mail: cdcinfo@cdc.gov

Children's AIDS Health Program
17 Henrietta Street
Toronto, ON
Canada M6N 1S4
Tel:416-878-6419
Toll Free: 1-866-530-AIDS (2437)
E-mail: info@LetsStopAids.org

Farha Foundation
576 Sainte-Catherine Street East, 1st Floor
Montréal, Québec
Canada H2L 2E1
Tel: 514-270-4900
Fax: 514-270-5363
E-mail: farha@farha.qc.ca

Level V > Sources and Resources: HIV/AIDS

Level III
The Seven Steps to Social Action:
Taking It to the Next Level

Level IV
The How-To Guide:
The Global Citizen's Toolbox

Level V
Sources And Resources,
End Notes

Fife House
571 Jarvis Street
2nd Floor
Toronto, Ontario
Canada M4Y 2J1
Tel: 416-205-9888
Fax: 416-205-9919
E-mail: info@fifehouse.org

Global AIDS Alliance
413 K Street NW, 4th Floor
Washington, DC
USA 20005
Tel: 202-789-0432
Fax: 202-789-0715
E-mail: info@globalalliance.org

Global Network of People living with HIV/AIDS (GNP+)
P.O. Box 11726
1001 GS Amsterdam
The Netherlands
Tel: +31 20 423 4114
Fax: +31 20 423 4224
E-mail: infognp@gnpplus.net

Global Youth Coalition on HIV/AIDS
307 West 38th Street, Suite 1805
New York, NY
USA 10018
Tel: 1-212-661-6111
Fax: 1-212-661-1933
E-mail: info@youthaidscoalition.org

TAKE MORE ACTION! How To Change The World

HOME	**LeveL I**	**LeveL II**
Preface, Contents	Global Citizenship: Around the World, Across the Street	Becoming Global Citizens: A Question of Choice

International HIV/AIDS Alliance
Queensberry House
104-106 Queens Road
Brighton BN1 3XF
United Kingdom
Tel: +44 1273 718900
Fax: +44 1273 718901
E-mail: mail@aidsalliance.org

The Marley AIDS Advocacy Project
372 Styer Road
Glenmoore, PA
USA 19343
Tel: 610-458-5906
E-mail: marleyAIDS@comcast.net

National Association for People With AIDS (NAPWA)
8401 Colesville Road
Suite 750
Silver Spring, MD
USA 20910
Tel: 240-247-0880
Fax: 240-247-0574
E-mail: info@napwa.org

National Minority AIDS Council (NMAC)
1931 13th Street, NW
Washington, DC
USA 20009-4432
Tel: 202-483-6622
Fax: 202-483-1135; (202) 483-1127
E-mail: info@nmac.org

Student Global AIDS Campaign
1225 Connecticut Ave NW, Suite 401
Washington, DC
USA 20036
Tel: 202-296-6727
Fax: 202-296-6728
E-mail: info@fightglobalaids.org

UNAIDS
20 Avenue Appia
CH-1211 Geneva 27
Switzerland
Tel: +41-22-791-3666
Fax: +41-22-791-4187
E-mail: unaids@unaids.org

Unite for Children Against AIDS Campaign
UNICEF House
3 United Nations Plaza
New York, New York
USA 10017
Tel: 212-326-7000
Fax: 212-887-7465 or 212-887-7454
E-mail: information@unicefusa.org

The United States President's Emergency Plan for AIDS Relief
U.S. Department of State
2201 C Street NW
Washington, DC
USA 20520
Tel: 202-647-4000

LeVeL III	**LeVeL IV**	**LeVeL V**
The Seven Steps to Social Action: Taking It to the Next Level	The How-To Guide: The Global Citizen's Toolbox	Sources And Resources, End Notes

U.S. Agency for International Development
Ronald Reagan Building
Washington, DC
USA 20523-1000
Tel: 202-712-4810
Fax: 202-216-3524
E-mail: pinquiries@usaid.gov

World Health Organization
525 23rd Street NW
Washington, DC
USA 20037
Tel: 202-974-3000
Fax: 202-974-3663
E-mail: postmaster@paho.org

YouthAIDS/PSI
1120 Nineteenth Street NW
Suite 600
Washington, DC
USA 20036
Tel: 202-785-0072
Fax: 202-572-4694
E-mail: youthaidsinfo@psi.org

YouthCO AIDS Society
1104 Hornby Street, Suite 205
Vancouver, British Columbia
Canada V6Z 1V8
Tel: 604-688-1441
Toll free: 1-877-YouthCO
Fax: 604-688-4932
E-mail: information@youthco.org

TAKE MORE ACTION! How To Change The World

HOME Preface, Contents	LEVEL I Global Citizenship: Around the World, Across the Street	LEVEL II Becoming Global Citizens: A Question of Choice

CLIMATE CHANGE

Acterra: Action for a Sustainable Earth
290 Santa Rosa Ave.
Mountain View, CA
USA 90043
Tel: 650-321-1994

C Level
5 Shirley Mews, 2 Shirley Street
Hove, BN3 3WJ
United Kingdom
Tel: 870 765 9891
E-mail: info@clevel.co.uk

Campus Greens
P.O. Box 536
Lombard, IL
USA 60148
Tel: 630-347-3562
E-mail: info@campusgreens.org

Center for Environmental Citizen
200 G Street, NE #300
Washington, DC
USA 20002
Tel: 202-547-8435
Fax: 202-547-8572
E-mail: Cec@envirocitizen.org

Climate Action Network - International
c/o US Climate Action Network
1326 14th St. NW
Washington, DC
USA 20005
Tel: +1-202-609-9846
Fax: +1-202-536-5503
E-mail: info@climatenetwork.org

Earth Team
PO Box 4686
Walnut Creek, CA
USA 94596
Tel: 925-274-3669
E-mail: info@earthteam.net

Free the Planet
218 D Street SE
Washington, DC
USA 20003
E-mail: info@freetheplanet.org

Friends of the Earth
1717 Massachusetts Avenue, NW, 600
Washington, DC
USA 20036-2002
Tel: 877-843-8687 (toll free)
Fax: 202-783-0444
E-mail: foe@foe.org

TAKE MORE ACTION! How To Change The World

HOME	LEVEL I	LEVEL II
Preface, Contents	Global Citizenship: Around the World, Across the Street	Becoming Global Citizens: A Question of Choice

Global Green USA Headquarters
2218 Main Street, 2nd Floor
Santa Monica, CA
USA 90405
Tel: 310-581-2700
Fax: 310-581-2702
E-mail: ggusa@globalgreen.org

Greenpeace International
Ottho Heldringstraat 5
1066 AZ Amsterdam
The Netherlands
Tel: +31 20 7182000
Fax: +31 20 5148151
E-mail: supporter.services@int.greenpeace.org

National Environment Trust
1200 18th St. NW, Fifth Floor
Washington, DC
USA 20036
Tel: 202-887-8800
Fax: 202-887-8877
E-mail: netinfo@envirotrust.com

The Otesha Project
72 Riverdale Ave
Ottawa, ON
Canada K1S 1R2
Tel: 613-237-6065
E-mail: info@otesha.ca

Sierra Club
National Headquarters
85 Second Street, 2nd Floor
San Francisco, CA
USA 94105
Tel: 415-977-5500
Fax: 415-977-5799
E-mail: information@sierraclub.org

Stop Climate Chaos
2 Chapel Place
London
EC2A 3DQ
UK
Tel: +44 (0)20 7729 8732.
E-mail: info@stopclimatechaos.org

LeVeL III	**LeVeL IV**	**LeVeL V**
The Seven Steps to Social Action: Taking It to the Next Level	The How-To Guide: The Global Citizen's Toolbox	Sources And Resources, End Notes

Toronto Environmental Alliance
30 Duncan Street, Suite 201
Toronto, Ontario
Canada M5V 2C3
Tel: 416-596-0660
Fax: 416-596-0345
E-mail: tea@torontoenvironment.org

U.S. Environmental Protection Agency
Ariel Rios Building
1200 Pennsylvania Avenue, N.W.
Washington, DC
USA 20460
E-mail: climatechange@epa.gov

United Nations Environment Programme
United Nations Avenue, Gigiri
PO Box 30552, 00100
Nairobi, Kenya
Tel: (254-20) 7621234
Fax: (254-20) 7624489/90
E-mail: unepinfo@unep.org

Youth Environmental Network
300-945 Wellington St. West
Ottawa, ON
Canada K1Y 2X5
Tel: 613-728-9810 ext. 233
E-mail: info@yen-rej.org

TAKE MORE ACTION! How To Change The World

HOME	LEVEL I	LEVEL II
Preface, Contents	Global Citizenship: Around the World, Across the Street	Becoming Global Citizens: A Question of Choice

LeVeL III
The Seven Steps to Social Action:
Taking It to the Next Level

LeVeL IV
The How-To Guide:
The Global Citizen's Toolbox

LeVeL V
Sources And Resources,
End Notes

RACISM AND MINORITY RIGHTS

Act Now To Stop War and End Racism (A.N.S.W.E.R)
Coalition Contact Information
National Office in Washington DC
1247 E St. SE, Washington, DC
USA 20003
Tel: 202-544-3389
E-mail: info@internationalanswer.org

Anti-Defamation League
Department: RL
P.O Box 96226
Washington, DC
USA 20090-6226
E-mail: webmaster@adl.org

Anti-Racist Action Toronto
P.O. Box 291, Station B
Toronto, Ontario M5T 2T2
Tel: 416-631-8835
E-mail: ara@web.net

Artists Against Racism
Box 54511
Toronto, Ontario M5M 4N5
Tel: 416-410-5631
E-mail: info@artistsagainstracism.com

TAKE MORE ACTION! How To Change The World

HOME	LEVEL I	LEVEL II
Preface, Contents	Global Citizenship: Around the World, Across the Street	Becoming Global Citizens: A Question of Choice

Canadian Race Relations Foundation
4576 Yonge Street, Suite 701
Toronto, Ontario M2N 6N4
Tel: 416-952-3500
Toll free: 1-888-240-4936
Fax: 416-952-3326
E-mail: info@crr.ca

Colours of Resistance
c/o Student-Worker Solidarity
QPIRG at McGill
3647 University Street, 3rd Floor
Montréal, Québec H3A 2B3
E-mail: cor@mutualaid.org

**Eliminating Racism
and Creating Equality (E.R.A.C.E)**
227 Third Avenue North
Franklin, TN
USA 37064
Tel: 1-651-791-7977
E-mail: erace@erace.com

Harmony Movement
255 Duncan Mill Road, Suite 705
North York, Ontario M3B 3H9
Tel: 416-385-2660
Fax 416-385-2644
E-mail: info@harmony.ca

Kick It Out
PO Box 29544
London
EC2A 4WR
Tel: 020 7684 4884
Fax: 020 7684 4885
E-mail: info@kickitout.org

Minority Rights Group International
54 Commercial Street
London E1 6LT, UK
Tel: +44 (0)20 7422 4200
Fax: +44 (0)20 7422 4201
E-mail: minority.rights@mrgmail.org

**National Conference
for Community and Justice**
760 N. Frontage Road
Suite 105
Willowbrook, IL
USA 60527
Tel: 630-789-6709
Fax: 630-789-6718

Office of the United Nations
High Commissioner for Human Rights
UNOG-OHCHR
1211 Geneva 10
Switzerland
Tel: +41 22 917 9000
E-mail: infoDesk@ohchr.org

Project Change
Address: 4110 Redwood Road, Suite 351
Oakland, CA
USA 94619
Tel: 510-875-5596
Fax: 510-569-9161
E-mail: sstrong@projectchange.org

World Against Racism Foundation
735 Upper Notch Road
Lincoln, VT
USA 05443
Tel: 802-453-5694
Fax: 802-453-6757
E-mail: webmaster@endracism.com

**Youth Against Racism
Multicultural Association
of Nova Scotia**
1113 Marginal Road
Halifax, Nova Scotia B3H 4P7
Tel: 902-423-6534
Fax: 902-422-0881
E-mail: lisa@Mans.ns.ca

Youth Forums Against Racism
Tel: 613-232-5751, ext. 249/240
E-mail: yfar@unac.org

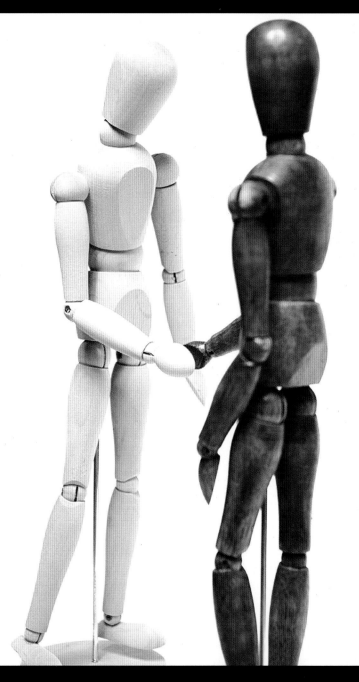

TAKE MORE ACTION! How To Change The World

HOME	LEVEL I	LEVEL II
Preface, Contents	Global Citizenship: Around the World, Across the Street	Becoming Global Citizens: A Question of Choice

GENDER INEQUALITY

The Association for Women's Rights in Development (AWID)
215 Spadina Ave., Suite 150
Toronto, Ontario
Canada M5T 2C7
Tel: (+1) 416-594-3773
Fax: (+1) 416-594-0330
E-mail: contact@awid.org

Canadian Feminist Alliance For International Action (FAFIA)
151 Slater Street, Suite 408
Ottawa, ON
Canada K1P 5H3
Tel: 613-232-9505
Fax: 613- 822-5089
E-mail: info@fafia-afai.org

Coalition for Women's equality
257 Slater Street
Ottawa, Ontario
Canada K1A 0M6
Tel: 1-800-463-6868

Equality Now
PO Box 20646
Columbus Circle Station
New York, NY
USA 10023
Fax: 212-586-1611
E-mail: info@equalitynow.org

Feminist Majority Foundation
1600 Wilson Boulevard, Suite 801
Arlington, VA
USA 22209
Tel: 703-522-2214
Fax: 703-522-2219
Or
433 S. Beverly Drive
Beverly Hills, CA
USA 90212
Tel: 310-556-2500
Fax: 310-556-2509

Level V > Sources and Resources: Gender Inequality

Level III	**Level IV**	**Level V**
The Seven Steps to Social Action: Taking It to the Next Level	The How-To Guide: The Global Citizen's Toolbox	Sources And Resources, End Notes

MADRE
121 West 27th Street, #301
New York, NY
USA 10001
Phone: 212-627-0444
Fax: 212-675-3704
E-mail: madre@madre.org

Maquila Solidarity Network
606 Shaw Street
Toronto, ON
Canada M6G 3L6
Tel: 416-532-8584
Fax: 416-532-7688

National Organization for Women
1100 H Street NW, 3rd floor
Washington, D.C.
USA 20005
Tel: 202-628-8669 (628-8NOW)
Fax: 202-785-8576

Oxfam Canada
250 City Centre Avenue, Suite 400
Ottawa, Ontario
Canada K1R 6K7
Tel: 613-237-5236
Fax: 613-237-0524
E-mail: info@oxfam.ca

UNIFEM Headquarters
304 East 45th Street
15th Floor
New York, NY
USA 10017
Tel: 212-906-6400
Fax: 212-906-6705

United Nations Development Programme Headquarters
One United Nations Plaza
New York, NY
USA 10017
Tel: 212-906-5000
Fax: 212-906-5364

United Nations Population Fund Headquarters
220 East 42nd St.
New York, NY
USA 10017
Tel: 212-297-5000

Women's Learning Partnership (WLP)
4343 Montgomery Avenue,
Suite 201
Bethesda, MD
USA 20814
Tel: 301-654-2774
Fax: 301-654-2775
E-mail: wlp@learningpartnership.org

YWCA USA
1015 18th Street, NW, Suite 1100
Washington, DC
USA 20036
Tel: 202-467-0801
Fax: 202-467-0802
E-mail: info@ywca.org

TAKE MORE ACTION! How To Change The World

HOME	Level I	Level II
Preface, Contents	Global Citizenship: Around the World, Across the Street	Becoming Global Citizens: A Question of Choice

PEACE AND SECURITY/CONFLICT

Amnesty International USA
5 Penn Plaza, 14th floor
New York, NY
USA 10001
Tel: 212-807-8400
Fax: 212-463-9193/212-627-1451
E-mail: admin-us@aiusa.org

The Canadian Peace Alliance
427 Bloor Street West, Box 13
Toronto, Ontario
Canada M5S 1X7
Tel: 416-588-5555
Fax: 416-588-5556
E-mail: cpa@web.ca

Canadian Human Rights Foundation
1425 René-Lévesque Boulevard West, Suite 307
Montréal, Québec
Canada H3G 1T7
Tel: 514-954-0382
Fax: 514-954-0659
E-mail: chrf@chrf.ca

Free The Children
233 Carlton Street
Toronto, Ontario
Canada M5A 2L2
Tel: 416-925-5894
Fax: 416-925-8242
E-mail: info@freethechildren.com

Level V > Sources and Resources: Peace And Security/Conflict

Level III
The Seven Steps to Social Action:
Taking It to the Next Level

Level IV
The How-To Guide:
The Global Citizen's Toolbox

Level V
Sources And Resources,
End Notes

Global Action to Prevent War
675 Third Avenue, Suite 315
New York, NY
USA 10017
Tel: 212-818-1815
Fax: 212-818-1857
E-mail: coordinator@globalactionpw.org

Human Rights Watch
350 Fifth Avenue, 34th floor
New York, NY 10118-3299 USA
Tel: 212-290-4700
Fax: 212-736-1300
E-mail: hrwnyc@hrw.org

Mines Action Canada
1 Nicholas Street, Suite 1502
Ottawa, Ontario K1N 7B7
Tel: 613-241-3777
Fax: 613-244-3410
E-mail: info@minesactioncanada.org

Nuclear Age Peace Foundation
322 Fourth Street NE
Washington, DC
USA 20002
Tel: 202-543-4100 ext 105
Fax: 202-546-5142

Peace Action
1100 Wayne Ave. Suite 1020
Silver Spring, MD
USA 20910
Tel: 301-565-4050
Fax: 301-565-0850

Peaceful Tomorrows
PO Box 1818
Peter Stuyvesant Station
New York, NY 10009
Tel: 212-598-0970
E-mail: office@peacefultomorrows.org

Seeds of Peace
370 Lexington Avenue, Suite 401
New York, NY
10017 USA
Tel: 212-573-8040
Fax: 212-573-8047
E-mail: info@seedsofpeace.org

War Child Canada
401 Richmond Street West, Studio 204
Toronto, Ontario M5V 3A8
Tel: 416-971-7474
Toll free: 1-866-WARCHILD
Fax: 416-971-7946
E-mail: info@warchild.ca

Youth Action for Peace
Avenue du Parc Royal, 3
Brussels-1020, Belgium
Tel: +32 (0)2 478 94 10
Fax: +32 (0)2 478 94 32

TAKE MORE ACTION! How To Change The World

HOME	Level I	Level II
Preface, Contents	Global Citizenship: Around the World, Across the Street	Becoming Global Citizens: A Question of Choice

INDIGENOUS RIGHTS

The Aboriginal Rights Coalition
National Office, ARC Ottawa
153 Laurier Avenue East
Ottawa, Ontario
Canada K1N 6N8
Tel: 613-235-9956
E-mail: arc@istar.ca

Aboriginal Youth Council
c/o National Association of Friendship Centres
275 MacLaren Street
Ottawa, Ontario
Canada K2P 0L9
Tel: 613-563-4844
Fax: 613-594-3428 or 613-563-1819
E-mail: nafcgen@nafc.ca

The Aboriginal Youth Network
Box 34007 Kingsway PO
Edmonton, AB
Canada T5G 3G4
Tel: 780-459-1884
Toll free: 1-800-459-1884
Fax: 780-458-1883
E-mail: siteadmin@ayn.ca

Assembly of First Nations
473 Albert Street, Suite 810
Ottawa, Ontario
Canada K1R 5B4
Tel: 613-241-6789
Toll-Free: 1-866-869-6789
Fax: 613-241-5808

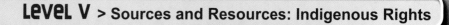
LeveL III
The Seven Steps to Social Action:
Taking It to the Next Level

LeveL IV
The How-To Guide:
The Global Citizen's Toolbox

LeveL V
Sources And Resources,
End Notes

Center for World Indigenous Studies
1001 Cooper Point Road SW Suite 140
Olympia, WA
USA 98502-1107
Tel: +1-360-586-0656
Fax: +253-276-0084

Cultural Survival
215 Prospect Street
Cambridge, MA,
USA 02139
Tel: 617-441-5400
Fax: 617-441-5417
E-mail: culturalsurvival@cs.org

**Indigenous Peoples Survival
Foundation**
P.O. Box 25,
Yonkers, NY
USA 10704
Tel: 914-237-4642
Fax: 914-237-4651
E-mail: chitral@indigenouspeople.org

**International Human Rights
Association**
of American Minorities (IHRAAM)
1-5765 Turner Rd., Ste. 117
Nanaimo, BC.
Canada V9T 6M4
Tel: 250-758-0449
E-mail: ihraam@usa.net

**International Work Group for
Indigenous Affairs (IWGIA)**
Classensgade 11 E
DK 2100 Copenhagen
Denmark
Tel: (+45) 35 27 05 00
Fax: (+45) 35 27 05 07
E-mail: iwgia@iwgia.org

Inuit Tapiriit of Canada
170 Laurier Street West, Suite 510
Ottawa, Ontario
Canada K1P 5V5
Tel: 613-238-8181
Toll-Free (Canada only) 1-866-262-8181
Fax: 613-234-1991
E-mail: info@itk.ca

Native American Rights Fund
1506 Broadway
Boulder, Colorado
USA 80302-6296
Tel: 303-447-8760
Fax: 303-443-7776

**The Native American Women's
Health Education
Resource Center**
PO Box 572
Lake Andes, South Dakota
USA 57356-0572
Tel: 605-487-7072
Fax: 605-487-7964
E-mail: nativewoman@igc.apc.org

TAKe MORe ACtiON! How To Change The World

| **HOMe** Preface, Contents | **LeveL I** Global Citizenship: Around the World, Across the Street | **LeveL II** Becoming Global Citizens: A Question of Choice |

Ojibway & Cree Cultural Centre
273 Third Avenue, Suite 204
Timmins, Ontario
Canada P4N 1E2
Tel: 705-267-7911
Fax: 705-267-4988
E-mail: info@occc.ca

Office of the United Nations
High Commissioner for Human Rights
UNOG-OHCHR
1211 Geneva 10, Switzerland
Tel: +41 22 917
E-mail: InfoDesk@ohchr.org

Secretariat of the Permanent Forum on Indigenous Issues
United Nations, 2 UN Plaza
Room DC2-1772
New York, NY
USA 10017
Tel: 1 917 367 5100
Fax: 1 917 367 5102
E-mail:indigenouspermanentforum@un.org

Level V > **Sources and Resources: Indigenous Rights**

Level III	**Level IV**	**Level V**
The Seven Steps to Social Action: Taking It to the Next Level	The How-To Guide: The Global Citizen's Toolbox	Sources And Resources, End Notes

Survival
6 Charterhouse Buildings
London EC1M 7ET
UK
Tel: +44 20 7687 8700
Fax: +44 20 7687 8701
E-mail :info@survival-international.org

Unrepresented Nations and Peoples Organization
UNPO Secretariat
P.O Box 85878
2508 CN The Hague
The Netherlands
Tel: +31 (0)70 36 46504
Fax: +31 (0)70 3646608
E-mail: unpo@unpo.org

UNESCO
7 place de Fontenoy
75352 Paris 07 SP
France
Tel: +33 (0)1 45 68 10 00
Fax: +33 (0)1 45 67 16 90
E-mail: bpi@unesco.org

TAKE MORE ACTION! How To Change The World

HOME	LeVeL I	LeVeL II
Preface, Contents	Global Citizenship: Around the World, Across the Street	Becoming Global Citizens: A Question of Choice

YOUNG PEOPLE AND VIOLENCE/CRIME

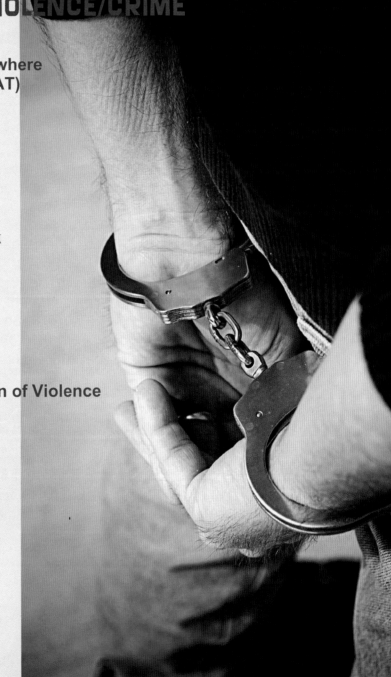

**Canadians Against Violence Everywhere
Advocating Its Termination (CAVEAT)**
P.O. Box 26044, LMRPO
Langley, British Columbia
Canada V3A 8J2
Tel: 604-530-5829
Fax: 604-530-5831
E-mail: bc@caveat.org

The Canadian Safe School Network
111 Peter Street, Suite 409
Toronto, Ontario
Canada M5V 2H1
Tel: 416- 977-1050
Fax: 905- 977-9514
E-mail: info@canadiansafeschools.com

Center for the Study and Prevention of Violence
Institute of Behavioral Science
University of Colorado at Boulder
439 UCB Boulder, Colorado
USA 80309-0439
Tel: 303-492-8465
Fax: 303-443-3297

Challenge Day
2520 Stanwell Drive, #160
Concord, CA
USA 94520
Tel: 925-957-0234
E-mail: office@challengeday.org

Level V > Sources and Resources: Young People And Violence/Crime

| **Level III** The Seven Steps to Social Action: Taking It to the Next Level | **Level IV** The How-To Guide: The Global Citizen's Toolbox | **Level V** Sources And Resources, End Notes |

Leave Out ViolencE (LOVE)
64 Fulton Street, Suite 801
New York, NY
USA 10038
Tel: 212- 608-7070
E-mail: love@leaveoutviolence-us.org

The National Crime Prevention Council
Teens, Crime, and the Community
1000 Connecticut Avenue, NW
13th Floor
Washington, DC
USA 20036
Tel: 202-466-6272
Fax: 202-296-1356
E-mail: tcc@ncpc.org

National Crime Prevention Strategy
National Crime Prevention Centre
Bank of Montreal Building
269 Laurier St. W, 9th Floor
Ottawa, Ontario
Canada K1A 0P8
Tel: 613-941-9306
Toll free: 1-877-302-6272
E-mail: prevention@ps.gc.ca

National Youth Violence Prevention Resource Centre
PO Box 10809
Rockville, MD
USA 20849-0809
Tel: 1-866-SAFEYOUTH
Fax: 301-562-1001
E-mail: NYVPRC@safeyouth.org

Students Against Violence Everywhere (SAVE)
322 Chapanoke Road, Suite 110
Raleigh, NC
USA 27603
Tel : 866 -343-SAVE
Fax: 919-661-7777
E-mail: cwray@nationalsave.org

YouCan! Youth Canada Association
223 Main Street
Saint Paul University
Ottawa, Ontario
Canada K1S 1C4
Tel: 613-230-1903
Toll free: 1-888-4youcan
Fax: 613-235-5801
Toll free fax: 1-877-309-5969
E-mail: info@youcan.ca

Youth Assisting Youth
5734 Yonge Street, Suite 401
Toronto, Ontario
Canada M2M 4E7
Tel: 416-932-1919
Toll free: 1-877-932-1919
Fax: 416-932-1924
E-mail: mail@yay.org

Youth Crime Watch of America
9200 South Dadeland Boulevard,
Suite 417
Miami, Florida
USA 33156
Tel: 305-670-2409
Fax: 305-670-3805
E-mail: ycwa@ycwa.org

TAKE MORE ACTION! How To Change The World

HOME	LEVEL I	LEVEL II
Preface, Contents	Global Citizenship: Around the World, Across the Street	Becoming Global Citizens: A Question of Choice

SUBSTANCE ABUSE

American Council on Alcoholism (ACA)
1000 E. Indian School Rd.
Phoenix, AZ
USA 85014
Tel: 1-800-527-5344
Fax: 602-264-7403
E-mail: info@aca-usa.org

Canadian Centre on Substance Abuse
75 Albert Street, Suite 300
Ottawa, ON
Canada K1P 5E7
Tel: 613-235-4048
Fax: 613-235-8101
E-mail: info@ccsa.ca

Council on Substance Abuse
828 Forest Avenue
Montgomery, AL
USA 36106
Tel: 334-262-1629
Fax: 334-262-6725
E-mail: csancadd@bellsouth.net

Global Youth Network Team
Prevention, Treatment and Rehabilitation Unit
United Nations Office on Drugs and Crime (UNODC)
Address: P.O. Box 500, A-1400
Vienna, Austria
Fax: +43-1-26060 5928
E-mail: youthmail@unodc.org

Level III
The Seven Steps to Social Action:
Taking It to the Next Level

Level IV
The How-To Guide:
The Global Citizen's Toolbox

Level V
Sources And Resources,
End Notes

Join Together
1 Appleton Street, 4th floor
Boston, MA
USA 02116-5223
Tel: 617-437-1500
Fax: 617-437-9394
E-mail: info@jointogether.org

**Mothers Against Drunk Driving
(MADD)**
MADD Canada
2010 Winston Park Drive, Suite 500
Oakville, ON
Canada L6H 5R7
Tel: 905-829-8805
Fax: 905-829-8860
E-mail: info@madd.ca

**National Council on Alcoholism
and Drug Dependence, Inc.**
244 East 58th Street 4th Floor
New York, NY
USA 10022
Tel: 212-269-7797
Fax: 212-269-7510
E-mail: national@ncadd.org

National Families in Action (NFIA)
2957 Clairmont Road NE
Suite 150
Atlanta, GA
USA 30329
Tel: 404-248-9676
Fax: 404-248-1312
E-mail: nfia@nationalfamilies.org

TAKE MORE ACTION! How To Change The World

HOME	LeVeL I	LeVeL II
Preface, Contents	Global Citizenship: Around the World, Across the Street	Becoming Global Citizens: A Question of Choice

National Institute on Drug Abuse (NIDA)
National Institutes of Health
6001 Executive Boulevard, Room 5213
Bethesda, MD
USA 20892-9561
Tel: 301-443-1124
E-mail: information@nida.nih.gov

Partnership for a Drug-Free America
405 Lexington Avenue, Suite 1601
New York, NY
USA 10174
Tel: 212-922-1560
Fax: 212-922-1570

Ryan's Cause
P.O. Box 6454
Laguna Niguel, CA
USA 92677

**SMART
(Self Management and Recovery Training)**
7537 Mentor Avenue, Suite 306
Mentor, OH
USA 44060
Tel: 440-951-5357
Fax: 440-951-5358
E-mail: info@smartrecovery.org

**Students Against Destructive Decisions
SADD, Inc.**
255 Main Street
Marlborough, MA
USA 01752
Toll free: 1-877-SADD-INC
Fax: 1-508-481-5759
E-mail: info@sadd.org

Youth Activism Project
P.O. Box E
Kensington, MD
USA 20895
Tel: 301-929-8808
Toll-free: 1-800-KID-POWER
E-mail: info@youthactivismproject.org

World Health Organization
Department of Mental Health and
Substance Abuse
Management of Substance Abuse
Team (NMH/MSD/MSB)
20, Avenue Appia
CH-1211 Geneva 27
Switzerland
Tel: +41 22 791 3494
Fax: +41 22 791 4851
E-mail: msb@who.int

Level III
The Seven Steps to Social Action:
Taking It to the Next Level

Level IV
The How-To Guide:
The Global Citizen's Toolbox

Level V
Sources And Resources,
End Notes

TAKE MORE ACTION! How To Change The World

HOME	Level I	Level II
Preface, Contents	Global Citizenship: Around the World, Across the Street	Becoming Global Citizens: A Question of Choice

CHILDREN'S RIGHTS

Amnesty International USA
5 Penn Plaza
New York, NY
USA 10001
Tel: 212-807-8400
Fax: 212-627-1451
E-mail: aimember@aiusa.org

**Canadian Coalition
for the Rights of Children**
c/o Canadian Child Care Federation
201-383 Parkdale Avenue
Ottawa, ON
Canada K1Y 4R4
E-mail: info@rightsofchildren.ca

The Children's Defense Fund
25 E Street NW
Washington, DC
USA 20001
Tel: 202-628-8787
Toll-free: 1-800-CDF-1200
E-mail: cdfinfo@childrensdefense.org

Children's Pressline
163 Amsterdam Ave PMB#149
New York, NY
USA 10023-5001
Tel: 212-501-1118
Fax: 212-501-1117
E-mail: cpl@cplmedia.org

Children's Rights Alliance
4 Upper Mount Street
Dublin 2
Ireland
Tel: (01) 662 9400
Fax: (01) 662 9355
E-mail: info@childrensrights.ie

Free The Children
233 Carlton Street
Toronto, Ontario
Canada
M5A 2L2
Tel: 416-925-5894
Fax: 416-925-8484
E-mail: info@freethechildren.com

**Global Children's
Organization**
P.O. Box 67583
Los Angeles, California
USA 90067
Tel: 310-581-2234
Fax: 310-934-0308
E-mail: gco@globalchild.org

**Global March
Against Child Labour**
L-72, 3rd Floor, Kalkaji
New Delhi-110 019
India
Tel: +91 11 4132 9025
Fax: +91 11 4053 2072
E-mail: info@globalmarch.org

Human Rights Watch:
Children Right's Division
350 Fifth Avenue, 34th floor
New York, NY
USA 10118-3299
Tel: 1-212- 290-4700
Fax: 1-212- 736-1300
E-mail:hrwnyc@hrw.org

International Bureau for
Children's Rights
1185 Saint-Mathieu Street
Montréal, Québec
Canada H3H 2P7
Tel: 514-932-7656
Fax: 514-932-9453
E-mail: info@ibcr.org

Kids Meeting Kids
Can Make A Difference
380 Riverside Drive
Box 8H
New York, NY
USA 10025
Tel: 212-662-2327
Fax: 212-222-1416
E-mail: Kidsmtgkids@igc.org

Office of the United Nations
High Commissioner for Human Rights
UNOG-OHCHR
1211 Geneva 10
Switzerland
Tel: +41 22 917 9000
E-mail: InfoDesk@ohchr.org

TAKE MORE ACTION! How To Change The World

| **HOME** Preface, Contents | **LEVEL I** Global Citizenship: Around the World, Across the Street | **LEVEL II** Becoming Global Citizens: A Question of Choice |

OneChild
1390 Major Mackenzie Drive East
Unit A7 Suite 106
Richmond Hill, Ontario
Canada L4S 0A1
Tel: 905-886-2222
E-mail: info@one-child.ca

Save the Children Canada
National Office
4141 Yonge Street, Suite 300
Toronto, Ontario
Canada M2P 2A8
Tel: 416-221-5501
Toll free: 1-800-668-5036
Fax: 416-221-8214
E-mail: sccan@savethechildren.ca

Level III The Seven Steps to Social Action: Taking It to the Next Level	**Level IV** The How-To Guide: The Global Citizen's Toolbox	**Level V** Sources And Resources, End Notes

UNICEF
3 United Nations Plaza
New York, NY
USA 10017
Tel: 212-326-7000
Fax: 212-887-7465
E-mail: information@unicefusa.org

UNICEF Innocenti Research Centre
Piazza SS. Annunziata, 12
50112 Florence, Italy
Tel: 39055 20330
Fax: 39055 2033220
E-mail: Florence@unicef.org

Youth Advocate
Program International
4545 42nd Street NW, Suite 209
Washington, District of Columbia
USA 20016
Tel: 202-244-1986
Fax: 202-244-6396
E-mail: yapi@yapi.org

TAKE MORE ACTION! How To Change The World

HOME	LEVEL I	LEVEL II
Preface, Contents	Global Citizenship: Around the World, Across the Street	Becoming Global Citizens: A Question of Choice

A Final Word

Being a global citizen is not always easy. There will be times when you lose hope, especially when you are dealing with complex issues such as war, environmental degradation, or poverty in inner-city communities. It is easy to feel that nothing you do will make a difference. After all, you are just one person. *What difference can you make?*

We learned the answer to this question not long after we first became involved in social justice issues. We were attending an international youth conference where thousands of young people had gathered to learn about the challenges our world faces and brainstorm ways to help. By the last day, we felt inspired by what we had learned from one another, but also worried that our action plans would be too small to overcome the world's enormous problems—that they wouldn't make a dent.

For the closing ceremonies of the conference, all the participants gathered in the quiet stadium. One young person stood in the center of the room, holding a lit candle, and called out the one question that was on all of our minds:

"I am one person. What difference can I make?"

She then turned to the four people closest to her, and lit the candles in their hands. Those four walked out to the corners of the stadium, repeated the question, and each lit the candles of five people they met there. The same question was echoed by the group fifteen times, and each time, the flame was passed forward. In this way, the firelight spread from one person to thousands until finally every candle was lit, and the whole stadium was aglow.

It was a simple but powerful statement. While it may seem naïve, it's important to recognize that every major social change comes about in this way, through very small, simple actions that spread like wildfire.

As an informed and inspired global citizen, be the first one to light the flame. A better world begins with you.

TAKE MORE ACTION! How To Change The World

HOME	LEVEL I	LEVEL II
Preface, Contents	Global Citizenship: Around the World, Across the Street	Becoming Global Citizens: A Question of Choice

ABOUT FREE THE CHILDREN

FREE THE CHILDREN
children helping children through education

Free The Children is a unique international youth organization that empowers young people through representation, leadership, and action. Founded in 1995 by Craig Kielburger, Free The Children has grown into the world's largest network of children helping children, having involved more than one million young people around the world in its projects.

Over 130 million of the world's poorest children do not attend school, and two-thirds of them are girls. Because education is the best way to end poverty and the exploitation of children, Free The Children has raised funds to build more than 500 schools in 16 developing countries, providing daily education to over 50,000 children. With Free The Children, young people have also collected and shipped 207,500 school and health kits and more than $15 million US in medical supplies to children in 40 countries of the developing world, including Afghanistan, Sierra Leone, Ecuador, India, China, Kosovo, Kenya, Togo, Brazil, Haiti, Nicaragua, Tanzania, Mexico, and the Philippines, among others. Alternative income programs sponsored by Free The Children have empowered 23,500 poor women and their families with the means to send their children to school.

As a voice for young people, Free The Children takes a stand on children's rights issues on local, national, and international levels. Youth representatives address students, educators, unions, religious groups, businesses, and government groups on social issues affecting children.

Free The Children is a group of passionate young people from all ages who wish to change the world! There are many ways for you, your school, or youth group to become involved and make a difference in the lives of children around the globe:

- Start a Free The Children chapter in your school.
- Fundraise to build a classroom or a school in a developing country.
- Research important issues such as child labor, children in armed conflict, and child poverty in Canada, and educate others about what they can do to help.
- Participate in a Free The Children campaign for children's rights.
- Attend one of Free The Children's leadership academies and conferences, which take place in Toronto and Arizona each year.

Visit **www.freethechildren.com** for more information on how to become involved, including how to start a Free The Children chapter, 101 fundraising ideas, fact sheets on important global issues and profiles of youth who have changed the world.

TAKE MORE ACTION! How To Change The World

| HOME
Preface, Contents | LEVEL I
Global Citizenship:
Around the World, Across the Street | LEVEL II
Becoming Global Citizens:
A Question of Choice |

ABOUT ME TO WE

Me to We is about living socially conscious and empathetic lives, engaging in daily acts of kindness and building meaningful relationships with others. Living Me to We means committing one's self to always considering the benefits for 'We' in our actions, from small choices to major life decisions. On a global scale, it means recognizing our ability to have a positive impact on our planet and in the lives of those around the world most in need.

Me to We is a new kind of social enterprise for people of all ages, offering socially conscious, ethically-minded alternatives to their usual daily choices. Through our media, products and leadership experiences, we direct support to Free The Children's work of empowering youth to create global change. Every trip, t-shirt, song, book, speech, thought and smile adds up to a lifestyle that's part of the worldwide movement of We.

• Me to We Books share stories that transform your life and your world. Readers aren't just purchasing a book; they're becoming a part of a movement.

• Me to We Leadership inspires youth to action through interactive workshops, seminars and international week-long leadership academies, showing the world that we truly are the generation we've been waiting for.

• With their experiences as humanitarians, activists, entrepreneurs, leaders and more, Me to We Speakers inspire and captivate more than 350,000 people each year to inspire others to create change.

• Me to We Trips opens a world of learning and adventure. Participants are immersed in new cultures, volunteer alongside local communities, develop friendships, and support development in places like Kenya, Ecuador, India, China or Arizona-Mexico.

• Me to We Music spotlights social issues through the universal language of music, bringing fresh sounds, energy and a positive message to festivals, concerts or other events.

Together, we can create a worldwide community of 'we thinking' and 'we acting,' where socially conscious choices are the norm and helping our global community drives the simple decisions we make each day. Visit metowe.org for all the latest updates!

Visit **metowe.org** for the latest updates!

TAKE MORE ACTION! How To Change The World

| **Home**
Preface, Contents | **Level I**
Global Citizenship:
Around the World, Across the Street | **Level II**
Becoming Global Citizens:
A Question of Choice |

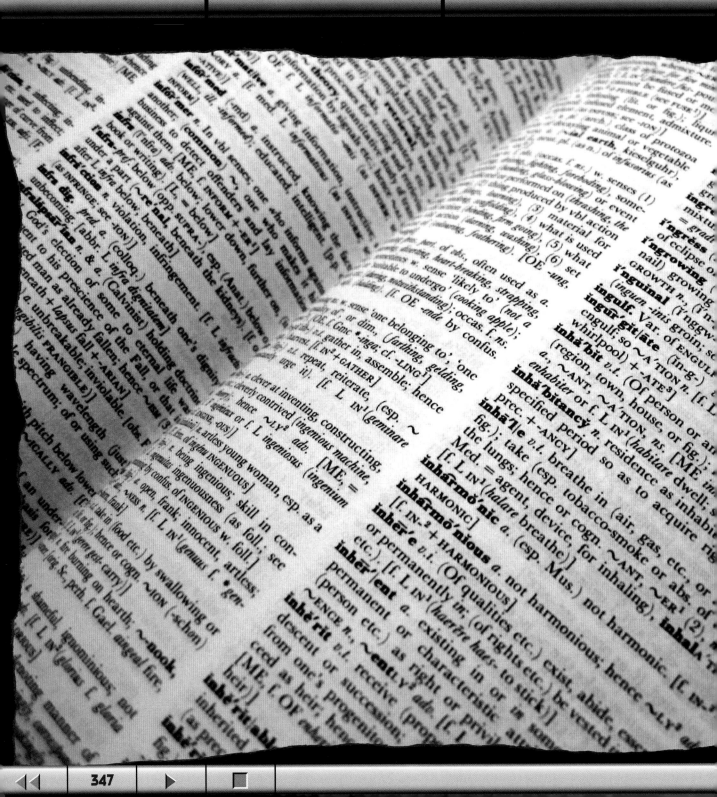

Level III
The Seven Steps to Social Action:
Taking It to the Next Level

Level IV
The How-To Guide:
The Global Citizen's Toolbox

Level V
Sources And Resources,
End Notes

GLOSSARY

Agenda: a list or plan of things to be discussed or accomplished.

Branding: the act of giving a company or organization a particular design or symbol in order to promote its products, services, or message.

Bridge-builders: leaders who negotiate to resolve conflicts between members to ensure that the team stays focused and works as a cohesive unit.

Budget: an estimate of the amount of money that will be spent for various purposes in a given time.

Citizen: one who is granted specific rights and responsibilities as a member of a state or nation.

Contingency Funds: money put aside to cover unexpected costs.

Core Group: three to five passionate and committed people who work together to plan and co-ordinate research and actions for an issue, making it a high priority in their lives.

Doers: leaders who take action to set the team in motion, leading by example, motivating people toward the main goal.

Ecological Footprint: all the productive land required on a continuing basis to provide all the resources consumed and absorb all the wastes created by a population, no matter where in the world that land is located; how much Earth was affected in the production and the eventual disposal of a particular product.

Ethical: being in accordance with standards of right and wrong.

Facilitator: one who is responsible for ensuring that group members treat one another with respect and follow the agenda during meetings; a facilitator may also encourage group interaction.

Global Citizen: one who considers the global impact of one's words and actions, questions the status quo, strives for a more just and sustainable world, and celebrates diversity and solidarity.

Global Citizenship: the responsibilities, rights, and privileges of being a member of the global community.

Globalization: the increased mobility of goods, services, labor, technology, and capital throughout the world.

HTML: acronym for Hypertext Markup Language, a computer programming language used to create and display hypertext files (from which text, graphics, and sound can be accessed by

TAKE MORE ACTION! How To Change The World

| **HOME** Preface, Contents | **LeveL I** Global Citizenship: Around the World, Across the Street | **LeveL II** Becoming Global Citizens: A Question of Choice |

selecting a specially marked word on the screen) on the Internet.

Java: a computer programming language designed to develop applications, especially ones for the Internet that can operate on different platforms.

Lobbying: trying to influence people, especially legislators.

Media outlets: businesses or companies focused on communicating news and events to the public, such as newspapers, magazines, and television and radio stations.

Metatag: an Hypertext Markup Language (HTML) command that defines keywords within Web documents (see also HTML).

Minga: a group of occasional volunteers who contribute their specific talents to the team during big actions; a term inspired by the indigenous societies in Central and South America who come together to accomplish important projects quickly, efficiently, and as a unified community.

Mission: the particular objective of a group.

Mission statement: a written outline of the group's objective.

Monitoring and evaluation plans: materials prepared before an action, including feedback forms, surveys, and tallies, that allow a group to measure its success in quantity and in quality.

Networking: meeting with friends or colleagues to exchange ideas or further one's interests.

Passion Booster: a visible, tangible reminder of one's mission, which stirs memory and rekindles passion about an issue.

Prayer: in a petition, what is being requested.

Press Kits: a packaged set of promotional materials, such as photographs and background information, for distribution to the press, as at a news conference.

Public Service Announcements (PSAs): advertisements or commercials promoting a social message and broadcast on radio and television stations.

LeveL III The Seven Steps to Social Action: Taking It to the Next Level	**LeveL IV** The How-To Guide: The Global Citizen's Toolbox	**LeveL V** Sources And Resources, End Notes

Racism: prejudice or discrimination against a person or group because of a difference of race or of cultural or ethnic background.

Reasoners: leaders who analyze the team's goals and actions, and determine the best possible way to achieve the goals given specific conditions and circumstances.

Search Engines: a piece of software used to find and access files or Web sites; examples include Google, Windows Live Search and Yahoo!.

Site Map: a visual or textually organized model of a Web site's content that allows the users to navigate through the site to find the information they are looking for; a kind of interactive table of contents, in which each listed item links directly to its counterpart sections of the Web site.

Solidarity: unity or fellowship arising from common responsibilities and interests.

Sound Bite: a short, catchy phrase or slogan that communicates a group's message.

Status Quo: the way things are; the existing state of affairs.

Substance Abuse: excessive use of a drug, alcohol, or other chemical agent that may lead to social, occupational, psychological, or physical problems.

Sustainable Consumption: meeting your needs with minimal negative social and environmental impacts, while maximizing positive impacts; actions that meet your needs without sacrificing the needs of future generations.

Thesis: in a speech, a proposition or statement to be proved or to be maintained against objections.

Values: beliefs that individuals or groups hold about what is really important or just, and that guide choices and behaviour.

Visionaries: leaders who dream of the team's goals and potential; those who develop new ideas for approaching problems or tasks.

  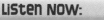

TAKE MORE ACTION! How To Change The World

HOME	LEVEL I	LEVEL II
Preface, Contents	Global Citizenship: Around the World, Across the Street	Becoming Global Citizens: A Question of Choice

LeveL III
The Seven Steps to Social Action:
Taking It to the Next Level

LeveL IV
The How-To Guide:
The Global Citizen's Toolbox

LeveL V
Sources And Resources,
End Notes

SELECT BIBLIOGRAPHY

Campaign 2000, "It Takes a Nation to Raise a Generation: Campaign 2007 Report Card on Child and Family Poverty."
http://www.campaign2000.ca/rc/rc07/2007_C2000_NationalReportCard.pdf.

Dingerson, Leigh and Hay, Sarah H. *Co/Motion: The Guide to Youth-Led Social Change*. Washington DC: Alliance for Justice, 1998.

Health Canada, "The Scoop."
http://www.hc-sc.gc.ca/hecs-sesc/tobacco/youth/scoop.html#never.

Human Rights Watch, "Racism and the Administration of Justice."
http://www.hrw.org/campaigns/race/criminal_justice.htm.

Human Rights Watch, "World Report 2007." http://www.hrw.org/wr2k7/wr2007master.pdf.

Human Rights Watch, "World Conference Against Racism Backgrounder."
http://www.hrw.org/campaigns/race/background0727.htm.

Indian and Northern Affairs Canada, "Backgrounder: Aboriginal Title in Canada's Courts."
http://www.ainc-inac.gc.ca/pr/info/tcc-eng.asp.

International Institute for Democracy and Electoral Assistance, "Democratic Dialogue: A Handbook for Practitioners."
http://www.idea.int/publications/democratic_dialogue/index.cfm.

International Labour Organization, "The end of child labour: within reach."
http://www.ilo.org/dyn/declaris/DECLARATIONWEB.DOWNLOAD_BLOB?Var_DocumentID=6176.

International Rehabilitation Council for Torture Victims, "What is Torture?"
http://www.irct.org/Default.aspx?ID=19.

TAKE MORE ACTION! How To Change The World

| HOME
Preface, Contents | LEVEL I
Global Citizenship:
Around the World, Across the Street | LEVEL II
Becoming Global Citizens:
A Question of Choice |

Jones, Ellis et al. *The Better World Handbook: From Good Intentions to Everyday Actions*. Gabriola Island, BC: New Society Publishers, 2001.

Kahn, Si. *Organizing: a Guide for Grassroots Leaders*. Silver Spring, MD: National Association of Social Workers, 1991.

King Jr., Martin Luther, "I Have a Dream."
http://news.bbc.co.uk/1/hi/world/americas/3170387.stm.

MADD Canada, "Alcohol, Trauma and Impaired Driving."
http://www.madd.ca/library/madd_alcohol_facts.pdf.

Mandela, Nelson, "I am Prepared to Die."
http://www.anc.org.za/ancdocs/history/rivonia.html.

Myers, David G. *Social Psychology*, 7th ed. New York: McGraw-Hill, 2002.

The Native Women's Association of Canada, "Discrimination Against Aboriginal Women Rampant in Federal Prisons, Claims the Native Women's Association of Canada."
http://www.elizabethfry.ca/submissn/prelease/nwac/nwac.pdf.

Oxfam Quebec, "The World is Still Waiting."
http://www.oxfam.ca/news-and-publications/publications-and-reports/the-world-is-still-waiting/.

Rainforest Action Network, "Why We Do It: Build Sustainable Economies."
http://ran.org/why_we_do_it/sustainable_economies/.

Statistics Canada, "A Profile of Youth Justice in Canada."
http://www.statcan.ca/english/freepub/85-544-XIE/0019785-544-XIE.pdf.

Steffen, Alex, ed. *Worldchanging: A User's Guide to the 21st Century*. New York: Abrams, 2006.

LeVeL III
The Seven Steps to Social Action:
Taking It to the Next Level

LeVeL IV
The How-To Guide:
The Global Citizen's Toolbox

LeVeL V
Sources And Resources,
End Notes

Stockholm International Peace Research Institute, "SIPRI Yearbook 2007: Armaments, Disarmaments and International Security."
http://yearbook2007.sipri.org/mini/yb07mini.pdf/download.

UNAIDS, "2006 Report on the global AIDS epidemic."
http://www.unaids.org/en/KnowledgeCentre/HIVData/GlobalReport/#english.

UNESCO Institute for Statistics, "Literacy."
http://www.uis.unesco.org/ev.php?URL_ID=6401&URL_DO=DO_TOPIC&URL_SECTION=201.

UNICEF, "A League Table of Child Poverty in Rich Nations."
http://www.unicef-icdc.org/publications/pdf/repcard1e.pdf.

UNICEF, "The State of the World's Children 2007: Gender equality."
http://www.unicef.org/sowc07/report/report.php.

United Nations, "Universal Declaration of Human Rights."
http://www.un.org/Overview/rights.html.

United Nations Office on Drugs and Crime, "Trafficking in Human Beings."
http://www.unodc.org/unodc/en/human-trafficking/index.html.

Welton, Neva and Wolf, Linda. *Global Uprising: Confronting the Tyrannies of the 21st Century*. Gabriola Island, BC: New Society Publishers, 2001.

World Health Organization, "Children and Young People are at the Centre of the HIV/AIDS Epidemic." http://www.who.int/child-adolescent-health/HIV/HIV_epidemic.htm.

United Nations Framework Convention on Climate Change, "Uniting on climate 2007: a guide to the Climate Change Convention and the Kyoto Protocol."
http://unfccc.int/files/essential_background/background_publications_htmlpdf/application/pdf/pub_07_uniting_on_climate_en.pdf.

TAKE MORE ACTION! How To Change The World

HOME	Level I	Level II
Preface, Contents	Global Citizenship: Around the World, Across the Street	Becoming Global Citizens: A Question of Choice

ACKNOWLEDGEMENTS

This book represents the collective efforts of an extraordinary team of individuals we are honored to call friends. Our gratitude to Deepa Shankaran and Laoghan Hendra for their dedication to the Take Action! series and their inexhaustible patience throughout the writing process. A huge thank you also to Marisa Antonello and the team at TurnStyle Imaging for their creativity.

Thank you to Eva and Yoel Haller for their love, Michelle Douglas for her commitment, Virginia Benderley for her wisdom, René Malo for his conviction, John Gaither for his thousands of hours spent volunteering and Dr. Dorothea Gaither for her insight. Thank you as well to Nancy Christopher, Janice Schoening, and Chris Besse for their support and assistance on the original Take Action! project.

Our work would not be possible without the help of Free The Children's supporters and board of directors, both in Canada and in the United States. We would like to especially thank David Sersta, Ed Gillis, Gregory Harmandayan, Kathy Sarafian, Adrian Horwood, Charlotte Empey, Amy Eldon Turteltaub, Beverly Cooper Neufeld, David Cohen, Ernan Roman, Hal Schwartz, Jessica Mayberry, Juliet Bryan-Brown, Prof. Jonathan White, Josh Cohen, Mary Lewis, Megan Singh, Monica Yunus, Richard Prins, Lara Steinhouse and Stephanie Kay.

Our gratitude goes out to all the organizations and individuals who believe in Free The Children's mission. We would like to extend special thanks to Oprah Winfrey and Katy Davis from Harpo and Caren Yanis, Tim Bennett, Annie Streer, Christina Timmins and Susan Thome from the Angel Network. We are thankful for the encouragement and support of Leonard Kurz and the Kurz Family Foundation; Julie Toskan-Casale from the Toskan Casale Foundation; Linda Rosier, Joe Catalano and the Colours of Freedom team; the Howie Stillman Young Leadership Fund; ONE X ONE; the Solo Family Foundation; the Boyd Foundation; the Journey Foundation; the Sanam Vaziri Quraishi Foundation; the Walter & Duncan Gordon Foundation; the Shapanski Family Foundation; The National Speakers Bureau; Michelle Lemmons and The International Speakers Bureau; the J.W. McConnell Family Foundation; Gerry Connelly, Allan Hux, Mark Lowry and the Toronto District School Board students, principals and teachers; Charlie Coffee; Bob French; Clive Metz; the Apostolopoulos family; the Joyal family; the Weiss Family; the Heimark family; the Rubin family; and Bob Lato and the Toronto Catholic District School Board.

We are privileged to count as friends Susan Antonacci and our friends at Canadian Living; everyone at the Toronto Star; Odette and Cristelle Basmaji; the entire team at National Bank Financial; Kim Mathewes from Klear Communications; Pi Media Partners; the i2 Foundation; the Skoll Foundation; the Singh Foundation; Buzz Hargrove and the Canadian Auto Workers Union; David Krieger and the Nuclear Age Peace Foundation; dozens

TAKE MORE ACTION! How To Change The World

HOME	LEVEL I	LEVEL II
Preface, Contents	Global Citizenship: Around the World, Across the Street	Becoming Global Citizens: A Question of Choice

of remarkable educators including Greg Rogers, Mary-Eileen Donovan, Mark Fenwick, Nancy DiGregorio and Chris Spence; Karla Wilson and the School Voyageurs team; Larry Moore and the Ontario Library Association team; Lorraine Frost, Ron Common, Dennis Mock and the educators at Nipissing University; Veronica Atkins, Abby Bloch, Jacqueline Eberstein and the Robert C. and Veronica Atkins Foundation; Susanne Boyce and Karen Barzilay at CTV; and Mark McInnis, Faith Feingold and Jessi Cruickshank at MTV.

Much appreciation goes out to all our corporate and organizational partners, including 8 Perf Pictures, DDB/Rapp Collins, Investors Group, National Public Relations, Telus and Young Presidents' Organization. We are grateful for the continued support of the Baby Girl Project, Canada AM, Dupree, Miller & Associates, Inc., GDTV, the Hamilton-Wentworth District School Board, the Hamilton-Wentworth Catholic District School Board, McMaster University, the National Children's Museum, OMNI Television, OTG Financial, Persistence of Vision Films, Simon & Schuster, Inc., Speakers Spotlight, Student Vote, Torys LLP, Transcontinental Media, Upper Canada District School Board, Viacom, Western Academy of Beijing and World Medical Relief.

Thank you to Marion Stewart, Joseph Koch, Jane Goodall, David Baum, Glen Kishi, Karen Radford, Jennifer Clarkson, Mark Caswell, Joan Brehl, Tim Broadhead, Patrick Johnston, Lis Travers, Donna Cansfield, Premier Dalton McGuinty, Rebecca Amyotte, Steve Miller, Sue Allan, Walter Green, Chris and Tania Carnegie, Terry Reeves, Judith Cunningham, Kate Dernocoeur, Liz Dowdeswell, Kathy Southern, Patricia Karen Gagic, Elaine Silver, Kim Phuc, Vito Maltese, Leo Ciccone, Dr. Mark Wise, Steve Miller and Janelle McFarlane.

We are, as ever, grateful for the hard work of the staff at Free The Children and Me to We, especially the many years of work of Dalal Al-Waheidi, Renée Hodgkinson, Lloyd Hanoman, Peter Ruhiu, Michelle Hambly, William Li and Victor and Wendy Li. A special thank you goes to Roxanne Joyal for her unwavering efforts on behalf of Free The Children and the children of Africa over the past eleven years.

We cannot sufficiently sing the praises of the amazing team of staff and volunteers who are the soul of Free The Children, Leaders Today and Me to We: Adam Baden-Clay, Agnes Mutahi, Afton Eddy, Aimee Polonsky, Alanna Box, Alem Tedeneke, Alexandra Clemmensen, Allison Sandmeyer, Ammana Haleem, Amy Peasgood,

LeveL III	**LeveL IV**	**LeveL V**
The Seven Steps to Social Action: Taking It to the Next Level	The How-To Guide: The Global Citizen's Toolbox	Sources And Resources, End Notes

Amy Schlein, Anab Jafri, Andreas Friis, Angelique de Montbrun, Ann Endress, Anna Crosskill, Annie Ly, Aprille Radam, Ashley Hilkewich, Ashley McEachern, Barry Corbedd, Bartek Kosinski, Bessie Ly, Beth Campbell, Bina Hwangbo, Bonnie Kay, Breanna Wright, Brooke Thompson, Caitlin Henry Macgregor, Cait McKinney, Carolina Arcila, Caryl Canzius, Catherine McCauley, Cayley Moffat, Charlotte Herrold, Chelsea Weinberg-Lynn, Cheryl Player, Chris Mallinos, Christian Corbeil, Cosmin Neamtu, Courtney Peck, Dan Kuzmicki, Dan Mossip-Balkwill, Daniel Yu, Dana Crawford-Dignard, Darren Tseng, David Johnson, Debbie Gray, Devora Winston, Don Lane, Drew Davidson, Edmond Chiu, Elysia Blake, Emily Finnie, Emily Payne, Erin Barton-Chery, Erin Blanding, Eugene Lai, Gabriela Larenas, Garrry Norman, Giustina D'Elia, Grace Hanley, Hannah Chen, Heather Barkley, Heather Hittner, Hilary Kilgour, Ingvild Vardheim, Jackie Plessl, Jacqueline Pilon, Janice Sousa, Jason Fung, Jen Farkas, Jesse Jewell, Jey Subramaniam, Joanna Maracle, John Gaither, John N'Drangu, Jonah Kanter, Jon MacIndoe, Jordana Weiss, Joseph Ngugi, Josh Wang, Justin Lawrence, Kailea Switzer, Kasia Popowicz, Kate Likely, Kate Richardson, Kathryn Meisner, Katie Goodman, Kevin Glowinski, Kieran Bergmann, Kimberly Hewitt, Kim Plewes, Krystal Loverin, Lauren Roach, Leandra Mendoza, Leen Latif, Lekhena Peou, Lena Eastes, Leysa Cerswell, Lilly Cheng, Linda Kent, Long Le, Louise Kent, Luke Nares, Maria Angela Pacheco, Marianne Woods, Marina Motova, Marissa Ali, Martine Mangion, Mary Eileen Donovan, Matt Ng, Matt Tod, Megan Barton, Megan Sullivan, Meghan Gamble, Melissa Yaw, Michael Smith, Michel Chickwanine, Mike Spagnolo, Nabeela Rahman, Nick Gichimu, Nick Magnone, Nicole Baden-Clay, Oliver Madison, Rann Sharma, Rob Benvie, Robin Wiszowaty, Roxanne Joyal, Russ McLeod, Ryan Hollinrake, Sally Hakim, Sara Panton, Sapna Goel, Sarah Aquilina, Sarah Wetmore, Sarah Young, Scott Baker, Scott McPherson, Shelby Pearce, Shobha Sharma, Stacey Sleightholm, Stefanie Shea, Stefanie Tan, Steve Tran, Sunita Chaudry, Tatiana Yu, Terri Brown, TJ Arch, Vi Vu, Wangu Chege, Whitney Burton, William Qi, Yohan Matthew and everyone overflowing with LEV3L passion. And a tribute to Joe Opatowski, our friend whom we all miss dearly.

Finally, our family deserves a heartfelt thank you, especially our Mimi, who remains our biggest fan. Of course, we would not be where we are today without the love and support of our parents, Fred and Theresa. Thank you for everything, Mom and Dad!

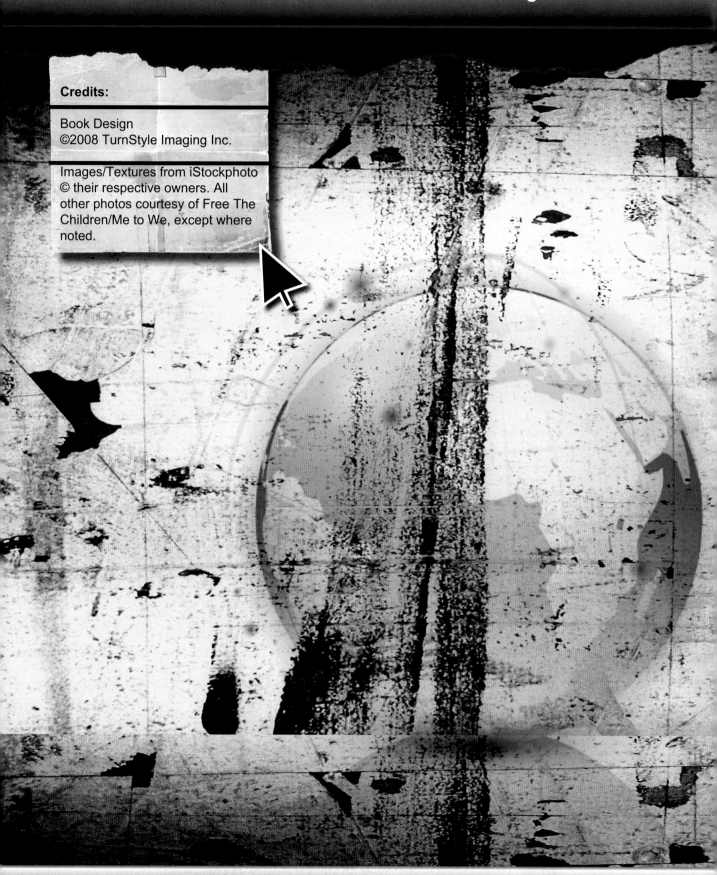

TAKE MORE ACTION! How To Change The World

me to we
BOOKS

Me to We Books share stories that transform your life and the world around you. Our award-winning and best-selling collection includes exciting non-fiction and biographies, curriculum for teachers and inspiring how-to guides. Me to We Books connects a wide range of readers to the latest thinking, stories, trends and issues in social responsibility. Readers aren't just purchasing a book; they're joining a movement.

Free the Children
Written by Craig Kielburger on his return from Asia, *Free the Children* is the story that launched a movement. It tells the remarkable story of his encounters with some of the most disadvantaged children on earth, trapped in poverty and exploitative child labour. Winner of the prestigious Christopher Award, it has been translated into eight languages.

Take Action!: A Guide to Active Citizenship
Written by Craig and Marc Kielburger, *Take Action!* is a colourful, step-by-step guide to active citizenship that equips young people with the tools they need to make a difference. Includes the 7 Steps to Social Involvement, 101 Fundraising Ideas and sections on working with the media, public speaking and setting goals. Ideal for grades 8-10.

Take More Action
Written by Marc Kielburger, Craig Kielburger and Deepa Shankaran, *Take More Action* is an advanced guide to global citizenship, empowering young adults to bring about social change. Brilliantly illustrated and full of powerful quotes, *Take More Action* includes invaluable material on character education, ethical leadership and global citizenship. Ideal for grades 10 and up.

The Making of an Activist
Warning: this book will change you. With vivid images and inspiring words, travelogues, poems and sparkling artwork, *The Making of an Activist* guides you on a journey of positive change, painting an intimate portrait of passionate young activists. Explore the book. Catch the spark.

It Takes a Child
Illustrated and adapted by Turnstyle Imaging with Craig Kielburger, *It Takes a Child* is a fun, vibrant look back at Craig's adventures in taking global action. Craig takes young readers along on his eye-opening journey throughout the developing world, learning about global issues and making many new friends along the way. Suitable for all ages.

Visit www.metowe.com to order your books today!